Ethics and Value Perspectives

To Dave and Penni
In memory of Howard Goldstein (1922–2000)

Ethics and Value Perspectives in Social Work

Edited by

Mel Gray and Stephen A. Webb

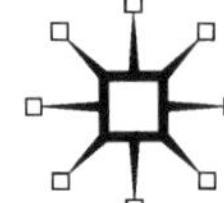

First published 2010 by
PALGRAVE MACMILLAN

Palgrave Macmillan in the UK is an imprint of Macmillan Publishers Limited, registered in England, company number 785998, of Houndmills, Basingstoke, Hampshire RG21 6XS.

Palgrave Macmillan in the US is a division of St Martin's Press LLC, 175 Fifth Avenue, New York, NY 10010.

Palgrave Macmillan is the global academic imprint of the above companies and has companies and representatives throughout the world.

Palgrave® and Macmillan® are registered trademarks in the United States, the United Kingdom, Europe and other countries

ISBN 978-0-230-22145-1 ISBN 978-0-230-31357-6 (eBook)
DOI 10.1007/978-0-230-31357-6

A catalogue record for this book is available from the British Library.

A catalog record for this book is available from the Library of Congress.

10 9 8 7 6 5 4 3 2 1
19 18 17 16 15 14 13 12 11 10

Contents

Acknowledgements vii
Notes on Contributors viii

Chapter 1 **Introduction: Ethics and Value Perspectives in Social Work** 1
Mel Gray and Stephen A. Webb

PART I PROFESSIONAL PERSPECTIVES 17

Chapter 2 **Codes of Ethics** 19
Elaine Congress

Chapter 3 **Codes of Conduct** 31
Paul Webster

Chapter 4 **Ethical Decision-making** 41
Donna McAuliffe

Chapter 5 **Ethical Dilemmas in Practice** 51
Stefan Borrmann

Chapter 6 **Faith-based Approaches** 60
Phillip Gilligan

PART II MORAL PERSPECTIVES 71

Chapter 7 **Ethic of Care** 73
Brid Featherstone

Chapter 8 **Ethics of Responsibility** 85
Sonia Tascón

Chapter 9 **Discourse Ethics** 95
Stan Houston

Chapter 10 **Virtue Ethics** 108
Stephen A. Webb

Chapter 11 **Postmodern Ethics** 120
Mel Gray

PART III SOCIAL PERSPECTIVES 133

Chapter 12 **Anti-racist Practice** 135
Haluk Soydan

Chapter 13 **Human Rights and Social Justice** 148
Jim Ife

Chapter 14 **Anti-oppressive Practice** 160
Lena Dominelli

Chapter 15 **Participation and Citizenship** 173
Aila-Leena Matthies

PART IV SPIRITUAL PERSPECTIVES 183

Chapter 16 **Islam and Ethics** 185
Terry Lovat

Chapter 17 **Christianity and Ethics** 196
Russell Whiting

Chapter 18 **New Age Ethics** 207
Dick Houtman and Stef Aupers

Chapter 19 **Conclusion: Practising Values in Social Work** 219
Mel Gray and Stephen A. Webb

References 224
Index 251

Acknowledgements

This book represents a contribution to what has been described as the 'ethical turn' in social work, and in the social sciences more broadly. As editors it is therefore most encouraging and commensurate to be able to acknowledge the generosity, tolerance, commitment and unflagging encouragement of a number of people who have helped us to complete this book. We would like to thank all the contributors to this book for making our work on this project most pleasurable and deeply rewarding. When it comes to the manner of relating ideas, practices and values to each other, our ability to marshal these has very much been dependent on the deep understanding these various contributors have made. We have been fortunate in being able to work closely with such a distinguished and intellectually engaging group of contributors. Our joint engagement in this undertaking has led to a collection of chapters which range from some traditional terrain in social work to innovative and cutting-edge perspectives that have previously been unexplored. From professional to moral, social and spiritual perspectives, we hope that we have opened up areas of reflection that will lead to a deeper engagement with ethics and values, an enrichment of social work practice in day-to-day engagement with clients but, most of all, a commitment to a modern profession that has intrinsic social value. Guiding us along the way were the invaluable help and support of the editorial team at Palgrave. Catherine Gray's has provided us with great succour. Her professionalism and detailed understanding of social work provided the context in which this work was born and came to fruition. Her dedication to and support for the project took us to the finishing line, and Kate Llewellyn and Khanam Virjee helped us across it, with our copy-editor Juanita Bullough ensuring that the final product was free from error and distraction. Thanks to Mel's son Barry Jon Gray for the cover design. She would also like to thank Dave for his unquestioning love and support and celebration of this achievement. Stephen is forever grateful to Penni, whose love and understanding nourishes and completes him. She is simultaneously his singular and his plural:

> Sharing comes down to this: what community reveals to me, in presenting to me my birth and my death, is my existence outside myself ... Being-in-common does not mean a higher form of substance or subject taking charge of the limits of separate individualities ... The limit of the individual, fundamentally, does not concern it, it simply surrounds it. (Jean Luc Nancy, *The Inoperative Community*)

Notes on Contributors

Stef Aupers is Associate Professor of Sociology at Erasmus University Rotterdam, the Netherlands. Much of his research deals with tendencies of 're-enchantment' in the modern world. He has published in Dutch and international journals on religion, New Age spirituality, conspiracy culture, and Internet culture. He is currently working on a monograph on online computer gaming and on a translation of his dissertation, *Under the Spell of Modernity: Sacralizing the Self and Computer Technology* (forthcoming 2009).

Stefan Borrmann, PhD is Professor for International Social Work Research at the University of Applied Science in Landshut, Germany. He is chair of the *Society for International Cooperation in Social Work (SICSW)*. During winter 2004/5 he was a visiting scholar in the School of Social Welfare at the University of California at Berkeley where he conducted a survey on ethical dilemmas in social work. He has published two monographs about social work with violent youth groups, one on theories of social work and another on social work history and research. His main research interests are theories of social work, social work ethics and professional youth work.

Elaine Congress, MSW, DSW is Professor and Associate Dean at Fordham University Graduate School of Social Service in New York. She serves on the Permanent Ethics Committee for the International Federation of Social Workers (IFSW), as well as the IFSW team at the UN. She has published extensively on social work ethics, social work education, and cultural diversity, including, most recently, *Social Work with Immigrants and Refugees* (with Fernando Chang-Muy, 2009) and *Teaching Social Work Values and Ethics*, 2nd edn (with Phyllis Black and Kimberley Strom-Gottfried, 2009).

Lena Dominelli is Professor of Social Work and Head of Social, Community and Youth Work at Durham University, UK. She has been a practitioner, researcher and educator in social work for many years. She has published extensively in various fields, including globalization, community development, social policy, working with ethnic minorities, working with women, and working with sexually abused children. Her most recent book is *Introducing Social Work* (2009).

Brid Featherstone is Professor of Social Work at the University of Bradford, UK. She has worked as a social worker in the field of child welfare and has a particular interest in applying feminist theory to child welfare policies and practices. She is a founder member of the international network on gender and child welfare. Recent publications include *Working with Men in Health and Social Care* (with Mark Rivett and Jonathan Scourfield, 2009) and *Contemporary Fathering* (2009).

Philip Gilligan is a Senior Lecturer in Social Work at the University of Bradford, UK. He qualified as a social worker in 1976 and worked as a practitioner, manager and practice educator in Derbyshire, Kenya, Rochdale, Kirklees, and Bradford, before becoming a full-time lecturer in 2004. He has worked in statutory and voluntary agencies, including a faith-based organization. His research interests focus on the impact of religion and belief in social work and on child protection and safeguarding practice, in particular.

Mel Gray is Professor of Social Work and Research Professor in the Australian Institute for Social Inclusion and Wellbeing, University of Newcastle, New South Wales, Australia. She has published extensively on social work and social development. Recent books include *Indigenous Social Work around the World* (with Michael Yellow Bird and John Coates, 2008), *Social Work Theories and Methods* (with Stephen Webb, 2008) and *Evidence-based Social Work* (with Debbie Plath and Stephen Webb, 2009). She is Associate Editor of the *International Journal of Social Welfare.*

Stan Houston qualified as a social worker in 1981. He then spent the following 16 years practising in a range of child and family social work settings in Belfast, Northern Ireland. In 1997, he entered higher education. Since then, his interests have focused on the application of critical social theory and moral philosophy to social work practice and research, particularly in the field of child welfare.

Dick Houtman is Professor of Cultural Sociology at Erasmus University Rotterdam, the Netherlands and member of the editorial boards of *Politics and Religion* and *Journal for the Scientific Study of Religion.* One of his principal research interests is the contemporary spiritualization of religion, about which he published in *Journal for the Scientific Study of Religion* (2002, 2007, 2009) and *Journal of Contemporary Religion* (2006, 2009). A volume titled *Religions of Modernity,* co-edited with Stef Aupers, has recently been submitted for publication.

Jim Ife is Emeritus Professor at Curtin University, Perth, Australia, where he was Head of the Centre for Human Rights Education until 2006. Prior to that, he was Professor of Social Work and Social Policy at Curtin University and at the University of Western Australia. His areas of interest are community development and human rights. Recent publications include *Community Development*, 3rd edn (2006), *Human Rights and Social Work*, 2nd edn (2008), and *Human Rights from Below* (forthcoming, 2009).

Terry Lovat is Professor of Education at the University of Newcastle, New South Wales, Australia. His major research areas are in Islam and values education. He has managed many research projects in these areas, including one on Islam and Muslim schooling in Australia. He has published widely and been a regular keynote speaker at national and international conferences in the area of Islam. He was recently invited by the government of the Ukraine to address a conference about his work on values education and Muslim youth.

Aila-Leena Matthies is social work professor at the University of Jyväskylä, Finland, at the university's second campus in Kokkola. Her research focuses on citizen participation and the role of NGOs in the context of various welfare states. Currently, she is co-ordinating a European Participation research network and a research project on participatory welfare services in Finnish rural areas. From 1996 to 2007 she was Professor of Social Work at the University of Applied Sciences in Magdeburg, Germany.

Donna McAuliffe is a Senior Lecturer in the School of Human Services and Social Work, Griffith University, Queensland, Australia. She has a diverse social work practice background and has worked in academia since 1999, developing her specialization in the field of professional ethics. She is the Convenor of the National Ethics Group for the Australian Association of Social Workers, and regularly provides continuing professional education on ethical decision-making for practitioners and managers in community and government organizations.

Haluk Soydan is Research Professor and Director of the Hamovitch Center for Science in Human Services at the USC School of Social Work in Los Angeles. He has a PhD in sociology from Uppsala University in Sweden. Before joining USC 2004, he served for ten years as Research Director at the National Board of Health and Welfare in Stockholm. His scientific publications include more than two dozen books and a large number of journal articles.

Sonia Tascón is a lecturer at the Australian Centre for Human Rights Education, RMIT University, Melbourne, Australia, and adjunct lecturer for the Centre for Human Rights Education, Curtin University, Perth, Australia.

The 'ethics of the Other' constitutes the backbone of her research and writing, particularly in relation to ways to formulate an ethics of hospitality to strangers. Her current interest is in finding ways to conceive of communities as constructed by difference as much as by sameness.

Stephen A. Webb is Professor of Human Sciences and Director of the Australian Institute for Social Inclusion and Wellbeing, University of Newcastle, New South Wales, Australia. He is author of several books, most recently *Social Work in a Risk Society* (Palgrave Macmillan, 2006), *Social Work Theories and Methods* (with Mel Gray, 2008) and *Evidence-based Social Work* (with Mel Gray and Debbie Plath, 2009). He is co-editor (with Mel Gray) of the four-volume *International Social Work* (2009), which includes a selection of seminal social work texts.

Paul Webster is a social work practitioner and doctoral student at the University of Sussex, UK. His chapter is based on aspects of his doctoral research on social work ethical theory. Committed to the importance of combining critical theory with day-to-day practice, he seeks to combine his early academic training in moral and political philosophy with his extensive work experience in nursing, health, social care, social work and social work education.

Russell Whiting is a Lecturer in Social Work at the University of Sussex. His social work experience has been with children and families but his interests in social work are broad. Since his days as an Erasmus student, he has been interested in social work practice outside the UK and he has a particular interest in the relationship between religion and social work. Most recently he has published '"No Room for Religion or Spirituality or Cooking Tips": Exploring Practical Atheism as an Unspoken Consensus in the Development of Social Work Values in England', *Ethics and Social Welfare* 2(1), pp. 67–83 (2008) and 'For and Against: The Use of a Debate to Address the Topic of Religion and Spirituality in Social Work Education', *Journal of Practice Teaching in Health and Social Work* (forthcoming).

1

Introduction: Ethics and Value Perspectives in Social Work

Mel Gray and Stephen A. Webb

Key Concepts

Ethics is a branch of philosophy which addresses questions about morality, such as what is the fundamental nature of morality and the way in which moral values are determined.

Professional ethics are close to the Greek meaning of ethics as duty-bound rules and procedures concerning the right conduct of the social worker and the moral standards of the profession.

Deontology is an ethical theory deriving from the philosophy of Immanuel Kant which places emphasis on individual autonomy and choice and concerns itself with guiding individuals to make the right choices through discerning moral duties, obligations, rules and principles.

Teleology refers to ethical theories concerned with ultimate purposes or end states. Utilitarianism and consequentialism are teleological ethical theories.

Utilitarianism is an ethical theory which holds that, given a number of possible courses of action, you should choose the one that will be of most benefit to the greatest number.

Consequentialism refers to an ethical theory which gives weight to the consequences of our actions and moral decisions.

How Important Are Ethics Today?

Here is a harrowing but true story. A young man who was a prisoner in a Nazi concentration camp in Poland was raped by a guard. The guard, knowing that any prisoner who appeared without a cloth cap on the morning roll call would be immediately shot, stole the victim's cap. If the victim were shot for not wearing the cap, the rape would remain concealed. Discovering it had been stolen, the prisoner knew that his only chance to live was to find another cap before the roll call. He stole the cap of another concentration camp inmate, asleep in bed, and therefore lived to tell the tale. The prisoner without the cap was shot at roll call. Roman Frister (2000), the prisoner who stole the cap, describes the death of his fellow inmate as follows:

> The officer and the kapo walked the lines of prisoners ... I counted the seconds as they counted the prisoners. I wanted it to be over. They were up to row four. The capless man didn't beg for his life. We all knew the rules of the game, the killers and the killed alike. There was no need for words. The shot rang out without warning. There was a short, dry, echoless thud. One bullet to the brain. They always shot you in the back of the skull. There was a war on. Ammunition had to be used sparingly. I didn't want to know who the man was. I was delighted to be alive. (p. 301)

Thankfully, social work students are unlikely to ever have to confront such moral situations. However, as we will note, some of the moral dilemmas they have to face in reaching professional judgements have a similar underlying structure to that described by Frister. In social work moral dilemmas are the rule rather than the exception. Social workers often agonize over moral dilemmas. Not only is the subject matter of social work ethics hard to grasp but, more importantly, the practical realities of reaching moral judgements are challenging and extremely complex. Learning about social work ethics requires not only high standards of scholarship but also makes demands on one's experiential and emotional resources. Social workers often have to choose to do either one thing or another. Because of the way practice and the organizational context are arranged, he or she cannot do both in relation to clients. Front-line practitioners face situations where there is often a moral conflict between what seems to be the right course of action.

For example, returning to the above scenario, what does morality say the prisoner ought to have done in that situation? How does he justify taking one moral decision over another? Frister's staggeringly honest account tells us something about the value of life. It has no price. In the camps, raw survival mattered more than anything else. Does the pricelessness of life mean that he was justified in doing anything to save his own life? As we shall see below, for some morality is supposed to be universal and categorical. Closer to our present-day situation the tortures, violations and humiliations at Abu Ghraib Prison and Guantánamo Bay detention camp, as part of the so-called 'War on Terror', are vivid reminders of the pressing relevance of ethics in modern societies. The photographs of the torture, arguably as part of that torture, not only express the American conquerors' glee of victory but also serve to intensify the excruciating shame of that experience for the Iraqi prisoners. Are Abu Ghraib and Frister's story provocative examples of morality being little more than a relative and situational convenience? Are such extreme examples unrepresentative of how morality takes place in everyday life, or are they indicative of the true nature of the human condition once all normal aspects are stripped back? Where does the common 'we' lie and where can the universal 'us' be found in these wicked atrocities? The recurring tragedies of Palestine, Somali, Kosovo, Congo, Chechnya, Pakistan, Afghanistan and Iraq show that we have been unable to dismantle or discourage recourse to an essentializing nationalist, imperialist or tribal 'we' that ultimately functions with the self-identity of an 'I'.

Those who believe that ethics have special significance in these late modern times will find much of value in this book. The book is aimed mainly at social work students and practitioners. It affirms social work as a *valuable* and *evaluating* activity with intrinsic worth that has an important role to play in society. It has intrinsic worth because social work activities rest on a 'constitutive human good' and an appreciation of the importance of shared values that transcend self-interest. 'Good social work' is conceived as morally good when achieved within the relationship of social worker and client. Its worth lies in its capacity to benefit and enrich the lives of others. In short, social workers are strong evaluators. They have an *appreciation* of the value of the good life, or what Nietzsche called 'the value of value'. Their appreciation of value through shared *value-driven* activity makes distinctive forms of *valued* relationships possible, through which the good of *valuable* activity is both confirmed and ramified. This is what we call the work of 'the virtuous social worker' (Gray & Lovat, 2007; McBeath & Webb, 2002). However, we suggest that readers in social work will benefit from the sort of ethical inquiries and case examples offered in this book. A key aim of the book is to arrive at an account of the values for social workers who have definite attachments and intuitions about the nature of their work. But this does not mean that the material offered in this book will merely repeat the values and judgements that the reader would have from the start. For, as Aristotle stressed, most people, when asked to generalize, make claims that do not reflect the complexity and the content of their actual values. Students and practitioners need to learn what they really think about values. As Martha Nussbaum (1986) states, 'When, through work on alternatives and through dialogue with one another, students have arrived at a harmonious adjustment of their beliefs, both singly and in community with one another, this will be an ethical truth, on the Aristotelian understanding of a truth' (pp. 10–11). By this Nussbaum means that students arrive at an ethical truth through the logic of argument and debate. For social workers to bridge the gap between personal values and theory, it is frequently valuable to work from texts, leading the people involved in the dialogue through an elucidation and assessment of someone else's complex position on the problem in question. This gives a degree of detachment and, if we, as editors, have made our selection of texts carefully enough, readers will be able to explore the major parallels, as well as alternatives, to enrich their own value perspectives. Research consistently shows that social workers are keen 'value activists', so it is crucial that their evaluations and judgements are represented in a book that acknowledges the diversity and scope of available value perspectives. It is widely accepted that social work is not value-free. Values imbue everything that is done in social work and the entire practice of front-line delivery of services and practice interventions. This book will demonstrate how value is inescapable in social work, how the processes of evaluation in social work can never be avoided. Beyond the technical competency and skills required of social workers, effective interventions are guided by the application of values. This means that values and the practices flowing from them play a key role in shaping social work intervention.

How to Use This Book

The range and scope of ethics and value perspectives that are offered in this book, we believe, much more accurately than many in this field of study and practice, represent the various tensions and contradictions that are experienced by students and practitioners in their day-to-day learning and front-line work. This introductory chapter lays the groundwork for demonstrating the importance of studying ethics and value theory in social work. The book includes several new perspectives, for example, Islam and New Age perspectives and moral approaches based on the ethics of responsibility and the ethic of care, which make the volume the most contemporary and up-to-date on aspects of values for social work. The book will help students and practitioners alike to reassess the limitations of contemporary approaches to social work ethics which circumscribe a narrow values agenda. It will open up thinking about values and ethics to a much fuller range of ethical and value perspectives in social work. Social work students and practising professionals have received very little and sometimes inconsistent preparation around how to resolve dilemmas arising from a clash of values or from their own beliefs and, more importantly for anti-oppressive practice, how to respond to the needs of those groups and individuals for whom an alternative value perspective, i.e. to the dominant Western worldview, is of major importance (Gray, Coates, & Yellow Bird, 2008).

Social work's problems with dealing with diversity have also impacted adversely on service users for whom differing perspectives have central significance. There are very obvious dangers associated with being unaware of alternative and even competing ethical and value perspectives. It seems that the failure to address value diversity in terms of alternative perspectives is a missed opportunity for social work to build on positive, strengths-based approaches found elsewhere in education and practice. Hence this book not only underlines the significance of values and value education for social work but also contributes to a value pluralism that embraces both solidarity and difference. In order to embark on this new route of recognizing a range of value perspectives in social work, we need a clearly formed and articulated set of values, ethical standpoints and evaluative criteria for these. If we are to argue for a system of perspectives, which allows for the clearer articulation of difference, in a plural rather than dual or unitary form, we must do so from the basis of thinking across different value perspectives that have cultural, societal and historical currency. Social work is distinctive in that it is one of the few modern professions that fully endorses a commitment to respecting the plurality of values. This book is the first to convey the value of moral pluralism in social work, and thus should appeal to a broad audience. If values are plural, then professional decisions between them will be complex. We contend that the attraction of moral pluralism for social work is that it seems to allow for the complexity and conflict that is part of practising values on the front line. Moreover, as the case examples in this book show, sometimes it may not be possible to make a rational choice between two values. As well as the exploration of complex value themes, a further strength of the text lies in the international authorship. It is the first book on ethics and value perspectives in social work to bring together such a wide range of international authors who offer insight into the diversity of ethical and value perspectives in social work. We would venture to say that this is the most impressive and outstanding line-up of social work writers on ethics that has been brought together in one single collection, spanning three different continents. Though the book is aimed primarily at students, and we hope that it will prove a useful resource to carry through courses from the beginning to the advanced level of study, it also has wider appeal for educators and practitioners, and students of applied professional ethics generally. We are sure all will find something meaningful in the chapters which follow to broaden their perspective on ethics and values in social work.

In short, the book aims to engage students with a range of values to critically reflect on and compare and contrast ethics across diverse dimensions. The principal object of studying the material in this book is to enrich one's own understanding of central ethical problems that are as pressing today in social work as they have always been. These questions help to mark out the territory of value perspectives in social work as an area of professional inquiry. The variety of value perspectives discussed by these writers who have played a leading role in developing them in social work will provide students with a first-hand look at their importance, how they came about and were developed for social work. Each chapter has a similar structure, beginning with an introduction to the ethical or value perspective, an outline of key ideas informing the perspective, an overview of social work literature pertaining to the perspective, a discussion of its application to social work practice, and a conclusion. Study aids include a glossary of key terms – key concept boxes – at the beginning of each chapter and study questions at the end. The book concludes with a list of references to prior work in this important field of study in social work, which should prove an excellent resource to students, practitioners, educators, fellow professionals, and researchers alike. It reflects a wide-ranging, growing literature on established and emergent ethical theories and value perspectives in social work.

Rationale for Selection of Perspectives

Ethical perspectives in social work are invariably overlapping and in tension with each other. Researchers interested in ethics and values conduct their work in a kind of perpetual living dialogue with protagonists from different perspectives, with each new perspective gaining vitality and meaning by drawing on or reacting against other perspectives. It is integral to the very idea of ethics in social work that every perspective, without exception, is subjected to scrutiny and challenge. Many of the ideas contained in this book have been subject to wide-ranging analysis and discussion in social work and this sort of close scrutiny is regarded as an ongoing process of critical engagement. The uniqueness of ethics and values in contemporary social work is reflected in the four discrete parts into which we have carefully grouped the texts:

- Professional perspectives
- Moral perspectives
- Social perspectives
- Spiritual perspectives

We identify the important dimensions by gathering together some of the most influential authors and relevant texts in the social work literature on ethics and values. This book – organized into four parts – is a presentation of international researchers' significant and distinctive contribution to social work ethics and values. One of the aims of the book is to provide an intellectual map of the development and key parameters of ethics and values in social work. Wherever possible, we have tried to group the material with a certain thematic relevance in mind. The intellectual map not only conveys overlapping subject matter of ethics and values in social work but also points to the significance of major themes in contemporary practice. While this books marks out the distinctiveness of ethics and values in social work, the field can only be partially identified, since no list of contents can properly accommodate every aspect of the significant contributions in this field. Moreover, given the vastness of the actual subject matter in ethics and values and the limitations on material we were able to include, it is difficult to claim any overarching comprehensiveness. Therefore, our attempt to present key themes of relevance in social work ethics and values must not be confused with presenting a definitive representation of all possible content. For example, in Part IV on spiritual perspectives we carefully chose the areas of Christianity, Islam and New Age for the following specific reasons:

1. From our teaching experience on social work values courses these three domains are most representative of students' interests, ethical dilemmas, classroom debate, and choice of essay or dissertation topics.
2. There is an emerging but limited literature in these areas that is not replicated in the areas of Buddhism, Judaism or Hinduism.
3. They are currently most topical and pressing in political, religious-cultural and social affairs.

Nevertheless, Chapter 6 by Philip Gilligan on faith-based practice addresses multi-faith issues for social work and draws attention to debate about representative student and client experiences that are mapped out as inclusive or exclusive. However, as editors it is important to remind the reader that there is inevitably a feeling of unease about the themes and content omitted from a text such as this. We therefore wish to make it plain that the range and coverage in this book makes no claim to finality.

The Language of Ethics

In moral philosophy various terms are used to describe the moral aspects that are important when making moral judgements or acting morally. Some refer to the nature of the moral decisions we make and form part of the criteria or language used to justify our decisions: duties and obligations, moral rules and principles, and moral character and disposition. Others describe the type of mindset we need to behave morally: moral sensitivity, moral conscience, and moral compassion. Still others refer to processes by which we might gain moral sensitivity, awareness and reflection: moral education or the inculcation of moral values. Various ethical theories give weight to different aspects of or criteria for judging whether our decisions and actions are right or wrong, good or bad.

The distinction between morals and ethics

The terms 'morals' and 'ethics' have different derivations, with the former similar to the Greek word meaning 'custom' and the latter to that meaning 'habit'. This gives us an idea of the social significance of morality in the sense that without it human life would not be possible. It conveys the idea that with moral awareness and moral education we develop good habits and thus behave ethically towards one another, i.e. in keeping with broad ethical standards and values. In philosophy ethics is the study of moral philosophy. Philosophy in its Greek derivation means 'love of wisdom', thus ethics is the love of knowledge about the moral life and the study of what this means. It has spawned several ethical theories, the most established of which are deontology, utilitarianism, consequentialism, and virtue ethics. The word deontology derives from the notion of duty. As we shall see below, a focus on duty in moral philosophy is the approach most identified with German philosopher Immanuel Kant, who believed that we could find universal, categorical and transcendental values that could apply to all people everywhere, like the duty to respect one another. Another term that arose from Aristotle's ethics is teleology, which has to do with end states, the ultimate purpose of goodness pursued in ethics. This was a central concern of the nineteenth-century founders of utilitarianism – Jeremy Bentham, John Stuart Mill and Henry Sidgwick – who sought, following Aristotle, to develop the idea that the criterion of goodness in any given action is that it produces the greatest possible amount of pleasure. This ethical hedonism – love of pleasure, however, is not confined to the self, i.e. it is not self-centred or egoistic, but involves a due regard to the pleasure of others, and can, therefore, be regarded as a universal principle. Aristotle had concerned himself with promoting ideas about morality which would lead to the ultimate end of promoting human flourishing. Utilitarians retain the principle that nobody should act in such a way as to destroy their own happiness, in Aristotelian terms, to prevent their own flourishing. However, G.E.M. Anscombe, in her essay 'Modern Moral Philosophy' written in 1958, suggested that the central error of existing moral theories is that they fail to take into account the importance of consequences in thinking about morality. She coined the term 'consequentialism'.

Aristotelian ethics fell by the way as Western philosophers sought to find rational grounds for morality and became increasingly tied to liberal notions of individual autonomy and free choice. But recently there has been a revival of interest in Aristotle who is most strongly associated with virtue ethics. It is to a fuller examination of these ethical theories that we now turn.

Introducing Ethical Theories

Any course or module on social work ethics and values will inevitably involve some introductory consideration of the different ethical theories that inform debates and discussion. The ethical approaches most commonly referred to in social work values and ethics texts come from the dominant moral theories in Western philosophy mentioned above. These can be divided into naturalistic theories, i.e. theories that try to find their base in human nature, and in human needs and interests – Aristotle's approach – and those that are non-naturalist, i.e. those that try to find transcendent or universal principles based on notions of what is right and good – the approach of Immanuel Kant.

Non-naturalistic ethical theories

Non-naturalistic ethical theories see ethics as transcendental and objective, i.e. they exist independently of human nature. Plato's philosophy typifies this approach. The most influential theory in this mode for social work comes from Kantian ***deontology***, in terms of which ethics involves acting out of a sense of duty or obligation. The professions have tended to follow this approach, which is why so much attention is paid within social work to its role – purpose or mission – in society. Once this is decided then codes of ethics are devised comprising professional obligations, rules and principles which all social workers are duty-bound to follow.

As we will see in the opening part on professional perspectives, respect for persons and individual autonomy expressed in the principle of self-determination are central to social work, and flow from a particular deontological and Kantian view of the individual as possessing rationality or the ability to reason and make their own choices. In most situations social workers would do their utmost to preserve and facilitate the client's right to self-determination, their purpose being to allow clients to make their own choices to the maximum extent that the situation and their competence permitted. The social worker tries to create an accepting context so that clients can exercise their own judgement and initiative whenever and wherever practicable.

In Western society, the right to self-determination expresses the conviction that people should be in control of their own destinies. Hence people's rights to make their own decisions and choices are the cornerstone of the liberal moral framework to which democratic Western societies – and the profession of social work – are committed. This right to self-determination is the key to other rights and privileges, such as confidentiality, informed consent, freedom from interference, and privacy. Since clients have the right to self-determination, the implication is that they should be encouraged to exercise this right, that they are responsible for their actions and for the realization of their desired goals. In fact, in social work decisiveness is applauded and indecision is frowned upon. However, the notion of self-determination is not without controversy. Perlman (1965) saw it as a myth, describing it as 'nine-tenths illusion, one-tenth reality' (p. 410). Hollis (1966) saw it as an 'unfortunate choice of words, implying ... an oversimplified notion of autonomy and self-sufficiency' (p. 95), believing that self-direction was a better term because it denoted the capacity to guide oneself, rather than absolute independence. For Spicker (1990), self-determination is impossible to reconcile with what social workers actually do. Although social workers try to be non-directive, in reality they cannot avoid influencing their clients. Social work intervention is partly a process of social influence which involves guiding clients in making appropriate choices, based on the Kantian belief that they have the right to choose and are capable of choosing for themselves. However, in the real world this is not always so. There is considerable agreement that social workers invariably exercise implicit or explicit control over their clients. Nevertheless, social workers constantly search for ways to avoid a heavy-handed approach and to reconcile themselves to the use of their professional authority.

The social work literature can leave you more confused than enlightened about the meaning of self-determination. Those authors who try to understand self-determination in relation to what social workers actually do in practice fail to acknowledge that because practitioners are not guided by their values this does not discount the importance of holding such values. The fact that our values seem to bear little direct relevance to social work in practice does not negate their importance. A moral stance which proposes that people ought to be allowed the freedom to choose is better than one which says that social workers have the right to manipulate and control clients in accordance with their professional knowledge, understanding and expertise in dealing with human problems. Without these guiding values people would become objects prey to the whims and fancies of social workers. It is precisely because social workers occupy positions of power and status that they need values which prevent them from exploiting clients. Understanding about the nature of their authority can help social workers appreciate the degree of influence which they have and values can guide them to use this influence in a moral rather than a paternalistic and manipulative way (Timms, 1983).

The notion of authority – and control – raises questions concerning 'conflicts of valid responsibilities' (Clark with Asquith, 1985, p. 41). As we will see in Chapter 1, in terms of existing ethical codes, social workers are responsible to society, to employers, to the profession, to their peers or colleagues, to clients, and to themselves. Potential problems and dilemmas arise when responsibilities, interests and demands conflict. The profession exerts powerful pressures towards social conformity. The social worker is expected to act responsibly by respecting relevant social and professional norms. In reality, professional autonomy denotes freedom to move within the boundaries of conduct legitimated by the profession and society, as shown in Chapter 3. A heavy-handed use of authority results in paternalism and manipulation, which Timms (1983) termed 'disvalues': 'Disvalues ... are those that actively indicate situations that ought to be positively avoided by social workers' (Timms, 1983, p. 46). Manipulation denotes a heavy-handed use of authority whereby clients are unwittingly led in certain ways by social workers who may believe that they are acting in their best interests. Ultimately, then, self-determination is a safeguard against the inappropriate manipulation of clients.

Self-determination typifies the strongly individualistic bias in social work values, which are often assessed in terms of their utility. The profession favours values that can be operationalized, i.e. that can be easily translated into ethical principles, rules or guidelines in keeping with its strong deontological leanings. Less emphasis is placed upon developing moral sensitivity and understanding. Hence, as we will see in Chapter 17, Biestek (1961) was one of the earliest writers to develop what Timms (1983) called the universalist 'list approach'. But as the chapters of this book show, we have developed way beyond this narrow approach to values and ethics in social work, embracing *inter alia* issues of social justice and rights, anti-discriminatory and anti-racist practice, religious and spiritual perspectives, and moral and political philosophy as we attempt to demonstrate the intrinsic nature of morality.

Naturalistic ethical theories

Naturalistic ethical theories come from Aristotle's attempts to base the conditions needed for human flourishing, the ultimate end of morality, in fundamental truths about human nature. For Aristotle science could tell us the facts about human nature and 'moral philosophy must answer to empirical facts about what makes people thrive' (Kristjánsson, 2007, p. 1). Both worked alongside politics, which was concerned with the kind of society needed for human flourishing. As we mentioned above, the theories of ethics which concern themselves with ultimate purposes are called 'teleological'.

Teleology derives from the Greek word *telos* and is concerned with ultimate ends or purposes. Teleological ethics hold that all things are designed for or directed toward a final result, i.e. that there is an inherent purpose or final cause for all that exists. As we saw in Aristotle's ethics, he holds that humans are directed towards *eudaimonia*, or human flourishing. Importantly, 'Aristotle's *eudaimonia* is a radically moralized notion; it is impossible to achieve *eudaimonia* without being morally good – without actualizing the moral virtues' (Kristjánsson, 2007, p. 15).

Utilitarianism is a form of consequentialism (see below) concerned with 'maximizing the good', i.e. giving precedence to decisions and actions which bring the greatest good – and the least harm – for the largest number of people. As in a democracy, majority interests count.

Consequentialism is a teleological theory which places importance on the consequences of our ethical actions or decisions. Consequentialism is usually understood as distinct from deontology, in that deontology derives the rightness or wrongness of an act from the character of the act itself rather than the outcomes of the action, and from virtue ethics, which focuses on the character of the agent rather than on the nature or consequences of the action itself.

Virtue ethics comes from the philosophy of Aristotle in terms of which morality stems from human character which is built by following the virtues. In terms of Aristotelian ethics, moral education is important and, through emulating the virtues, we can inculcate good habits into the young. In virtue ethics, a good act is one that ensues from the good intentions of the actor, i.e. the virtuous person, and virtuous acts are most likely to produce moral outcomes and lead to human flourishing. It is often claimed that virtue ethics, developed in Chapter 10, offers an alternative way of thinking about ethics than that based solely on reason and rational decision making (see Phoca & Wright, 1999). However, Aristotle, the founder of virtue ethics, saw reason as the primary intellectual virtue and believed that it was in our nature to have the ability to use our faculty of reasoning to discern a way of life in accordance with our human nature. For him, morality works with human nature, not against it, so he does not focus on the idea of free will, so important in Christian and Kantian ethics. He does not talk, e.g. about morality involving being in rational control of the emotions but seeks a fusion of head and heart: Aristotle implicates emotions in moral virtues because for him 'emotions have a cognitive component that is amenable to rational and moral evaluation' (Kristjánsson, 2007, p. 18) ... 'an emotional reaction is potentially an intelligent reaction, open to rational persuasion by the ... moral educator' (p. 19). Aristotle proposes 'a highly moralistic vision of human well-being ... [and was a] great believer in scientific order and rational explanations' (Kristjánsson, 2007, p. 7). For him, morality was not about devising and conforming to rules, but more about learning to cultivate a moral life. For Aristotle virtues are fixed character states: we could be trained to see in a moral way, to be sensitive to and aware of morality and its overriding importance. Virtue theorists, following Aristotle, suggest that philosophers should concentrate more in what makes good people and good societies.

A neo-Aristotelian ethics is focused very much on examining the kind of society needed for people to live full and meaningful lives. It fits well with social work's approach to human rights and social justice (see Chapter 13). It flows from a focus on fundamental *human* interests and needs. It fits well with social work's view of itself as a profession which helps people achieve their full potential, i.e. which helps them to actualize their capacities. This naturalistic ethics then asks what kind of structures and institutions are needed in society for people to realize, fulfil or actualize their potential. These concerns are very different from the questions of non-natural ethics, like Kant's deontological ethical theory, which 'depict ethics as something transcendentally pure and uncontaminated by the world of human desires' (Phoca & Wright, 1999, p. 124) and searches for universal rules and principles. Virtue ethics represents a different way of thinking in social work which has focused heavily, as we shall see in Chapters 1–5, on developing ethical principles and codes and rational ethical decision-making models – revolving around the client's right to self-determination – rather than on what it takes to be a good social worker who automatically does the right thing in the right place at the right time (Kristjánsson, 2007).

The difference between these three ethical theories tends to lie more in the way moral situations are approached than in the moral conclusions reached. For example, a consequentialist may argue that lying is wrong because of the negative consequences produced by lying, though a consequentialist may allow that certain foreseeable consequences might make lying acceptable. A deontologist might argue that lying is *always* wrong, regardless of any potential 'good' that might come from lying. A virtue ethicist, however, would focus less on lying in any particular instance and instead consider what a decision to tell a lie or not tell a lie said about the person's character and moral outlook.

Why Are Ethical Considerations Important to Social Work?

A book on ethics and value perspectives in social work is inevitably also a book about morality. We know that there are very different and competing ideas about the moral condition of humanity. For example, in the seventeenth and eighteenth centuries it was believed that moral agency consisted in being subject to a divine natural law and carrying out duties imposed by such law. God was the moral legislator. Rights were only regarded as derivative, being a mere means to the fulfilment of celestial duties (Haakonssen, 1996). By the beginning of the nineteenth century this perspective had been chipped away at with a subjective theory of rights gradually emerging. The morally autonomous individual, with rights, has risen from the vestiges of these competing ideas. Today, for many, it is the modern State and the individual conscience that are the joint moral legislators. For over 150 years social work has been keenly concerned with this untidy mass of things that relate to morality: moral decision, moral reasoning, moral character, and moral action, to name just a few. Morality has expanded its frontiers through its deployment in social work and has, to a large extent, claimed sovereignty over certain corners of social work discourse. 'Duty', 'rights', 'ought', 'virtue', 'justice' and 'good' are a few examples that spring to mind. Indeed, we can confidently claim that the moral life of individuals and societies has preoccupied the history of social work and is likely to continue to do so. True to its characteristically critical function, social work never rests content with an acceptance of prevailing norms and standards or values. It seeks to scrutinize these norms, to examine whether they are consistent and coherent, and to see how far they can be rationally justified. Social work is intimately concerned with what is considered to be good and evil, right and wrong. What is the relationship between the ethical principles we are encouraged to adopt in social work and personal values or self-interest? What connection is there, if any, between how we ought to behave as professional practitioners and how society regards individual morality? These are some of the fundamental issues with which social workers have been characteristically concerned and will continue to remain so.

But how did social work get involved in all of this talk about ethics, morality and values? To paraphrase Freud's observations on morality for social work, we can say that while morality 'is within us' as a social work profession it has 'not been there from the first'. In other words, it has a history and one that reflects the changing nature of the history of moral philosophy and the societies in which it is articulated. We can locate the preoccupation with ethics in British social work to the mid-1860s in the early pioneering work of the Charity Organization Society. This was a particular mixture of moral idealism that combined notions of the 'common good' for society and the moral character development of the individual with value sentiments of compassion and benevolence (Webb, 2007). Social work in late nineteenth-century Victorian England was fashioned distinctively against the background of moral, scientific and aesthetic outlooks. If morality is historically shaped it is likely to produce fashions and trends as well as orthodoxies. It constructs a normative ethical order and tries to establish a self-evident set of moral dispositions. This is one reason why we have 'codes of ethics' in social work that are taken as self-evident universals for the profession. 'Respect for persons' is one obvious example of the orthodoxy at work. To give a starker example, it is unlikely that you will come across a social worker who openly admits to adopting Machiavellian tactics in her work with service users. Values are created, some are legitimated and authorized, and others are repudiated with some remaining silent.

If morality changes over time there is also something that is stubbornly persistent about certain assumptions made in relation to the values it endorses, for example, the idea that a life worth living is one that necessarily involves self-reflection and critical scrutiny. This old adage holds as much today as it did for Socrates in Ancient Greece. We moderns embody the classical Socratic tradition of self-scrutiny as a continuous flow of asking and answering, of searching for meaning and understanding in experience. What is most important in the process of self-examination and crucial to the way we live our lives, is the fact that we may hold our desires and emotions, our motives and aspirations, in check. That is, we subject them to a form of moral scrutiny. Why we do this is one of the most challenging things that philosophers and historians have tried to grapple with. There is no obvious answer why a conscience or moral self-examination kicks in. Perhaps this is because forms of moral scrutiny are complex and multi-layered. What is most evident is that there is no one such thing called moral reflection. Richard Wollheim (1984) makes a compelling case for taking a pluralistic approach to ethics and values. He does this not because there is a wide variety of perspectives on values or a diversity of ethical standpoints. Rather, for Wollheim, it is because of the very nature of morality in our modern times. He says that the 'alleged unity of morality ... is a rationalization, a piece of secondary revision' (p. 197). In part he blames moral philosophy for this rationalization of a single discursive entity, as 'ethics', claiming that it has failed to recognize the richness of our moral sensibilities and how they are lived and enacted in their everydayness.

Professional ethics idealize morality by trying to give it clarity, a sense of purpose and cohesiveness that it often lacks. We, too, in social work must be careful not to make the same mistake by prescribing 'bleach-effect ethics' that are professionally sanitized in the regulatory claims made on the morality of the social worker. Clearly, tolerance has a very important role to play in all of this. Indeed, the very idea of the 'professional social worker' may militate against this tolerance in requiring a straitjacket set of dispositions and endorsing only a narrow set of behavioural competencies. When educators say that the better 'professional social worker' is 'A rather than B' this tends to be a narrow judgement. It implies that, for *all* purposes, A is better than B. It is our contention that the recent development of controversial

'Codes of Conduct' in UK social work hardens these narrow regulatory perspectives and is in fact much more to do with risk management strategies than professional ethics (Webb, 2006; see Chapter 3). Social work educators need to remain open and flexible about what constitutes the dispositions of a professional social worker. Are we prepared to accept, for instance, that the values a social work student has about, say, the excesses of social injustice towards minority groups, and which she has taken from a book – perhaps a very good book – in which all the arguments have been persuasively made, just may be no part of her morality, even though they are certainly values of hers? Are we also prepared to accept as routine that there is no single value perspective in social work but many, and there is no one ethical framework but a multiplicity of often competing perspectives?

In some important ways, this book critically engages with some of these tensions and complexities. It starts from the assumption that morality is not learnt or inherited and, if it is anything at all, it is an achievement. Secondly, because we have referred to value perspectives in the plural we are implying that values are historically contingent, elastic and context-bound. However, the contingency of values very much depends on the time scale we are talking about. As we have indicated above, some values are extremely persistent while others are more transitory. Nevertheless, we would wish to claim that values are not objective properties of people or institutions, nor are they simply subjective constructions, but instead are the complex effect of numerous interacting forces that belong to systems of appropriation and enrolment that are distributed as the 'circulation of goods' (Smith, 1988). You only have to think about the enormously varied critical reception to Salman Rushdie's *The Satanic Verses* since 1988 to understand the contingency of values. Professional social work values are no exception to this rule in that they are culturally derived (Gray et al., 2008). When faced with the contingency of values in social work, one has to acknowledge that an evaluative response is required which, though difficult, complex, interfered with, obstructed by ideology and never quite pure, is still worth pursuing. It is worth the battles and the difficulties because it is about something important in social work. We wish to applaud a form of critical engagement that takes value conflict, and what we call moral evaluations, as a starting point, then asks what is actually involved in the practice of social work values in professional contexts. It is this formative professional response to ethics and values that we turn to in Part I.

Part I
Professional Perspectives

Professions are shaped by the social and political realities of their time and by the societies of which they are part. Their orientations and practices are reflections of the prevailing ideologies and values of the greater society in which they are embedded. Ideological shifts in society lead to a re-evaluation of professional values and practices. Over the years, a diversity of 'value perspectives' has influenced social work practice but, perhaps the dominant or overriding focus – the *professional* ethical perspective outlined in Part I – was set in train in 1915 with Abraham Flexner's address to the US National Conference on Charities and Corrections: 'Is social work a profession?' His announcement that to be a profession social work required, among other things, its own scientific knowledge base, educational programmes and professional code of ethics set in motion a sequence of events out of which the social work's professional ethical system emerged.

As we discover in Chapter 2, social work's professional ethical perspective emerged with the first code of ethics developed in the 1920s. Today part of the paraphernalia of rational choice inheres in codes of ethics, codes of conduct and ethical decision-making frameworks, as we see in Part I on professional perspectives. Today social work increasingly has to contend with these rational–technical devices *sans* their moral and philosophical underpinnings since the study of moral philosophy has all but disappeared from the social work curriculum. In Chapter 2, Elaine Congress draws attention to the range of core values that underpin social work ethics but also demonstrates how codes of ethics – as modes of professional regulation – serve as a guide for practice and assist in the resolution of ethical conflicts.

Paul Webster in Chapter 3 shows us how, more recently, professional codes of ethics have been supplanted by codes of practice – also called codes of conduct – which herald an administrative legal approach to the regulation of individual conduct within the workplace, with separate codes for employers and employees, though the former are in place mainly to control the latter. One might see codes of conduct as attempts to bolster professional regulation, and to enforce disciplinary regimes in the workplace to ensure compliance. Thus codes of conduct trump codes of ethics. Here we might learn from Foucault in recognizing the relationship between ethics and power from a sociological perspective.

In Chapter 4, Donna McAuliffe shows how rational ethical decision-making frameworks, which feature prominently in the literature on social work ethics, work in conjunction with professional codes of ethics. McAuliffe writes that social work promotes various models of ethical decision-making in its literature on ethics and proposes that, no matter how many models, using different theoretical and conceptual foundations and structures and forms, are advanced, ultimately, the making of a decision is up to the individual social worker, who has then to be able to justify and live with that decision, often in the face of opposition. If social workers do not have a well-integrated and conscious awareness of their own individual decision-making patterns, and the forces that impact on this, and do not understand the importance of honest and critically reflective practice, then no number of models will make much difference.

In Chapter 5 Stefan Borrmann, based on empirical analysis, develops the argument that ethical choices are often complex and involve moral dilemmas where several courses of action are open to the social worker, none of which is any more or less right or wrong. He discusses the various consequences that moral dilemmas have for front-line practitioners who are expected to weigh up and balance a number of often competing courses of action.

One of the distinctive contributions Part I makes with the inclusion of Chapter 6 on faith-based practice is to draw attention to the potential tensions between professional codes of ethics and spiritual values. Implicit with the concept of professionalism is the connotation that the social worker must set aside personal values and interests in order to meet the ethical responsibilities attached to professional roles. Indeed, social workers who fail to put aside their personal life are often accused of being unprofessional or lacking a prerequisite professional distance that may bring about a conflict of interest with service users. For example, a social worker who is both a professional practitioner and a believer in, say, Islam or Christianity is potentially caught between two competing ethical perspectives. On the one hand she is required to adhere to a set of professional codes of ethics that are formalized and socialized in her professional training and, on the other, a non-formal set of beliefs or values that form part of her faith. The faith-based approach to social work inevitably raises questions about the relationship between religion and secular professional ethics, which have persistently engaged in criticism of particular religious practices, just as religions criticize secular practices. From here we can begin to construct a practical model that provides for a positive relationship between secular professional standards and faith-based religious practices.

2
Codes of Ethics

Elaine Congress

Key Concepts

Professional values are a particular grouping and ordering of values within a professional context. In social work such values tend to focus on human functioning, capabilities and development.

Codification is the process of collecting and restating the mandatory elements of a jurisdiction in certain areas. It involves the translation of ethical rules and principles into prescriptions for practice.

Ethical codes: in the context of a code that is adopted by a profession or governmental organization to regulate that profession, an ethical code may be styled as a code of professional responsibility that makes practitioners accountable. Codes are general guiding principles for professional practice.

Introduction

Since the Hippocratic Oath provided a standard of practice for physicians, professions have seen codes of ethics as important. Professional work, however, usually began with practice experience while, later, professional bodies codified principles to guide practice. Each country has had its own unique experience in developing codes of ethics for social work. In the US, the 1915 Flexner Report indicated that social work was not a profession because, among other things, it lacked an ethical code. This led to the drafting of the first US social work code in the 1920s by a chapter of the (North) American Association of Social Work, which preceded the National Association of Social Workers, based in Toledo, Ohio. The process of code development has been similar in many countries around the world, with social work practice usually predating codes of ethics. Professional social work associations in some developing countries are still in the process of devising codes of ethics for their social workers.

This chapter examines the rich tapestry of codes of ethics in social work. It comprises three parts. The first focuses on key concepts and the difference between values and ethics, and ethical codes, the core values of social work and their universality. The second provides an overview of the social work literature on the nature and purpose of ethical codes and the relationship between codes of ethics and laws. The third discusses codes of ethics around the world, including the International Federation of Social Workers' (IFSW, 2004) Ethical Statement of Principles, and the British (BASW) and US (NASW) codes of ethics, and examines commonalities between codes of ethics from different countries, the strengths and limitations of ethical codes and their future relevance.

Key ideas

From the social work literature, it is clear that often we use the terms social work values and ethics interchangeably despite their difference in meaning. Congress (1999) defines *values* as the 'relatively enduring beliefs of the profession' (p. 3) about what is right and correct, while she sees *ethics* as values put into practice, i.e. the behaviours that follow from our beliefs about what is right and correct (see also Timms, 1983). As US social work educator Helen Harris Perlman (1976) noted, our values have limited meaning unless we translate them into ethical practice. Most *codes of ethics* comprise general value-based statements of principle to guide professional practice. They have varying degrees of enforceability. In a few countries, and in most US states, government-issued licenses for social workers require adherence to the social work code of ethics based on social work's core values. These include respect for persons, self-determination, confidentiality, social justice, human rights, professional integrity, non-discrimination, and cultural competence (Abbott, 2002; IFSW, 2004).

Social work's core values

For the most part social work's core values convey an aura of certainty about what the profession stands for, but they belie controversy in their interpretation and application by practitioners in particular circumstances. More recently, the values of non-discrimination and cultural competence have been added to Biestek's (1961) and Timms's (1983) original lists of values comprising respect for persons, self-determination, individualization, confidentiality, and a non-judgemental attitude (now broadened to non-discrimination).

With the influence of critical theory, human rights and social justice were added to the social work repertoire and, as issues of professional malpractice began to surface, so too did the notion of professional competence and integrity. Most social work texts on values would include some or all of the following core values and principles in social work.

Respect for persons

The literature on social work values and ethics, including codes of ethics, usually express respect for persons as respect for the worth and dignity of the individual or the uniqueness of the individual, and the principle flowing from this value is individualization. It relates to self-determination and the belief in client autonomy (Timms, 1983; Webb & McBeath, 1989; Gray & Stofberg, 2000).

Self-determination

A core social work value is upholding the client's right to self-determination, i.e. the client's right to choose based on the belief that humans are rational beings able to choose for themselves (Biestek & Gehrig, 1978; Levy, 1983; Perlman, 1965; Spicker, 1990). It leads to a rational approach to ethical decision-making in social work with individuals choosing among options, which has led to criticism from those cultures with collective rather than individualistic value systems (Ejaz, 1991). Its converse is paternalism (see Reamer, 1983).

Confidentiality

An important ethical principle is that of maintaining client confidentiality (Collingridge et al., 2001; Rhodes, 1986; Timms, 1983). It assumes overwhelming importance in the US code of ethics but can be waived when there is perceived risk of harm to self or others. However, from an international perspective, many countries and cultures have differing views on issues of confidentiality. Confidentiality is not individualistic, but collective in many African and Asian countries (Gray et al., 2008; Healy, 2001). Differing beliefs of migrants on confidentiality quickly become evident in social work practice in the US (Chang-Muy & Congress, 2008; Congress & Lynn, 1994) and elsewhere (Gray et al., 2008).

Social justice

Despite lack of consensus about its meaning, the international definition of social work affirms social workers' duty to promote social justice (Rhodes, 1986; Solas, 2008). Social justice features prominently in the Canadian (CASW) and the Australian (AASW) codes of ethics. The US (NASW) code mentions it in relation to individual clients, while the New Zealand (NZASW) code proposes a dual focus in which social workers help clients find individual solutions, but at the same time work to change the structure of society.

Human rights

For some, human rights are more universal than social justice (see Chapter 13). According to Wetzel (2005), national and local cultural differences lead to a varying focus on human rights from country to country. For example, teaching about human rights is a recent addition to the US social work education curriculum (Congress & Healy, 2006; Mapp, 2008; Reichert, 2006; Perez-Koenig & Rock, 2001). In the NASW code of ethics, a concern for human rights only appears in the concluding section on responsibility to society (Ife, 2008).

Professional integrity

At all times, the profession expects social workers to conduct themselves in a professional manner in accordance with the standards of practice enumerated in the code of ethics. Professional integrity – or professional competence, e.g. the Australian code – is central to many codes of ethics, which stipulate the core characteristics and actions required of social workers. Some codes speak of the importance of agency conditions that support professional integrity, i.e. the Canadian code of ethics explicitly states that, 'If a conflict arises in professional practice, the standards declared in this Code take precedence' (CASW 1994, p. 7).

Non-discrimination

The earlier value of non-judgementalism, i.e. not prejudging clients based on prior preconceptions is – following the influence of anti-oppressive practice and feminism – now conceptualized as non-discrimination or tolerance of difference. In earlier conceptions of social work values, the principle of acceptance expressed this value in a positive way (Biestek, 1961; Timms, 1983). But unlike the connotations of 'acceptance of difference' in anti-oppressive or culturally sensitive practice, acceptance in its original use meant acceptance of the client as a human being with dignity and worth (see Chapter 17 for an understanding of the roots of this value in Christian humanism). Today, most codes of ethics have a provision about non-discrimination in terms of class, religion, race, gender, sexual orientation, age, ethnicity, culture, economic status, political beliefs, disability, and so on. The NASW code of ethics recently added migrant status in its anti-discrimination clauses. Similarly, the Australian code includes a section on preventing and eliminating discrimination based on national origin, race and culture (AASW, 1999, S4.1.2b). The Australian code makes a distinction between 'negative discrimination' that serves to prejudge people or treat them in a way that disadvantages them because of their background and 'positive discrimination' or affirmative action that gives formerly disenfranchized people preferential treatment in accessing needed resources. The

Australian code mandates against negative discrimination but condones positive discrimination when client's needs are compromised. An example of this might be the Australian social workers' advocacy for reconciliation and reparations for Indigenous people who have, historically, endured the most economic and social discrimination (AASW, n.d.; Briskman, in Gray et al., 2008).

Cultural competence

Since 1996, the NASW code of ethics has had a policy on cultural competence that mandates the development of cultural sensitivity – defined as awareness of cultural differences – in working with clients from a different background from that of the social worker concerned. Despite the fact that social workers have always worked with diverse populations in the US, the NASW only added this provision in 1997. The recent increase of anti-immigrant policies and practices has contributed to the inclusion of a provision about immigration status (Chang-Muy & Congress, 2008).

The universality of social work values

Despite debates from some quarters, a lack of empirical evidence on their universal applicability, for the most part, the social work profession regards these values as universal. Ann Abbott's (2002) landmark study examined the professional values of social workers in four different parts of the world, namely, the US, Asia, Europe, and Australasia. She grouped social work's values into four categories: respect for human rights, social responsibility, commitment to individual freedom (which she defined as social justice), and self-determination. She found that social workers shared two common values, namely, respect for basic human rights and self-determination. The Australasian sample, though small (n=29), showed the highest commitment to all four values. More recently, Dominelli (2004a) found that an overwhelming 96 per cent of social workers believed in maximizing self-determination and 72 per cent in promoting social justice, but a disturbing 16 per cent believed that social work values did not 'underpin their practice' (p. 163).

Overview of the social work literature

The nature and purpose of ethical codes

There is some agreement in the social work literature that codes of ethics serve several purposes. Among other things, they (1) provide a set of ethical standards for social work practice; (2) guide practitioners in resolving ethical dilemmas in practice; (3) protect the public from incompetent practitioners; (4) ensure professional self-regulation rather than governmental control; and (5) protect social workers from litigation (Congress, 1999; Dolgoff, Loewenberg, & Harrington, 2009). Although there have been some attempts to make code of ethics more easily translatable to practice – either by the addition of a special supplement to the code of ethics (Reamer, 1998a) or the inclusion of a special section on ethical decision-making (AASW, 1999) – most continue to be general statements of principles. They do not offer much guidance about how to decide between the conflicting values or principles they outline.

Banks (2006) maintains that most codes are 'principle based as opposed to character based, with a greater emphasis on Kantian (deontological) rights and duties ... than on utilitarian principles' (p. 85). For her, this deontological approach seems preferable to a teleological, consequential approach if social workers want to avoid relativism, thus compromising their moral stance. However, there has been much debate on this (Webb & McBeath, 1989). For example, for a deontologist, a code of ethics that included consequential caveats to human rights provisions might become a slippery slope for serious ethics violations. In reality, however, most code provisions include some exceptions, as for example the National Association of Social Workers (NASW) Code of Ethics (1999), which makes confidentiality an absolute value except when there is a perceived danger to the self or others. However, the whole idea of the application of codes of ethics and ethical decision-making as portrayed in social work is to – rationally – weigh and measure the consequences of our actions, to maximize good, and reduce harm, which is inherently a utilitarian ideal (Gray & Lovat, 2007, 2008; Robinson & Reeser, 2000; McBeath & Webb, 2002).

Relationship between codes of ethics and laws

A fundamental difference between codes of ethics and laws is that the latter are more enforceable. In many countries, social work practice is not licensed. Thus, codes of ethics are not legally enforceable legal documents. Even countries that license social work, like the US, Japan, and England, often do not base licensing laws on social work associations' codes of ethics. Hence, the provisions of ethical codes are usually not enforceable except among members of a professional association. Professional associations often have a means to adjudicate members who do not abide by their codes of ethics but, unfortunately, many social workers are not members of professional associations and some do not have the resources for this policing activity. An interesting consideration is how laws and ethical codes are related. At times, laws and ethical codes may be similar, while at other times there may be an ethical provision but no corresponding law. A third possibility is that there is a law but no ethical mandate, and a final option is that laws and ethical principles, as laid out in codes of ethics, may conflict. An example of the first occurs when both laws and ethical codes have statements about confidentiality, while in the second scenario social work codes forbid a particular practice, such as dual relationships with clients, but there is no corresponding legal provision. A third situation may occur when laws lay out the qualifications for social work practice, but qualifications are not included in codes of ethics. The fourth is often the most challenging, but an increasing reality in democratic countries with conservative leadership. A current example of this increasing conflict are the regressive laws regarding migrants, while social work codes stress the importance of non-discrimination, respect, and self-determination for all people.

Application to social work practice

There has been ongoing debate about the utility and relevance of social work codes of ethics, and as to whether social workers use codes of ethics in practice (Congress, 1992; Congress & Gummer, 1996; Jayaratne, Croxton, & Mattison, 1997; Holland & Kilpatrick, 1991; Kugelman, 1992; McAuliffe, 1999; Walden, Wolock, & Demone, 1990. Congress (1992) found that US social workers knew about the NASW code of ethics and applied it in making ethical decisions. Walden et al. (1990) found that social workers often made quick decisions without much attention to the code of ethics. Holland and Kilpatrick (1991) found that social workers did not use the code of ethics when dealing with ethical issues. Kugelman (1992) found that 'although cited, the code of ethics was not used in any organised or systematic fashion' (p. 75). Jayaratne et al. (1997) found that while social workers might be aware of the major provisions of the ethical code, such as avoiding sexual contact with clients, they knew less about, and were less likely to adhere to provisions pertaining to non-sexual dual relationships, especially with former clients. McAuliffe (1999) found that Australian social workers, although relatively familiar with the Australian code of ethics as 'a useful construct in laying down the basic values of the profession' (p. 19), did not use it when confronted with ethical dilemmas. For the most part, practitioners do not use the code of ethics in practice because they have difficulty with translating its abstract ethical principles into concrete decisions and actions, especially when faced with challenging ethical dilemmas (Congress, 1993; Reamer, 1998a).

Codes of ethics around the world

The IFSW Ethical Statement of Principles

The IFSW is an international professional social work organization with member associations from 84 countries. Its website includes codes of ethics from 18 countries in three official UN languages, namely, English, French and Spanish (IFSW, 2004). Most are from developed Western countries, where English is the dominant language or a strong second language.

The first part of the IFSW Ethical Statement of Principles includes the international definition of social work followed by a section on International Conventions, such as the Convention on Human Rights. It affirms the profession's core values, stating explicitly that social workers promote human rights and social justice. The second part outlines what constitutes professional conduct and lists several ethical challenges. These include loyalty to ethical prescriptions in the face of conflicting interests and functions, e.g. as helpers and controllers, conflicts between the duty to protect clients' interests and organizational – and societal – demands for efficiency and utility, and difficulties with meeting clients' needs in the face of limited social resources.

The British code of ethics

First developed in 1975, the British Association of Social Workers (BASW) code of ethics sets forth primary objective to make the ethical principles implicit in the practice of social work explicit to protect clients and other members of the society (Banks, 2002; BASW, 2002). Commentators, like Rice (1975) and Watson (1985), have emphasized the ethos of codes to 'create the spirit and standard of ethical reflection in ... [the] community' (Rice, 1975, p. 381). The British code of ethics cites five main values: human dignity and worth, social justice, service to humanity, integrity, and competence, and provides a detailed discussion of each. The practice section outlines social workers' responsibilities to service users, the employing organization, and the profession and in different roles, including manager, educator, independent practitioner, and researcher.

The NASW code of ethics

The issue of confidentiality receives a great deal of attention in the US code with the largest number of provisions, possibly because US social workers are more likely to be engaged in full- or part-time private practice than social workers elsewhere. Further, a detailed, explicit code of ethics is a safeguard against malpractice litigation. A large number of charges for code violations involve violations of confidentiality (Strom-Gottfried, 1999). There has been ongoing concern that the US code is too litigious without sufficient focus on other social work values. Since many social workers are engaged in psychotherapy – or clinical social work – the US code also emphasizes the importance of the client–worker relationship. In striving for concreteness, it includes a number of practice-specific scenarios, especially relating to private practice. Since social workers enter into a fiduciary relationship with their clients, they must act in a trustworthy manner (Kutchins, 1991). They must maintain appropriate professional boundaries to avoid harming and exploiting vulnerable clients. The US code has detailed provisions on dual relationships, which occur 'when social workers relate to clients in more than one relationship [whether] ... social, business, or sexual' (NASW, 2008, p. 15). With respect to sexual dual relationships, the code advises social workers to avoid sexual relationships not only with current clients, but also with former and future clients.

Other codes of ethics

Most codes are concerned about cultural differences. For example, the BASW code refers to cultural sensitivity and the US code views cultural competence as ethical practice. However, the New Zealand code is unique in that, while it does not include a focus on diversity, it does contain a Bicultural Code of Practice that supports Māori people's rights to independence. It advises social workers to support the role of the extended family and each Māori client's entitlement to a Māori worker. While there are codes from particular racial or ethnic groups, such as the South African Black Social Workers' Association code, it is not and has never been the official South African code. National professional social work associations develop most codes but, in the case of South Africa, the quasi-government Council of Social Work, which the South African Council of Social Service Professions (SACSSP, n.d.) replaced in the 1990s, devised the official code – for many years the one-page Code of Conduct.

Similarities and differences across codes

In her study of codes of ethics from 31 countries, Banks (2006) noted that there was great variability in length, with the 27-page US NASW (2008) code being the longest. While some countries have maintained approximately the same length and content for a number of years, others have changed significantly in size and content. There has been a tendency for countries to develop lengthier and more detailed codes of ethics over time. An example is the US code that grew from a one-page document with 14 aspirational statements in 1960 to 28 pages with 160 provisions in 1999, the last time the association revised the code. Depending on length, there was much variability in detail. Some relates to practice issues in the country concerned, e.g. in the US the focus on private practice led to specific provisions on advertising and fees. However, Banks (2006) also found many similarities in values and principles: Most codes began with a general statement of principles or values with common themes of respecting the unique value and dignity of each person, promoting self-determination, working for social justice and against discrimination, and maintaining professional integrity. The second part often focused on ethical principles or standards. For example, the NASW code begins with a declaration of seven core social work values, including service to humanity, social justice, dignity and worth of the person, importance of human relations, integrity, and competence, while the values identified by the Australian code of ethics are human dignity and worth, social justice, service to humanity, and competence. Both the basic concepts and terminology is similar possibly because many countries draw on the IFSW Statement of Ethical Principles or codes from other countries for guidance in developing their codes of ethics.

Congress and McAuliffe (2006) compared and contrasted the US and Australian codes and found that confidentiality receives much more emphasis in the former than the latter. The US NASW code has 18 provisions on privacy and confidentiality, while the Australian code has only seven. Collingridge et al. (2001) perceived confusion between the terms privacy and confidentiality, noting that in the US code, confidentiality was mistakenly elevated to a first-order ethical principle, while for Congress and McAuliffe (2006), despite overemphasis in the NASW code on confidentiality, the fundamental principles were privacy and respect for persons. The Australian code includes a provision that social workers must take into account the client's culture in terms of how the client wants her to apply confidentiality. This is especially important with regard to the self-determination of Indigenous people (Thorpe, 1996). Indigenous communities take a much broader view of the involvement of family and significant others in an individual's welfare (Gray et al., 2008). Nevertheless, difficulties in balancing professional and cultural demands remain (Bennett & Zubrzycki, 2003).

Another point of difference relates to conflicts of interest. Australian social workers are advised 'to set and enforce explicit, appropriate professional boundaries to minimize the risk of conflict, exploitation and harm' (AASW, 1999, p. 12). Similar to the US code, the Australian code advises social workers not to become sexually involved with current or former clients since 'a professional relationship invites trust and confidence in the practitioner role [and] ... involves an unequal distribution of power or authority in the social worker's favour' (AASW, 1999, p.12). The Australian code advises social workers to seek consultation before entering into a sexual relationship with a client. Neither the Australian nor the US code has any statute of limitation about sexual relationships with former clients, unlike the American Psychological Association (APA) or the Australian Association of Psychologists (ASAP), which have a two-year statute of limitation.

Sonnenberg (2003) explored differences between the English and German codes of ethics and found variability in approaches to values within one country, rather than between countries. Nevertheless, the English code had a greater emphasis on anti-discriminatory practice than the German code. In England, as with social work codes in other countries, some have argued that codes of ethics have become increasingly irrelevant, while others have taken the approach that they are particularly important now that there are so many threats to the social work profession. New public management focuses on technical skills and codes of conduct (see Chapter 3) rather that professional ethics. This could compromise the social worker's personal and professional autonomy and moral commitment. For Banks (2006), a code of ethics is an important part of the social work tradition. It provides opportunities for ongoing debate and discussion. Hence, she moves the focus of codes from guides to practice to avenues for dialogue and debate, as Rhodes (1986) did much earlier.

Conclusion

Codes of ethics are important for all professions. They provide a common frame of reference for social workers all over the world and a vehicle to enhance the profession's status. The common values of human rights and social justice, as articulated in codes of ethics and the IFSW Ethical Statement of Principles, set forth the mission of social work. Because of the intricacies and complexities of practice, codes of ethics, by definition, must be general. Translating general principles into daily practice is not easy. At times, the values themselves are in conflict. There are exceptions to most of social work's trusted values. For example, social workers can waive confidentiality when it poses a threat to their well-being or that of another person, as in the case of impending suicide or homicide. Promoting human rights may also present an ethical dilemma, as when one person's rights jeopardize those of another.

Many countries continually review their code of ethics in an effort to expand their detail and specificity. However, there is little evidence that codes of ethics reflect cultural differences or keep up to date with societal trends. For the most part, their focus is individualistic rather than community oriented. As many countries, but especially the US, have become more litigious, there is an increasing trend to use the code to avoid legal action. In a challenging economic climate, agencies are particularly concerned about the possibility of lawsuits. This has reinforced the view that the code is primarily a legal defence rather than a statement of moral principles by which social workers should conduct their professional life. With an increasing number of social workers in private practice in the US and a subsequent increase in the number of civil and criminal actions against private practitioners, the expansion of the NASW code in recent years has focused on private-practice concerns, such as registration, licensing and fees. This contrasts with codes in other countries. Thus, says Banks (2003b), codes have a broad purpose in describing social work practice within particular countries.

Brill (2001) sees codes of ethics as 'windows into [our] ... profession' (p. 223), but in modern-day practice, there are increased sources of guidance for social work on ethical issues, such as agency policy, procedural manuals and codes of conduct, national and international conferences, and expanded information available on the internet. To some extent, there is a danger that codes of conduct might supersede codes of ethics (see Chapter 3). In the final analysis, an ethical code can only do so much in articulating the core values and ethical principles of our profession. The onus is still on social workers to engage in a process of ethical decision-making based on the values and ethics of their profession (see Chapter 4).

Study Questions

1. What is the relationship between social work values and ethical codes?
2. What ethical codes should guide social work practice – IFSW Statement of Principles or national codes? Do they complement or contradict one another?
3. Is the social work code of ethics in your country compatible with the sociocultural values of your country, the social workers who live there, and the clients you serve?

3
Codes of Conduct

Paul Webster

Key Concepts

Codes of Conduct are statutory, regulatory measures that attempt to standardize practice. The difference between a Code of Ethics (discussed in Chapter 2) and a Code of Conduct (discussed in this chapter) lies in the locus of control. While a Code of Ethics is professionally based, a Code of Conduct is a statutory instrument.

Risk regulation: Codes of Conduct are risk-regulation standards. They are processes that attempt to avert risk and its consequences. The regulation is dependent on three processes: information gathering, behaviour modification and standard setting.

Disciplinary practice: Developed by French historian Michel Foucault, this term refers to institutional systems (e.g. schools or the Church) that monitor human behaviour through specific practices or rituals of surveillance, e.g. confessionals and examinations. In modern societies, Foucault argues that techniques are used to extend disciplinary practice to self-reflexive monitoring, e.g. diet and health.

Introduction

This chapter examines the concept of a Code of Conduct using the English General Social Care Council's (GSCC) regulatory code and statutory registration as an example. The compulsory registration of social workers in the UK is seen by some as a means of protecting standards, promoting the profession and embedding social work values. However, as Joan Orme and Gavin Rennie (2006) point out, the relationship between registration and regulation is not uncontentious. There is an 'anti-ethical' tendency in all codification, and this is exacerbated in a political environment that seeks to regulate the behaviour of those involved in the delivery of social care services. In effect, a code functions to control the 'street-level bureau-worker' (Lipsky, 1980) and works against professional autonomy. Reprised by Kathryn Ellis (2007) for social work provision, Lipsky's street-level bureaucratic framework also has some salience for social work ethics and codified conduct, which focus on individual (mis)conduct. Subjugation to a Code of Conduct has less to do with professional ethics and more to do with defensive and defensible practice. One might place a Code of Conduct at the extreme end of a continuum of ethical practice, with professional autonomy at the opposite side.

Though ethical codes *per se* – as basic lists of do's and don'ts – are seemingly not a bad thing, once deconstructed and politically located, a Code of Conduct is at best a precursor to ethics proper, i.e. the moral domain, since it marginalizes the practitioner's autonomy to engage with a practice of value. The difference between a Code of Ethics (see Chapter 2) and a Code of Conduct lies in the locus of surveillance and control. The former is professionally based and seeks to create a self-reflective 'insider' space for ethical deliberation, while the latter is statutorily driven and privileges 'outsider' scrutiny and external regulation and control. Karen Healy and Gabrielle Meagher (2004) document the insidious processes of deprofessionalization created by the routinization and technicalization of social work tasks. From a broader social policy perspective, Carole Smith (2004) notes the shift from old-fashioned, unconditional civic trust in professionals by society to a contractual confidence in public systems of accountability. The latter foregrounds institutionalized conditional confidence in regulatory systems, but this comes with some burdensome transaction costs imposed on the individual practitioner, reshaping moral identity. The codification of this process marks a subtle transformation from engagement with ethical desiderata to conformity with service standards, between what Richard Hugman (2003) calls acting well and acting correctly.

Key ideas

At the heart of social work lies a moral impulse towards the other. Its apex is in due care and minimum control of those in need. Social workers listen to the inner voice in incessant moral talk. The professional quest is for 'doing things properly' – *eupraxia* – in the 'comforting of the stranger' (Webb, 2006). A Code of Ethics should stitch together *eupraxia* – good conduct – defined as competent practice and the individual practitioner's moral voice in the promotion of care, compassion, justice and desert. To do so is to behave with professional integrity. The same aim could be said of a Code of Conduct. However, we may ask whether it is really about cultivating our moral impulse, ethically caring for and about distressed others in their fateful moments, or is it really just about the practitioner being prudent, risk-aversive and pragmatic? Defensive practice is not necessarily ethical practice (Orme & Rennie, 2006).

Elsewhere in this book, competing perspectives on ethical theory are offered. This chapter makes a connection between a Code of Conduct and what are referred to in moral philosophy as deontological – duty-based – and consequentialist – consequence-based – ethics. These are the cornerstones of all Codes of Ethics. So too with a Code of Conduct, but this has much more to do with external regulation of the social worker than with the care or protection of the client. Codes are a mixture of deontic duties and desired outcomes or consequences, which are given effect through the moral agency, motivation, disposition or 'character' of the individual practitioner. The deontological approach gives rise to a 'principle-based ethics' and paints a picture of professional ethical procedure as a rational, deliberative, deductive process of applying moral propositions or rules. This works in tandem with a consequentialist ethics wherein the moral agent tries to anticipate the consequences of applying particular principles or rules in any given situation. It is a predictive formula which presupposes that cause and effect are eminently controllable.

Chris Clark (1999) employs a 'lighthouse' metaphor to understand a code, likening it to a homely beacon which serves as a guide. As we saw in Chapter 2, this is generally how codes of ethics are viewed in social work. But a Code of Conduct carries with it a metaphor of surveillance and control, with the light beam firmly aimed at individual conduct rather than the needs and interests of clients and their significant others. A Code of Conduct has to do with trespass and transgression, and this divests it of its protective force. Behind every positive injunction to do something good lies a prohibition not to do something bad. All codes define failure and errant conduct as much as critical pathways to success or appropriate practice.

No matter how prescriptive it might be, a code of ethics cannot tell us what to do when we are faced with ethical dilemmas and must allow for some professional autonomy in deciding what it is best to do. But such latitude is absent from a Code of Conduct where we are basically tied to 'doing what we are told' by a disciplinary or regulatory regime. Hence, a Code of Conduct simply and forcefully tells us what we must and must not do. Once the choosing between and among options is removed, its ethical 'ethos' or ethical character is lost and replaced by 'consuetude', i.e. simple conformity and obedience to what's given. Simply being obedient offends our professional sensitivities and invokes connotations of unquestioning compliance and docility, but this is what a Code of Conduct demands of us. A liberal-humanist code of ethics struggles with this conflation, wrestling individual conscience with social mores and a universal professional ethics. Hence, for a Code of Conduct a searchlight metaphor is still appropriate but, unlike the welcoming beacon of a lighthouse, patrol-like, it sweeps the profession for infractions.

Social work is a socially mandated role charged with delivering a public bundle of distinctive ethical goods and services, which carries with it a particular deportment. This requires a preset array of professional habits, attitudes, commitment, behaviour and competence. The antithesis is misconduct or the 'failure to perform [this professional] ... role in conformity with relevant scientific and ethical standards, whether through negligence, incompetence or corrupt intent to secure an illegitimate advantage' (Clark, 2007, p. 60). A Code of Conduct, then, involves not guidance and direction, but instruction, even compulsion and coercion, along a 'straight and narrow' path.

Overview of the social work literature

Many have argued that ethical theory, which privileges deontological and consequentialist approaches, has failed social work. They invoke a revised radicalism in the call to revitalize personal commitment and reawaken our moral responsibility as ethically charged practitioners. This approach calls into question the efficacy of codification as a construct for decision making. Transformative theoretical perspectives highlighting this 'attribution error' are supported by research findings, such as those of Amy Rossiter et al. (Rossiter, Prilletensky, & Walsh-Bowers, 2000), that codes of ethics are not much use. Indeed, they are not used in practice at all.

Most of the more code-specific theoretical literature predates the practical experience of state-regulated conduct and mandatory registration. The GSCC's code was published in 2002 and registration commenced in 2003. However, it should be noted that, due to poor take-up, most social workers did not register until 2005, when it became compulsory. Frederick Reamer (1998a) provides a historical overview of the evolution of social work ethics climaxing in their codification, portraying this as a positive step and hallmark of professional maturity and recognizable status. Others have focused on the changing context of work, the drive towards measurable performance-managed technical skills, the restructuring of welfare services, fragmentation of provision, privatization and the new consumerism, all of which are seen to undermine the more fluid, tacit claims of professionalism in the pursuit of protection of the public and those agencies which serve the public. There are several examples from the mainstream whose insights have continuing relevance to the 'professional maturity' versus 'proletarianization' debate (Banks, 2006, 2008a; Beckett & Maynard, 2005; Bowles et al., 2006; Clark, 1999; Hugman, 2005).

While not expressly focused on regulated conduct, two indicative texts worth highlighting are Richard Spano and Terry Koenig's (2007, 2008) dialogue with Paul Adams (2008), demonstrating how a code of ethics is just the starting, not the finishing line for a value debate. The one set of protagonists argue that a dogmatic personal world-view can be used to reinterpret a code, but should not, since a code is meant to provide a screen through which personal world-views must be drawn to determine their acceptability in social work practice. The other protagonist argues that a code itself is a particular dogmatic kind of orthodox world-view that discourages open discussion and suppresses dissenting opinion. Banks (2008a) makes a plea to avoid the piecemeal and simplistic application of moral philosophy to social work ethics in order to break out and move beyond the framing of 'difficult cases' in terms of a 'code mentality'. Broader social policy and agency agendas also need to be interrogated as a precondition of transformative practice and committed personal ethical fluency. The suggestion is that not to do so is to collude with the powers that be and the imposed given.

Aside from official publications, updates, press releases and regular but parochial commentary in the trade press, there has been a dearth of GSCC-specific literature. Orme and Rennie (2006) offer a critical comparison of the introduction of registration in Scotland (essentially the same as the GSCC's in England) and New Zealand, examining the motivation behind these moves. Echoing Stephen Webb's (2006) analysis of social work and the 'risk society', Kenneth McLaughlin (2007) argues that the stated GSCC intention of protecting the public, improving the quality of care and increased public confidence in the profession disguises the increase in regulatory control over the workforce, creeping intrusions that have met with little criticism to date. He notes that risk and its management are at the forefront of contemporary social policy: the underlying sentiment is a climate of fear and distrust in which there is a tendency to view people, whether client or social worker, as either vulnerable, dangerous or both. This risk-aversive regime has penetrated social work education.

Reid (2007) complains that social work lecturers are under pressure by their own institutions as a prerequisite of tenure to register with regulatory bodies and, through an analysis of ethical teaching norms, ponders whether the price is too high. Malcolm Cowburn and Peter Nelson (2008) explore the tensions of managing social work student admission procedures, safe recruitment, selection decisions, and social justice, offsetting them against disclosures of criminality.

Application to social work practice

McLaughlin's (2007) baseline claim, which captures a growing caucus of concern, invites further consideration. There are, at present, just a few relevant albeit small-scale empirical studies and surveys (for example, Community Care Special Edition, 2008; Meleyal, 2009), illustrating just how much is still to be garnered in order that speculative theorizing can be grounded in practitioner realities. As we saw in Chapter 2, there is already a 'binding' code of ethics in social work comprising about 125 value statements and principles for any social worker who voluntarily subscribes to the British Association of Social Workers (BASW, 2002), the professional organization in the UK. Now we also have a state-regulated code that foregrounds conduct. The employment of familiar language may overlap but its underlying meaning and purpose are quite different. One benign definition of regulation is that it is a sustained control exercised by a public agency over activities that are valued by the community. Less benignly, it is a process by which standards are set and enforced by bureaucrats who are somewhat aloof from those who are being monitored. Not benignly at all, regulation engineers external behavioural restrictions to prevent, or at least punish unwanted outcomes by those deemed unruly. As an adjunct to regulation, at this level a Code of Conduct becomes a technology of control for the regulator on behalf of the state.

One key theme to extrapolate from this perspective is that the centralizing risk-aversive political climate has become increasingly interfering and manipulative. It heightens governmental concern to monitor and control social work, questioning its legitimacy and credibility, dismissing traditional modalities of accountable self-management and substituting its own intrusive instrumentalities. It gives short shrift to a self-regulating professionalism, as not even a complementary adjunct so much as a failed irrelevancy. The notion of perfectly ethical social work, which a code of ethics elusively seeks, is supplanted by a notion of perfectly safe social work, which a Code of Conduct is determined to control through the emission of predictive text. The purpose of a Code here might be seen not just as an attempt 'to create constraints on professionals' behavior' (Spano & Koenig, 2007, p. 13) but more a blunt 'ideological enforcer' (Adams, 2008, p. 6). The official GSCC Code of Practice requires that all social workers must comply with it on pain of admonition, suspension or deregistration. The GSCC Code, with only 68 or so prescriptions, easily trumps the BASW Code of Ethics, not so much a double-indemnified identity as a kind of moral schism for those who are subject to both. We should pause to interrogate what this means for a practice of value.

The GSCC's compulsory registration and its concomitant Code of Practice has been in existence for some time now. The GSCC regulates through compulsion, force of law and the trappings of judicial process, around 96,000 qualified social workers and students in England who must comply with the provisions of its Code of Conduct. As the official verse goes, all social workers need to be registered, meeting standards of training, suitability and commitment to high standards. Registrants must:

- Protect the rights and promote the interest of service users and carers.
- Strive to establish and maintain their trust and confidence.
- Promote their independence while protecting them as far as possible from danger or harm.
- Respect their rights while seeking to ensure that their behaviour does not harm themselves or other people.
- Uphold the public trust and confidence in social care services.
- Be accountable for the quality of their work and take responsibility for maintaining and improving knowledge and skills.

They are accountable for maintaining these standards of conduct to the GSCC. Action can be taken against social workers who fall below these standards or who are not suitable to hold the responsibilities of being a social worker. Decisions are taken to protect the public interest and the 1.5 million or so people who use social care services.

It should perhaps be noted that this code of practice is a code about malfeasance, the identification of conduct which fails to follow statutorily determined injunctions. Each standard is broken down into exact prescribed enumerated behaviours. These list simple statements that purportedly describe professional conduct and the practice required of social workers in going about their daily work and their personal lives outside of their work. All this is expressed in the catch-all duty not to behave in a way in work or outside work which could call into question suitability to work in social care services (5.8). Quite a few are expressly about work procedures. So, for example, a social worker must:

- Follow risk assessment policies and procedures to assess whether the behaviour of service users presents a risk of harm to themselves or others (4.2).
- Adhere to policies and procedures about accepting gifts (2.7).
- Comply with health and safety policies (3.6).
- Maintain clear and accurate records as required by procedures established for their work (6.2).

The do's and don'ts, many of them quite banal, such as being respectful, reliable, honest, non-exploitative and non-neglectful, should be familiar enough to all social work practitioners and students in England and elsewhere. They are intended to confirm the professional standards required in social work and to ensure that social workers know what standards of conduct employers, colleagues, service users, carers and the public expect of them. Registrants are reminded that they should use the Code to examine their own practice and look for areas of improvement (GSCC, 2002).

Consider some relevant data for the period 2003–8 regarding non-compliance: Two hundred and fourteen people have been refused registration following declarations related to criminal convictions, health conditions or work-related disciplinary matters. Since the first conduct hearing in 2006, in the space of just over two years, 33 hearings took place, with 14 being removed from the register, three suspended and 16 receiving an admonition (GSCC, 2008). As a proportion of 96,000 registrants, it might be concluded that the actual number 'in trouble' of some sort at any given time is statistically insignificant. However, the level of scrutiny from all quarters is high. On the one hand, as a legally binding contract every social worker must accept and renew it at every moment while, on the other, the social worker who violates its precepts breaks the contract. Forty complaints about registrants are received on average each month. Very few of these end up being processed for a possible misconduct charge but there is a steady diet of fully-blown cases. Impeachment, branding, banishment and expulsion motifs are played out through loss of protection of legal title and right to work.

It might be argued that the frequency and rigour of high-profile conduct hearings prove that the public, clients and society in general may have confidence in 'the system' to remove dangerous, unsafe practitioners, or those whose behaviour besmirches the reputation of the profession or the agencies in which professionals practise. Any code of whatever hue not backed up by meaningful sanction is surely impotent. A majority of misconduct cases has involved unacceptably naïve if not blatant transgressions of professional boundaries in forming inappropriate personal relationships with service users (5.4). The second most common has involved dishonesty, followed by gross incompetence or inexcusable carelessness in going about work. At the very least, the social worker 'ought to have known better', invoking powerful notions of moral hazard, disgrace, stigma and treachery. Usually, where a single injunction of the Code has been breached others have also: the pattern is for findings of multiple and related transgressions. Prompt and timely expressions of contrition and remorse or other mitigating factors may succeed in reducing the tariff.

Tales from the field suggest that there is broad approval from service users for an effective Code of Conduct. If anything, the demand is for better access, more punitive decisions and extra powers to curtail misconduct from social workers (Community Care Special Edition, 2008). Why, then, should any genuine social worker look askance? I do not wish to dwell on the obvious truism that what constitutes instantiation of particular misconduct is always going to be highly normative and hegemonic. Evidently, some so-called social workers should always be accompanied with a health warning and it is as well that someone is playing the ever-vigilant guard in search of transgressions. The critical point is that our social work bona fides are only a prerequisite for authentic moral engagement, not the engagement itself, and this distinction can get lost. By its very monological nature, a Code of Conduct is itself expansive and colonizing, liable to encroach on, usurp and squeeze out ethos or ethics proper. It demarcates the boundary of accepted practice and can become an all-encompassing, obsessive substitute for professional ethical discourse.

We might consider the view that a Code of Conduct, such as the GSCC's, is really a response to a particular type of moral panic, where that hallmark social work gaze is turned back upon the profession itself. In a worst-case, Kafkaesque nightmare scenario the custodian surveils and pronounces from its 'panopticon' – a circular prison constructed so as to allow prisoners to be observed at all times from any angle – such is the inescapable forensic scrutiny of a Code of Conduct. Regulated conduct is not just about external discipline to inculcate good habits and exorcize bad ones. It is also about enforcing behavioural predictability, ensuring that practitioners function within the narrow confines of prescribed behaviour. It might be said that 'good' social workers have nothing to hide or fear once they have learnt what is required of them. A Code of Conduct reduces or narrows the range of acceptable behaviour or conduct and once desired habits are learnt, they need only be repeated. It works on the principle that no thought is required other than to think obedience. In removing the need to wrestle with ethical complexities, it arrests moral development. A Code of Conduct isolates the workplace as a site of fractious misconduct and is served by checklists, formal processes, policies, procedures, rules, regulations and instructions. The problem is that workplace discipline and obedience as prescribed in a Code of Conduct is conflated with being ethical. The Code of Conduct becomes a surrogate code of ethics. Its usurpation of professional ethical identity is totalizing and meets with little resistance since codes of ethics, which might act as a self-righting ethical counterbalance, are not much use in practice at all (Rossiter et al., 2000).

No longer strong evaluators with a deep awareness of ethical complexities, today's practitioners caught in the moral panic induced by risk-aversive environments, clamour for guidance on 'what to do' based on step-by-step ABC approaches (Community Care Special Edition, 2008). We end up believing that we are all potentially at risk. On the one hand, Lel Meleyal (2009) reports how, from the outset, codified regulation closes down professional debate for fear of saying the wrong thing, for being different, or standing out. On the other hand, rather than draw attention to others' misconduct, many practitioners have revealed that they have remained silent to protect erring fellow employees even though this, in itself, constitutes misconduct (Community Care Special Edition, 2008). The Code requires that registrants must not condone unjustifiable or unlawful discrimination by service users, carers or colleagues (5.6) and that they must inform the appropriate authority where the practice of colleagues may be unsafe or adversely affect care (3.5). A culture of deterrence and fear of retribution leads to moral paralysis.

Conclusion

This chapter has argued that a Code of Conduct militates against a lively and expansive ethical environment in social work. By default it pathologizes and scapegoats erring individuals without acknowledging the harsh managerial practices, poor supervision or the impossible situations social workers often have to confront. Of late, a couple of practitioners have successfully defended themselves on these grounds, showing how a well-argued misconduct case can exonerate the defendant, especially if the employer can be shown to have been negligent. However, these are rare events. As the Code requires, frontline social workers are obliged to use standardized procedures to challenge and report dangerous abusive discriminatory or exploitative behaviour (3.2), yet no senior manager of a plaintiff authority has been found to have engaged in misconduct and been struck off for abusing or harming service users, carers or colleagues (5.1). On the McLaughlin (2007) premise, this is no surprise, since the regime targets frontline practitioners. In the absence of a safe, healthy climate for honest and open discussion, formulaic deliberations masquerade as moral practice and replace critical ethical discourse. A Code of Conduct may be a necessary feature of our unhappy landscape but it is not a sufficient condition for a true 'practice of value' (Webb, 2006, p. 200).

Study Questions

1. How far can any code meaningfully capture all that is involved in being a morally active practitioner and, if it cannot, what does it foreclose?
2. Is it inevitable that a code of conduct will trump a code of ethics? If so, is this due to inherent flaws in the very idea of codification of ethics or to other dynamics?
3. If an authentic ethical identity is ensnared and fixed by the technologies of regulated conduct, how might genuine ethical dialogue and a practice of value be generated?

4
Ethical Decision-making

Donna McAuliffe

Key Concepts

Ethical decision-making is the process by which social workers engage in an exploration of values – that may be evident in the personal, professional, social and organizational spheres – in order to establish where an ethical dilemma might lie according to what competing principles, and what factors take priority in the weighing up of alternatives.

Critically reflective practice is about evaluating one's own performance. It is an important dimension of an integrated ethical decision-making framework. It is developed through an exploration of pre-existing values, socialized value patterning and the influence of personal and professional experiences. Incorporating critical reflection into ethical decision-making requires the social worker to explore the moral realm to clarify issues to do with duty, responsibility, obligation and rights.

The moral continuum is the mapping of ethical theory and perspectives along a continuum that incorporates deontological through to utilitarian thought and highlights the place of virtue ethics, ethics of care, ethics of responsibility, discursive ethics and postmodern ethics.

Introduction

It is well established that social work is a moral endeavour that rests, often tenuously, on a foundation of values intrinsically embedded in frameworks of social justice, human rights and anti-oppressive practice. As we have seen in previous chapters, these values find their way into formalized documents, such as ethical codes, standards of practice and codes of conduct, which attempt to dictate appropriate ways that social workers should behave in carrying out their professional duties. Debates about whether values can be 'taught' continue to play out in educational circles and academic literature, as do questions about whether values are 'universal' or culturally relative and locally specific (Webb, 2003). Against this backdrop of social work as 'not value-neutral', it is equally well understood that social workers make ethical decisions all day, every day. So, too, it could be argued, do accountants, veterinary surgeons, parents, doctors, builders, florists, nurses, teachers, engineers and politicians. Decision making is part and parcel of life, yet the consequences of decisions are likely to be very different depending on the nature, impact and outcome of the decision, and whether there is potential for harm, oppression or injustice. It is the latter form of decision that concerns us in this chapter. Those decisions which have moral consequences are termed 'ethical decisions'. A florist's decision to put together an arrangement with colours that clash is not an ethical decision, even though it might make someone unhappy. But a doctor who decides to discharge an elderly patient to an unsafe home environment or a social worker who decides not to remove a child from an abusive situation is clearly making an ethical decision, i.e. one that will have moral consequences. Decisions which are ethical in nature, and which often sit within the professional domain, concern the moral realm when they involve questions about rights, duties, responsibilities and obligations. When someone's rights are violated, the potential for harm increases. When a person does not fulfil obligations or responsibilities, the potential for injustice to be caused to another is heightened. Social workers constantly deal with a complex array of ethical issues and questions which generate difficult ethical dilemmas (see Chapter 5) in a practice environment characterized by continuous and rapid change. Practitioners need to have robust, rigorous and efficient ways of making ethical decisions whether they do this 'on the run' or have the luxury of time for deliberation.

They then need to be able to justify these decisions. This chapter poses the question of what makes the decisions that social workers are often called on to make sufficiently complex or important to warrant the burgeoning literature on ethical decision-making models. Furthermore, what claims do those who write about ethical decision-making processes make about the potential for improvement of effectiveness of options and outcomes if a practitioner does follow the steps of a particular model? Decision making is largely presented by these writers as a rational or technical process, i.e. as a series of logical steps to follow to arrive at a predetermined or anticipated conclusion that will ideally be in the best interests of all concerned. It is the *ethical* part of the decision-making process that provides the wildcard, because every social worker and client carries with them heuristics, attitudes, beliefs and personal values that can sway the analysis of a situation in unanticipated directions. The mere act of making ethical or moral decisions is fraught with uncertainty. The central argument put forward here is that when social workers' subjective interpretations of events take precedence – and the final justification is the one that can best be lived with in accordance with the social worker's personal and professional values – ethical decision-making becomes no more than an exploration of many sides of a story, including that of the client. Ultimately, one hopes – but certainly not always – the decision is grounded in what is just and good on some rationally justifiable premise. This chapter traces the history of ethical decision-making as a distinct body of social work literature and maps its development as a professional practice skill. It challenges social workers to acknowledge the importance of critical reflection and honest appraisal of socialized value positions. A case study shows that what might be a clear path forward for one practitioner engaged in an ethical conflict may not be so clear for others, even when all hold common social work values. Comment is also offered on the teaching of ethical decision-making in social work education. Recommendations are given for the development of a broader perspective that focuses more on understanding the critical principles underlying ethical decision-making than on rigidly defined processes used to reach resolution of an ethical problem or dilemma.

Key Ideas

Social work is moving with the times and entering a period of increasing complexity as the globalized world experiences economic turmoil, environmental change and demographic movement, all of which are placing pressures on the health and welfare systems in which most social workers work. Social workers are at the forefront of many systems that face difficulty, such as housing, mental health and income support, and are well placed to provide practical assistance to individuals, groups and communities at risk of impending disadvantage. Many of the decisions that social workers have to make involve the movement of resources from one place to another, and the constant weighing up of what constitutes the 'greater good' and to whom this analysis should justly apply. Social work walks a tightrope between deontology being concerned with absolutist notions of duty and obligation on the one hand and utilitarianism being attentive to consequences and committed to maximizing benefits for clients, especially those who are socially excluded and marginalized, on the other. The moral continuum between deontology and utilitarianism, as commonly constructed in moral philosophy and ethical theory, has been further expanded by explorations of the feminist ethic of care (see Chapter 7), virtue ethics (see Chapter 10) and communitarian and rights-based theories (see Chapter 13). Being able to speak the language of ethics to justify their stance on particular moral and ethical issues has enabled social workers to engage more fully with colleagues from diverse disciplines and professions, and thus reach a shared understanding of professional ethics to facilitate ethical decision making. Bioethical principles, such as autonomy, beneficence, non-maleficence and justice (Beauchamp & Childress, 2001) also provide a common language and aid for ethical decision-making for social workers in health and welfare services (Freeguard, 2007). The critical point here is that moral philosophy and ethical theory provides an invaluable knowledge base that enlarges social workers' thinking on and understanding of moral issues; creates a dialogical space for debate and discussion with others; and enhances their ability to justify the ethical decisions they make.

The ethical foundations of social work provide fundamental principles that connect social workers across continents. For example, as we saw in Chapter 1, the IFSW statement of ethical principles seeks to provide a unified professional value position centred on the promotion of human rights and social justice. Guided by these ethical principles and a growing body of literature on social work values and ethics, social workers have a starting point from which to explore competing value positions. For example, self-determination and autonomy are often, particularly in health or mental health settings, overridden by paternalism; recognition of diversity is often overshadowed by rigid condemnations of lifestyles or cultural customs that are outside the 'societal norm'; resources are often distributed according to who can afford to pay, or who has been in a position of being able to contribute, rather than equity based on need; and the right to participation of people in decisions that will affect their lives is often relegated to a tokenistic effort aimed at appeasement rather than genuine acknowledgement of the value of lived experience. Against this backdrop, social workers engaged in ethical decision-making have an uphill battle in many practice contexts. This is why it is so important that an understanding of ethical theory and principles is combined with an honest exploration of prejudices, biases and religious and spiritual convictions, which could lead to judgementalism, stereotyping and intolerance (see Chapter 6). Such self-reflection must precede any attempt at developing a decision-making process to work through options and consequences of ethical conflicts and dilemmas. Ethical decision-making, I would argue, is empty of meaning without the necessary prerequisites of knowledge and self-reflection that should form a major part of social work education. Furthermore, if social work students and beginning practitioners do not have a very clear understanding of the concepts of professional accountability, cultural sensitivity, the importance of consultation, and well-developed skills in critical reflection, they will not have the platform on which to build sound decisions about complex ethical issues (McAuliffe & Chenoweth, 2008).

Overview of the Social Work Literature

The literature on ethical decision-making in social work and the human services, counselling and therapy, community practice and within organizations has significantly increased since the early to mid-1990s. Given that the period of the 1980s–1990s has been described as the 'ethical theory and decision-making period' (Reamer, 1998b), it is perhaps not surprising that social work academics, predominantly from the US, generated a number of ethical decision-making models during that decade. More recent contributions to the ethical decision-making literature from the UK and Australia have challenged some of the premises on which many of those models were based, and have broadened the scope of analysis to incorporate structural concerns and acknowledgement of issues of power (Asquith & Cheers 2001; Bowles et al., 2006; Clifford & Burke, 2009; McAuliffe & Chenoweth, 2008). Many attempts have been made to analyse the constructions of the plethora of ethical decision-making models available as they have significant differences in philosophical foundations and focus and are not easily categorized. Chenoweth and McAuliffe (2008) distinguish between process, reflective and cultural models in their 'inclusive model' of ethical decision-making in which they attempt to combine the best of the available models. They construct their inclusive model on the previously mentioned platforms of accountability, cultural sensitivity, consultation and critical reflection. In developing their 360-degree model Bowles et al. (2006) distinguished between rational-cognitive models; virtue ethics models focusing on the personal qualities of the practitioner; prescriptive models combining theories about duties, virtues and outcomes; and transcultural integrative models emphasizing the cultural dimension.

What is interesting as we look at the development and range of ethical decision-making models over time, is that the core elements of good decision-making processes lie at their heart. The essential steps that social workers are encouraged to work through to reach a principled decision are, in fact, very similar. Whether we are looking at the ETHIC model developed by Congress (1999), the highly reflective Mattison (2000) model, the feminist model for ethical decision-making (Hill, Glaser, & Harden, 1995), the 'tracking harms' (Robinson & Reeser, 2000) model, the determination of 'ethical traps' (Steinman et al., 1998) model or the transcultural integrative model (Garcia et al., 2003), we find a great deal of common ground. Even looking outside social work to ethical decision-making models from other professions, we see that the 'ethical grid' developed by Seedhouse and Lovett (1992) from medicine focuses on equal respect for persons, creation of and respect for autonomy, and minimizing harm. The 'comprehensive model' proposed by Miner (2006) from psychology emphasizes human well-being, duty of care, cultural inclusion and the importance of dialogue. In the field of business, it is recognized that ethical decision-making at an organizational level must take account of cultural factors (Robertson & Fadil, 1999). What is starting to happen in more recent times in social work, however, is an adding of depth to established models and an extension of the ways in which ethical decision-making must be relevant to context. Take for example one of the most widely cited texts on ethical decision-making in social work, originally developed by Loewenberg and Dolgoff (1988), whose controversial 'ethical principles screen' involves the rank ordering of seven principles. Despite the debate and uncertainty about the value of this model, the text is now moving into its ninth edition. A recent article by two of its authors, Harrington and Dolgoff (2008), published in *Ethics and Social Welfare,* addresses the issue of ethical hierarchies, and concludes that they are highly contextual, meaning that ways that social workers prioritize ethical principles will vary with circumstances and inevitably be influenced by their personal values. The authors clarify that their ethical hierarchy should be used only to stimulate debate. It is 'a helpful starting place for classroom or workplace discussions [and] ... it is constructive for social work educators, practitioners, and students to arrange their own priority listings of ethical principles' (Harrington & Dolgoff, 2008, p. 193). This is a significant move forward, since ethical principles cannot be given rank-order priority in the real world of practice. Every situation is different and each social worker has a personal value position, despite his or her professional values and ethics.

This brings us to the question of whether ethical decision-making models are in fact useful or more of a hindrance than a help. The literature certainly suggests that while some models are overly simplistic, excessively prescriptive or lacking in depth, there are valid reasons for continuing to develop decision-making models. They give students and practitioners a starting point from which to develop their own more integrated decision-making processes with time and experience. As Banks (2008b) points out, 'while ethical decision-making models often seem mechanistic and artificial – more suited for use in the classroom than the home, street or social care institution – they do help raise awareness of the myriad factors and perspectives involved in any professional decision' (p. 7). She goes on to say:

> the development of new critical models is important: [The profession needs] models that move beyond simplistic, rational deductive accounts of moral reasoning; that take account of the co-constructions of issues and problems; that leave room for emotional and culturally sensitive responses; and encourage reflexivity on the part of professionals to see themselves as engaged participants rather than neutral and impartial decision makers. (p. 7)

Clifford and Burke (2009) believe that, while ethical decision-making models have their place, there is a need to incorporate an 'anti-oppressive approach to ethics ... [It] is an obligation which should be embraced regardless of any specific decision that may be required or indeed of any specific problem that may arise' (p. 185). What we are seeing in the progression of literature, then, is an adding of layers to the core, meaning that social work is embracing a much more complex analysis of ethical decision-making than mere reliance on the simplistic reductionism often seen in earlier models. It is this complexity that we must grapple with as we move to explore how an ethical decision-making process could be applied to practice.

Application to Social Work Practice

Ethical decision-making is a process by which a social worker arrives at an option for action (that may also include inaction) on the basis of a weighing up of information, exploration of values (personal, professional, social and organizational), and investigation of relevant laws, protocols, ethical codes and cultural viewpoints. A decision ultimately reached may depend on which way the balance tips in relation to logic, emotion, moral conscience or possible repercussions. This is why no two social workers can be guaranteed to make the same decision in a given case, and why there can be no predictable 'right' outcomes even if an ethical decision-making model were followed to the letter. The following case illustrates some of the ways in which these differences can play out.

> Danielle works in an agency that provides counselling services to families who have difficulties with parenting and relationship issues. The caseloads for staff are high, the work is complex and there is little opportunity for supervision of practice. Danielle has worked closely with another social worker, Rosie, for the past four years. They are close friends as well as colleagues, and enjoy a mutually supportive working relationship. Rosie lost her partner to an aggressive form of cancer six months ago. She has two small children, a high mortgage and little extended family support. She has been desperately trying to maintain control of her emotions at work, but has been feeling detached from clients and has begun to cancel appointments and avoid families that she finds too taxing. She has asked Danielle on a number of occasions to cover particular clients for her, and has taken many days off work, leaving other staff to manage her cases. Danielle has tried to help, and Rosie has pleaded with her not to let management know that she is not coping for fear that her contract will not be renewed. It is well known that management of this agency do not consider that staff should allow personal issues to interfere with their work, and there is little sympathy for anyone not pulling their weight in the team. Danielle is feeling stressed and is having difficulty sleeping. She lies awake at night worrying about her own, as well as Rosie's clients, and realizes that Rosie is not performing well at her job. She knows that these vulnerable families are not receiving quality service, and has to decide whether to continue to keep Rosie's confidence, or alert management to the problems in the interests of the welfare of the clients of the service.

The first question that must be asked is whether this is an ethical situation, and if it is considered so, what elements make this the case. Is this an issue that has anything to do with rights, duties, obligations or responsibilities? The clear answer here is that there are concerns about the rights of clients, the duties and responsibilities of staff and the obligations of management. It would be unlikely that it could be argued that this is not an ethical issue. An ethical problem this may well be, but the second question is whether this situation constitutes an ethical *dilemma*. The common definition of an ethical dilemma is a situation in which there are clearly competing principles at stake, one issue up against another, and there is no clearly defined course of action (see Chapter 5). Rothman (2005) terms this sorting-out of competing ethical principles an 'ethical dilemma formulation', which is a useful concept in the early stages of decision making. If there is a clear course of action, there is no 'dilemma' as such, even though the situation might well still have ethical dimensions. It is at this point, before we have crossed the threshold into ethical decision-making, that four social workers may reach two different conclusions (is this or is this not an ethical dilemma), based on four sets of reasoning.

Social worker A might very clearly look at this situation and immediately conclude that the competing principles are 'confidentiality (in relation to Rosie) vs disclosure (to management)'. Social worker B might look at the same situation and conclude that the competing principles are 'collegial relationships (in relation to Rosie) vs duty of care (in relation to clients)'. Technically both would be correct, and both would be unable to determine which principle to uphold, thereby placing them in an ethical bind. For these social workers, there is evidence of a dilemma that requires further thought. Social worker C might look at this situation and conclude that there is no dilemma. Support of colleagues, particularly when such a tragic event has occurred, is undisputed. Loyalty and confidentiality win out and there is no question of not continuing to support Rosie and manage the caseload demands as best as is possible, preferably covertly, given the management culture. After all, Social worker C knows what it is like to have been in a similar situation in the past herself, and has strong values about workplace support. Social worker D also sees no ethical dilemma here. There is no place for impaired practice in a service that deals with distressed families. Clients have a right to quality service and if this were not being provided, for whatever reason, management would have a responsibility to act. Therefore, Social worker D believes that Danielle has an obligation to report Rosie in the best interests of the clients of the service. It is not Danielle's responsibility to cover for Rosie, manage clients that are not part of her caseload, or keep secrets that impact on the functioning of the agency.

Social workers A and B have further work to do to reach a decision about maintaining the confidence of a colleague in the face of a hostile management, as opposed to allowing management to exercise a duty of care to clients through disclosure of the extent of Rosie's inability to perform her job to the best of her ability. At this point, the process-oriented, rational ethical decision-making models would guide the social workers in the direction of ethical codes that refer to the best interests of clients, issues in relation to impaired practice, limits of confidentiality, predominance of duty of care, and loyalty to the employing agency. What ethical codes also point to, however, are reciprocal rights of workers to receive support and supervision from managers who are cognizant of the stresses of practice, and collegial relationships based on trust and mutuality. In this situation, ethical codes may provide information, but may not point to a clear way forward. Some ethical decision-making models focus on legal parameters and the assessment of risk. What if a client were to take legal action as a result of poor service? What if Danielle were seen to be a contributor to Rosie's continued impaired practice by covering up the problems? What if the service were to lose funding as a result of unwanted media attention should it become known that clients were disadvantaged? At any of these points, social worker A or B could decide that the pendulum has swung in a particular direction, making what needs to be done quite clear.

The more reflective models of ethical decision-making would urge Danielle to discuss her ethical dilemma with Rosie, who is a legitimate party to the dilemma. The ethical dilemma might well be resolved at this very early point if Rosie were to hear the impact that her situation was having on her friend and colleague, and decide for herself that it was her responsibility to better manage this situation and approach management to seek support in her time of crisis. Feminist models of ethical decision-making would recommend active engagement of clients or legitimate others in discussions about the ethical dilemma where this is appropriate. Reflective models also encourage consultation with others who may have expertise, and require the decision maker to engage in critical reflection about past experiences that might invoke patterned value responses. The social worker who had personal experience of trauma that was not managed constructively by employers would perhaps be less likely to trust management responses to perceived impaired practice. The social worker who was held responsible in another agency for not providing supervision to staff might well have a different view on management's duties. Added to all of these factors are other issues that creep in to further complicate matters. What of Rosie's children and the impact on them should she lose her job, her income, or her house? What of the reputation of the agency in a competitive environment where ongoing funding is often tied to client feedback on service outcomes and quality? All of these issues would be considered and weighed up. Social workers A and B would reach a conclusion about what to do only after much reflection amid the complexity. They would ultimately reach a decision that they could live with should it reach the front pages of a major newspaper, or should they be held accountable to an ethics committee, or should they be called on to justify their decision to their employer or to the relevant authority.

Good ethical decision-making is principled rather than pragmatic. It is congruent with appropriate practice in that it empowers rather than discriminates. It exposes structural or power-based inequities, rather than entrenches oppressive systems and practices. It upholds the principles of social justice and human rights, and values accountability, transparency and integrity. The social worker who develops an integrated process of ethical decision-making is a practitioner who consults wisely, has an internalized understanding and healthy critique of ethical codes, holds knowledge from both theory and practice wisdom, and has a well-developed ability to engage in critical reflection. Ethical decision-making then becomes a part of the professional repertoire of skills that can be translated to any field of practice or any context of employment. The challenge for social work education is to assist emerging practitioners to consider these important elements of ethical decision-making as essential parts of their practice framework. Ethical practice is not tangential to, but rather an integral part of, the social worker's professional identity, i.e. the core of the social work 'self'.

Conclusion

This chapter has highlighted the importance of ethical decision-making as a key part of social work practice, given that social workers work daily with situations that involve the moral realm. Ethics has to do with the rights, duties, obligations and responsibilities of all parties to a situation and the social worker must learn to balance competing principles in order to arrive at decisions that are congruent with the values of the profession. The point has been made in this chapter that ethical decision-making models, of which there are many in the social work literature, do little more than lay out a technical process. It is the ability of a social worker to engage with contextual factors and complexity in a critically reflective way that moves decision making to a higher level skill built on a sound foundation of core values.

Study Questions

1. Do the ethical principles outlined by the IFSW provide a sound foundation for ethical decision-making, or are there other ethical principles that should be included?
2. What are the most important elements of good ethical decision-making, and on what basis should a decision ultimately be reached?
3. Do ethical decision-making models help or hinder social work practice?

5

Ethical Dilemmas in Practice

Stefan Borrmann

Key Concepts

An ethical dilemma is defined as a situation in which a social worker has to decide on a course of action in which the legitimate wants of one or more person are neglected because they are in direct opposition to another person's legitimate wants. If these competing legitimate wants are based on the same level of need, one can call it an ethical dilemma.

Intrinsic values are the natural health-giving properties of organisms, which are influenced by internal – physiological – and external – environmental – factors. They are not entities in themselves, but properties that vary under different conditions. These variations in the value conditions can be defined as human needs.

Moral spheres: There are three interdependent moral spheres: the private, the professional and the public. The private moral sphere is ruled by norms regardless of the person's role in society. The professional moral sphere is constituted by norms particular to each profession. The public moral sphere refers to matters of public interest involving rights and duties.

Moral realism is a theory which holds that there are true moral statements which report objective moral facts. Aristotle is a moral realist who believes that it is the job of moral philosophy to act on scientific facts about human nature.

Introduction

Social work is a value-based profession which deals with issues of extreme complexity. Since the problems confronting social workers are often complicated by the competing interests of those involved in particular situations, it is not surprising that ethical dilemmas are common in social work practice. Following on from Chapter 4, which examined ethical decision-making in social work, this chapter considers the nature of ethical dilemmas from a moral-realist perspective in relation to the three interdependent moral spheres in which social workers' ethical deliberations take place: the private or personal, professional and public or social (Banks, 2006; Bunge, 1989), all of which are contingent on the dominant social and cultural norms of the wider society. The private moral sphere is governed by social norms regardless of the person's role and position in society. The professional is constituted by norms particular to professions, which must be seen to be in the public's interest and cohere with the norms of the public moral sphere, i.e. social norms relating to the rights and duties of citizens. There is some disagreement, however, about how these levels interact:

> On the one hand, individualists are bound to claim that there is no difference between the three moral spheres because every moral norm regulates the behaviour of individuals. On the other hand, holists are likely to hold that professional and public morals hover above personal morals and are independent of the latter. (Bunge, 1989, p. 160)

Both positions – individualist and holist – contain some truth because they refer to individual behaviour. However, neither can bring all three spheres into a coherent whole unless individual rights are combined 'with professional and civil duties in such a way that performing the latter makes it possible for the former to be exercised' (Bunge, 1989, p. 160). MacIntyre (1985) maintains that a shared morality needs a mutually agreed-upon conception of human nature and the purpose of human existence. Without this there could be no agreement on the moral basis of society, no universal ethical principles and no way of finding common values. Moral philosophy seeks to find a rational grounding for ethics and to provide rational arguments for taking a stance on particular moral issues:

> Ethical arguments ... cannot be settled by an appeal to higher authority or any general conception of what is good or right. The arguments may be equally logical and valid in their own terms, but their basic premises – the points from which they start – are incommensurable, and there is no way in which the issues they raise can be settled within the term of conventional ethical debates. (Hugman & Smith, 1995, p. 9)

Here Hugman and Smith (1995) see ethical dilemmas as beyond the purview of rational deliberation. Even though ethical decision-making frameworks are very popular in social work (see Chapter 4), and might give the impression that there is a solution to every ethical situation, they cannot relieve social workers of the angst of making difficult ethical judgements, which necessarily confront their beliefs, decisions and actions and in which their personal values, moral beliefs, professional ethics and social norms necessarily play a significant role. This chapter aims to provide a framework for understanding ethical dilemmas and presents a case study to highlight their intractability.

Key Ideas

The literature on social work ethics offers several definitions of ethical dilemmas. Here are three examples:

> An ethical dilemma is usually defined as a choice in which any alternative results in an undesirable action. When, for example, we have promised confidentiality to a client, who tells us something that endangers others, we have an ethical dilemma. If we uphold the confidence, we may contribute to harming others. If we violate the confidence, we violate our trust. Whatever we do, we seem to be 'in the wrong'. (Rhodes, 1991, p. xii)

> An ethical dilemma may arise when a practitioner is faced with two or more competing values, such as justice and equality, or confidentiality and protecting life. (Dolgoff et al., 2009, p. 8)

> Ethical dilemmas occur when the social worker sees herself as facing a choice between two equally unwelcome alternatives, which may involve a conflict of moral values, and it is not clear which choice will be the right one. (Banks, 2006, p. 13)

Rhodes uses the phrase 'undesirable action', Dolgoff et al. 'two or more competing values' and Banks 'conflict of moral values' to refer to the nature of ethical dilemmas. How might our strong professional value-base help us find our way through ethical dilemmas? What role do professional ethical codes play? What moral theories might we draw on? Sarah Banks (2006) discerns two categories of ethical theory which have influenced approaches to values and ethics in social work: the first focuses on principles of action, including deontology (Kantianism), consequentialism, utilitarianism and anti-oppressive practice (see Chapter 12) and the second on the moral agents and their relationship with one another, including the ethics of care (see Chapter 7), virtue-based ethics (see Chapter 10) and postmodern ethics (see Chapter 11). The following approach of moral realism fits into the first category.

Moral realism

The leading idea of the ethical theory of moral realism is that values are grounded in human nature. People attach positive value to anything they need for their personal well-being and, primarily, for their survival. Therefore, human needs and wants are the root of values and the function of norms is to protect these needs. The 'good' and the 'right' are sometimes objective, as when they relate to biological needs, and at other times subjective, as when they pertain to psychological and social needs. However, judgements about what is 'good' and 'right' are always relative to people and their environment (Bunge, 1989). Mario Bunge's (1967, 1989, 1996, 1998) theory of moral realism was applied to social work by Swiss scholar Werner Obrecht (2001, 2005). He makes an important distinction between intrinsic and instrumental values and their link to human needs (Bunge, 1989; Obrecht, 2005). Beginning with *intrinsic values*, they are the health-giving properties of organisms, which are influenced by internal – physiological – and external – environmental – factors. They are not entities in themselves, but properties that vary under different conditions. A human need arises when there is a deviation from an organism's ultimate state of well-being, which is recognized by the central nervous system and motivates the organism to act so as to compensate for the deviation. *Human* needs differ from animal needs in that humans are capable of learning and self-conscious reflection and thus, over time, grow and adapt, developing new methods, strategies and plans to fulfil their needs (Bunge, 1989). There are three types of interdependent human needs: biological or physiological, biopsychological and biopsychosocial. To maintain their state of well-being, all these needs must be met. However, there is a hierarchy of needs with biological or survival needs, i.e. the need for food and shelter, as higher on the hierarchy than social needs, i.e. the need for social support (Maslow, 1943; Obrecht, 2005). Since needs are conditions of the organism, they are part of the human being's intrinsic make-up and, as such, are universal. All human beings have the same needs and have to obtain the resources necessary to fulfil their needs. The desire to satisfy needs is defined as a legitimate *want*. Everything that is helpful to satisfy human needs has *instrumental* value and is, therefore, legitimate. In many cases, these instrumental resources are closely connected to several philosophical values, such as the value of human life, social justice, non-discrimination, freedom, and so on, which are included in the manual of *Human Rights and Social Work* developed by the IFSW, IASSW and UN Human Rights Commission (United Nations Centre for Human Rights, 1994; see Chapters 12 and 13). They all have in common the onus they place on society to ensure the satisfaction of human needs, even though the ways in which different groups of human beings go about trying to meet their needs differs from country to country, social group to social group, and culture to culture.

What are the implications of Bunge's moral realism for social work ethics? The first implication is that human needs are universal and thus constitute an appropriate justification for ethical action: 'I acted to fulfil a human need.' Rights ensure that human needs are met. For Bunge, moral norms relating to the satisfaction of human needs and wants are essential for social coexistence and constitute legitimate grounds for the generation of human rights, which are limited only by the rights of others: 'every one of my liberties ends where someone else's begins: Your right is my duty, and your duty is my right' (Bunge, 1989, p. 103). Importantly, for Bunge, rights are tied to duties and human beings have a duty to promote the rights of others so as to enhance their well-being. This is a deontological, rights-based ethics which treats duties, obligations and rights as objective facts because they are universal. Everyone has rights, duties and obligations to one another.

In terms of the ethical theory of moral realism, ethical dilemmas can be defined as situations in which a social worker has to decide on a course of action in which the legitimate wants of one or more persons are neglected because they are in direct opposition to another person's legitimate wants. It tells us that when there are competing or conflicting interests, those involved in the dilemma must work together to decide what kind of human needs are involved. Contrary to Hugman and Smith's (1995) claim cited above that ethical issues defy logic, moral realism permits the ordinary rules of logic to be applied straightforwardly to moral statements. Legitimate wants based on biological human needs are more urgent to fulfil than the ones based on psychological or social needs. And in the same way that we would evaluate a factual belief we can say that an action is *false* or *unjustified* when it hinders someone from fulfilling their biological needs. But this is where the logic ends. In a situation where there are competing issues that are based on the same level of need and resulting legitimate want, where neither moral realism nor ethical decision-making frameworks offer a solution, we would be faced with an ethical dilemma.

Overview of Social Work Literature

The social work literature on ethical dilemmas can be categorized into four areas. The first includes literature on ethical dilemmas in social work in general, how they arise, what they are and how they are connected to ethical issues other professions also face (Banks, 2006; Hugman, 2005). The second area includes literature that describes ethical dilemmas in social work practice, including empirical research about the areas in which social workers are most likely to face dilemmas, such as confidentiality or conflicting interest with professionals of other professions (Borrmann, 2007; Linzer, Conboy, & Ain, 2003). But the vast majority of the literature in this area is about ethical dilemmas in certain fields of social work practice, such as AIDS and HIV (Reamer, 2001a; Silverman & Rice, 1995), case management or aged care (e.g. Larkin, 2007). The third area includes literature about how social workers *actually* deal with ethical dilemmas (Borrmann, 2005; Linzer et al., 2003; McAuliffe & Sudbery, 2005). This literature is often based on empirical research and does not necessarily involve a detailed discussion about how social workers *should* deal with dilemmas. This is the main focus of the final fourth area, which deals with what social workers actually can or should do when they are facing ethical dilemmas. The literature in this area includes various forms of ethical decision-making models (see Chapter 4) that follow a rational problem-solving framework. It also includes literature suggesting different critically reflective approaches to ethical dilemmas (e.g. Gray & Gibbons, 2007; Meacham, 2007).

Application to Social Work Practice

It is in the nature of a profession like social work, which has to deal with competing interests and complex problems, that ethical dilemmas arise (Borrmann, 2007; Linzer et al., 2003; McAuliffe & Sudbery, 2005). In 2005, while I was a visiting researcher at the School of Social Work at the University of California at Berkeley, I conducted an empirical study on ethical dilemmas in social work practice in the field of HIV and AIDS (Borrmann, 2007). All the participants in the study had been faced with complex ethical dilemmas. Most involved issues of confidentiality and privacy (68 per cent), followed by issues of self-determination, especially where clients lacked the capacity to make their own decisions (64 per cent) and conflicts between social workers and other professionals arose (56 per cent). The following case study concerns a female social worker, MSW, aged 40, working in a hospital. She had 15 years' practice experience, mostly as a clinical social worker. The department in which she worked provided medical and socio-psychological services to HIV-positive men, women and children. She herself worked exclusively with the 150 HIV-positive women in the clinic. However, many of them had children and, therefore, she also had to provide family-oriented services. As a social worker in an HIV clinic, it was her job to carry out psychosocial assessments, counselling, coordinating case conferences and advocacy in the community. She recalled a particular case.

We have an HIV-positive mother of a 10-year old child. The mother is probably going to die in the next year and her daughter has HIV too but she is doing well on the medicines. So the daughter is positive too, but does not know her own status and she gets her care here. Ten years old. She does not know her mother has AIDS or that her partner is HIV-negative. The three of them live together. As a social worker, I had to talk with her frankly about who would take care of her child when she dies. For years she refused to set up legal planning, because it requires the judge to ask the mother publicly to declare her HIV status so that the guardian understands the situation. So now we are trying to encourage her to disclose her status because she wants to appoint her partner. But she doesn't want to declare her HIV status because she is afraid he will reject her. If she does nothing and she dies, the child becomes a ward of the state. That's sorrowful for the child. So this is our problem. We think the best thing is: disclose the status, we will give you mental health support, family support, everything you need. We have the resources to help you, as a family, adjust to this information. Let's go to court, let's make it legal; it gives the child a sense of security. That's a very valuable psychological thing for this child. This is what everyone wants. Except for the patient ... We agreed as a team not to talk to the partner. And we are going to continue to work with her to persuade, educate, convert. I understand my role as a social worker to help the client understand the pros and cons of her decision. And I will give her my recommendation. I feel it is my responsibility. I cannot be completely neutral. I don't think it is ethically correct for me to just simply be objective: here are the pros, there are the cons, what is your decision? I believe it is my ethical responsibility to recommend what is best for the family.

How does this case example add to our understanding of ethical dilemmas? As already noted, from a moral-realist perspective, an ethical dilemma is defined as a situation in which a social worker has to decide on a course of action in which the legitimate wants of one or more people are neglected because they are contradictory to another person's legitimate wants at the same level of need. In this particular case, the legitimate wants, defined as the ways or the resources someone uses to satisfy their needs, refer to the psychosocial needs of the persons involved. This means that we cannot rank the want of one person higher than the others. And it is obvious that in the given situation the social worker has to make a decision. If she does nothing she would rate the confidentiality of her patient higher that than the child's or the partner's right to know or and, more crucially, the child's right to security.

There are at least four people involved: the mother, daughter, partner and social worker. The ethical dilemma concerns the conflict between the mother's desire not to disclose her HIV status and the needs of those close to her. She was reluctant to disclose her status, fearing that her partner would reject her. Thus far, due to her non-disclosure, she and her family had adjusted well to her illness. Her decision to keep the information to herself can be seen as a legitimate want. But the social worker believed that the mother's wants were overshadowing the child's needs. What should the social worker do? She clearly had a strong sense that she needed to do something to protect the child's interests to avoid her becoming a state ward.

The daughter, however, is in a different position. Since she is not aware of the facts regarding her mother's prognosis, she feels no immediate need to change the current situation, despite the mother's impending death. She believes she is part of a stable family and has no idea that she could become a ward of the state. It is highly likely, however, that the partner would seek custody for the child, though only after a protracted legal battle if the mother failed to make appropriate legal arrangements. The partner is in a similar situation to the child, and the social worker believes that his needs and interests must also be considered. Presently, he is being excluded from the decision-making process by the mother.

Mindful that confidentiality is a value, which generates tough ethical dilemmas in social work practice, the case could be clear from a legal perspective: the mother, not the daughter or the partner, is the client and the social worker must respect her desire not to disclose her HIV status. This is the mother's choice. Therefore, the social worker is obliged to maintain confidentiality. The social worker is, however, in a special situation, since she has a professional ethical obligation to make a decision that takes the interests of all involved into account. Interestingly, she has paid little attention to the norms the professional sphere provides for a social worker, i.e. the code of ethics:

> No. I don't rely on the Code of Ethics in a concrete way. Maybe I should. I don't know. I have a lot of confidence in my own ethical framework and I am familiar, also I have not memorized it, with the Code. And I have a lot of confidence in my colleagues' ethical conduct and framework. And so, maybe I should look more at the Code of Ethics but I don't.

Instead, she draws on her professional judgement and that of her (non-social work) colleagues that it is morally wrong to exclude the child and partner from the decision-making process. Furthermore, she thinks that she could help in her professional social work role in this particular situation. She continues to struggle with the dilemma, trying to find a way to support everyone involved:

> We think the best thing is: disclose the status, we will give you mental health support, family support, everything you need. We have the resources to help you as a family to adjust to this information.

But the social worker is bound to the ethical principle of confidentiality as long as her client desires this. Still the ethical dilemma remains ...

Conclusion

In contrast to the utilitarian or deontological approaches to ethics, moral realism can be helpful in identifying the inner logic of ethical issues and problems, some of which can be solved by deciding on what's right and in persuading the client to do the right thing. But this only applies to ethical issues in which legitimate wants relating to identifiable human needs are involved. In this chapter, we have examined the complexity of ethical dilemmas, which defy solution. Perhaps in such cases, there are no right answers, only choices (Gray & Gibbons, 2007). It is clear, then, that moral realism is most helpful in explaining how to resolve moral conflicts within a professional context. However, critics have suggested that it does not help explain how these conflicts arose in the first place. Social workers who face ethical dilemmas consistently in front-line practice might well have to make do with the golden rule articulated by Charles Handy (1994) that there are dilemmas that cannot be solved so much as managed. As we saw in the case discussed above, even though the social worker chose confidentiality over disclosure, the ethical dilemma remains.

Study Questions

1. What is the difference between human needs and legitimate wants?
2. Analyse the case example. What additional legitimate wants can be involved on the site of the stakeholders involved? Can this ethical dilemma actually be solved?
3. Take your national code of ethics. Compare the human needs mentioned in this chapter with the code.

6
Faith-based Approaches

Philip Gilligan

Key Concepts

Faith is the confident belief or trust in the truth of a person, idea or thing. The word faith can refer to a particular religion or to religion in general. It involves future events or outcomes that do not need to rest on logical proof or evidence. Faith is often used in a religious context where it *universally refers to a trusting belief in a transcendent reality or a supreme divine being.*

Religion is an organized set of beliefs and practices relating to spirituality that are shared by a faith community.

Spirituality is a search for meaning, and purpose and connection with self, others, the encompassing universe and ultimate reality (see also Chapter 18).

Fundamentalism refers to a belief in and strict adherence to a set of basic religious principles sometimes as a reaction to traditional religious and modern social and political tensions. It can be a feature of all types of religion.

Introduction

Faith-based social work is characterized by the recognition and acknowledgement of faith and faith-based values as significant sources of motivation and guidance. These may enhance professional values, but may also draw practitioners into direct conflict with secular values within the mainstream. This chapter explores the religious or faith-based origins of social work, the nature of faith-based practice, contemporary faith-based issues, and the global spread of social policies aimed at increasing the involvement of faith-based organizations in service delivery. It also seeks to highlight some of the dilemmas involved.

Religious or faith organizations – and individuals who subscribe to spiritual or religious beliefs, notably particular types of Christianity – had a sometimes dominant influence on the origins of social work, at least as constructed in English-speaking (Anglophone) countries and colonial contexts. Their influence continues but varies across contexts. For example, in postcolonial contexts, Western – Christian – and non-Western traditional religious values sometimes conflict with local cultures and at other times exist side by side in a hybrid belief system (see Gray et al., 2008). Faith-based social work practice extends the range of interventions and challenges to the bureaucratic services provided by statutory agencies. Social work with asylum seekers and refugees in Britain and elsewhere provides a stark example of this, with statutory agencies implementing oppressive legislation, while faith-based organizations provide sanctuary for those whom the authorities seek to detain, exclude and deport (Cemlyn & Briskman, 2003; Hayes & Humphries, 2004). However, there is the risk that faith-based organizations may 'abuse' their position as service providers, while also being exploited by neoliberal social policies which charge them with major responsibilities in the absence of adequate resources (De'Ath, 2004; Jordan with Jordan, 2000). It is sometimes inappropriate to give faith-based organizations responsibility for particular tasks, most notably risk assessment of clergy suspected of abusing children (see Plante, 2004). Organizations may prioritize their reputation over the needs of individuals (see Bryant, 2004) or religious conversion of service users (see e.g. www.teenchallenge.co.uk/content/view/23/49/ or www.caringforlife.co.uk/). They may advocate spirit possession (see Gilligan, 2008; Stobart, 2006) or oppressive views of gay men and lesbian women (see Hicks, 2003; Trotter, Kershaw, & Knott, 2008), or deny the equal rights of women or other groups (see Busuttil & ter Haar, 2002).

Key Ideas

There is no single faith-based approach to social work. However, approaches arguably fall into two contrasting types: 'fundamentalist or exclusive' and 'liberal or open' approaches.

Fundamentalist-exclusive

Fundamentalist-exclusive approaches begin with the view that the experience of, or adherence to, a faith is an essential starting point, not only for eventual spiritual salvation, but also for a fulfilled and satisfying life in the present. Acceptance of the faith may be seen as an essential component in being able to move on from current difficulties or overcoming past trauma. In such approaches, faith is an integral part of practice which is likely to involve at least an invitation to service users to accept aspects of it. Faith is seen as beneficial, protective and potentially life-changing and becomes part of, perhaps fundamental to, practitioners' repertoire of interventions. For example, the Social Work Christian Fellowship (SWCF) in the UK states that it 'seeks to develop Biblical thinking, challenge secular assumptions, and promote Christian perspectives in policy-making and practice', while its aims include encouraging 'Christians working in social work and social care settings to integrate their personal faith with their professional practice' (see www.swcf.org.uk/aims.html). Meanwhile, the North American Association of Christians in Social Work (NAACSW) says that its goal is to provide members with 'the ability to tap the resources of faith to provide more effective and faithful social work services', while the Catholic Social Workers National Association (CSWNA) describes its mission as being 'to promote implementation of Catholic social teachings in social work practice as we support competent professional social workers living out their baptismal call by being the hands and feet of Christ' (see www.cswna.org/).

Pressure groups, such as the British Humanist Association (BHA), argue that organizations whose motivation is a manifestation of their beliefs are in danger of discriminating against potential employees and clients. They cite the example of the Salvation Army, whose mission is 'to proclaim his [Jesus Christ's] gospel, to persuade people of all ages to become his disciples and to engage in a programme of practical concern for the needs of humanity' (BHA, 2007, p. 6).

Liberal-Open

Faith-based agencies adopting more liberal-open approaches, while they usually involve individuals and organizations who profess faith, express the part it plays very differently. Faith is seen as a motivation for action, but not necessarily as an essential part of that action. Practitioners may believe that their faith requires them to act and to provide services, but they will do so without attempting to engage those people in their particular faith or any faith other than as beneficiaries of actions motivated by it. In such approaches, faith may sometimes appear almost incidental to face-to-face interventions. For example, in the UK, organizations like Barnardo's and the Children's Society, which provide many social work services to children and families, clearly acknowledge their faith-based origins. However, in policy statements, they are explicit in emphasizing their inclusiveness and, by implication, the absence of conditionality or proselytizing. Barnardo's, for example, tells prospective employees:

> In today's multi-faith society we continue to recognise and respect our Christian foundation, and we also embrace the changing society in which we live ... We welcome, value and need staff from many world faiths and philosophies, and the diversity and talent they bring. (Narey, 2007)

The Children's Society (2008) says:

> Our Christian values drive [our] ... work ... and are our motivation for working with children and young people ... We understand our Christian mission in terms of changing the society in which we live so that it models the values of the re-ordered world of the Kingdom of God. These values are love, justice and forgiveness.

Social workers are unlikely to quibble with this set of values, regardless of their particular outlook. The BHA (2007) suggests that such organizations, 'despite a religious foundation, do not (or no longer) discriminate on grounds of religion or belief in either employment or service provision, being motivated wholly or principally by the desire to provide a useful service' (p. 6).

Overview of the Social Work Literature

The nature of faith

Commonly held Western understandings of faith, together with the shared characteristics of different faiths, allow construction of what might be called faith-based approaches to social work practice. Faith involves numerous beliefs and perspectives. While there are many commonalities within and between sects, denominations and other religious groupings, there are also wide differences. The broad differences and commonalities between major world religions are relatively easy to identify. However, there are many important issues on which even co-religionists place different degrees of emphasis, which may have significance for individuals, but will often be relatively difficult for external observers to identify. They include matters such as the degree to which a particular faith is viewed by adherents as the only 'true faith' and the relative significance given to 'Good Works' *vis-à-vis* 'Belief'.

At the same time, some faiths, such as Islam or Sikhism, have no generally accepted spokespeople to offer collective viewpoints and the official statements of institutional religions do not necessarily reflect the beliefs of all adherents. Additionally, the nature of governance for different organizations is extremely varied. Generally accepted constructions of social work are contested. Nevertheless, Gray et al. (2008) note that social work is essentially a Western construction informed by a broad array of Western social and behavioural science theories, methods and approaches. It attracts individuals and organizations with complex, contrasting and sometimes contradictory motivations.

Western theology draws clear distinctions between concepts of religion, spirituality, faith and culture (see, for example, Canda & Furman, 1999; Gray & Lovat, 2008; Henery, 2003; Patel, Nalk, & Humphries, 1998). However, definitions tend to overlap and, especially among groups and communities where faith is central to their understanding of events and experience, distinctions made by outsiders may have little practical meaning for believers, including social workers and service users. As a result, there is some risk that overemphasis on theoretical distinctions diverts attention from actual beliefs guiding behaviour and providing frames through which events are understood (Goffman, 1975; Park, 1990).

Social work's religious origins

Malcolm Payne (2005) reminds us that social work is a Western idea that arises largely from activities in some Western European and North American societies in the late 1800s. Constructions of social work arise within a particular social, political and historical context, and thus change over time. Western social work has, perhaps, undergone several transformations from charity or philanthropy, or what Franklin (1986) calls its period of 'moral certainty', to 'rational enquiry', beginning with Mary Richmond's (1922) notion of ' social investigation'. Social work might have developed differently had it followed Jane Addams's ([1902] 1964) model of community-based 'cultural education'. But instead it pursued a science-based professional model and targeted clinical intervention. John Harris (2008) emphasizes that the construction of social work is always a 'conjunctural settlement', a 'combination of events and ideas in which the interests represented by different discourses are subordinated by a specific configuration of a dominant discourse for a period of time' (Harris & Kirk, 2000, p. 111). However, for the most part, the nature of social work remains contested and varies across sociopolitical contexts, though vigorous attempts are made to promote the dominant scientific and philosophical ideas of Western social work, despite calls for cultural relevance (Gray et al., 2008).

Social work's origins are distinctly Judeo-Christian. Payne (2005) traces the roots of British social care to religious influences from medieval Catholic Europe, particularly Augustinian and Thomist philosophy. In so doing, he emphasizes the difference between charity, welfare and social work, with the latter being a specific and paid professional activity. David Guttmann and

Ben-Zion Cohen (1995) note the influence of Jewish teaching on social work's conception of social justice, human rights and mutual responsibility. However, there is much debate on whether it is possible to identify a distinctly Jewish approach to social work (Chaiklin, 1982; Gidron, 1983; Mittwoch, 1983; Prager, 1988). Many Muslims would, meanwhile, see the concept of social work within Islam as arising from chapter 2, verse 177 of the Qu'ran:

> It is not righteousness that you turn your faces towards East or West; but it is righteousness to believe in Allah and the Last Day and the Angels and the Book and the Messengers; to spend of your substance out of love for Him, for your kin, for orphans, for the needy, for the wayfarer, for those who ask; and for the ransom of slaves; to be steadfast in prayers and practice regular charity ... Such are the people of truth, the God-fearing.

Sara Ashencaen Crabtree, Fatime Husain and Basia Spalek (2008) observe that 'the principles governing Islam itself are ... essentially compatible with social work values' (p. 52; see Lovat, Chapter 16). Similar observations can be made about other belief systems, including atheism or secular humanism and even, perhaps, social work itself.

Application to Social Work Practice

In the late twentieth and early twenty-first centuries, there has been a rekindling of recognition of the potential significance of religion and spirituality in social work practice (Canda, 1998; Crisp, 2008; Crompton, 1996, 1998; Furman et al., 2004; Furness, 2003; Gilligan, 2003, forthcoming; Gilligan & Furness, 2006; Gray, 2008a; Patel et al., 1998). This work includes a necessary critique of tendencies within mainstream literature and professional education to ignore the potential significance, both positive and negative, of faith and religion in difficulties faced by service users and in potential solutions to them.

In such a context, some social workers in Anglophone countries are increasingly confident about using religious or spiritually sensitive interventions in their practice, although the likelihood of their doing so varies with geographical location. In a sample of social work students in the US, Michael Sheridan and Katherine Amato-von Hemert (1999) found that 31.2 per cent had already recommended participation in a religious or spiritual programme to service users and 79 per cent approved of this practice. However, Philip Gilligan and Sheila Furness (2006) found that only 15.5 per cent of a British sample of student social workers had done so and that 65.5 per cent would not approve. In general both qualified social workers and students in Britain were less likely to consider such interventions appropriate. Pedro Rankin (2006), like Ed Canda (1998), emphasizes that spirituality is a neglected area of social work practice, which can provide strength and support for many service users, while Karla Krogsrud Miley, Michael O'Melia and Brenda Dubois (2004) suggest that:

> Affiliating with a community of faith provides a network of personal relationships and concrete support in times of need. Specifically, spiritual beliefs and practices strengthen the ability to withstand and transcend adversity and are virtual wellsprings for healing and resilience. (p. 235)

David Hodge (2001) notes the need to capture the 'subjective, often intangible nature of human existence' (p. 204). He offers a framework for assessing people's personal subjective spirituality as a real force in their lives. He suggests that an individual's relationship with 'the Ultimate' facilitates coping, promotes a sense of purpose, instils a sense of self-worth, and provides hope for the future, while rituals serve to ease anxiety and promote a sense of security and being loved. Hodge (2005) also advocates the collection of spiritual histories and the use of life maps in assessing a person's spiritual journey and relationship with God or a transcendental force, and the use of spiritual ecomaps and ecograms to focus on the individual's spiritual relationships.

Three contemporary moral issues

It is instructive at this point to reflect on the ways in which religious affiliation, faith and beliefs may profoundly influence attitudes and perspectives in relation to specific moral issues. For secular organizations and a secular profession with national accrediting bodies, such as the General Social Care Council (GSCC), the Australian Association of Social Workers (AASW) or the Council on Social Work Education (CSWE), such matters raise important questions regarding the extent to which individual conscientious objection can be accommodated, while for governments and professional and funding bodies the attitudes and behaviours of faith-based organizations may raise important concerns. This has recently been illustrated by the difficulties caused for, and by, faith-based agencies and individual practitioners in relation to three moral issues:

1. Adoption by same-sex couples

Adoption by same-sex couples has become an issue of contention within and between legislators and faith communities in several countries throughout the world. In the UK, faith-based agencies have needed to make decisions about whether to continue to offer services in a legislative context (Adoption and Children Act, 2002; Equality Act, 2006; Sexual Orientation Regulations, 2007), which may require them to act against their duty to God. At the same time, the government has had to consider whether to grant those providing previously acceptable and valuable services exemption from legislation, which the chief executive of the British Association for Adoption and Fostering (BAAF) describes as 'very important at a time when too many children wait too long in temporary care ... for an adoptive family or, in some cases, never have the chance of adoption at all' (Mulholland, 2005, p. 1, see also Community Care News, 2003a, 2003b; Furness & Gilligan, 2009; Hicks, 2003; Christian Institute, 2002a, 2002b; O'Donoghue, 2007; Price, 2008).

In Norway, as in other Nordic countries and some US states, strong opposition from sections of faith communities ensured that the right to adopt children was specifically forbidden to same-sex couples in the 1993 Registered Partnership Act (Eskridge & Spedale, 2006). However, the revised law which came into force on 1 January 2009 grants what have been called 'sex-neutral' marriage rights to all couples and has split opinion within the Church of Norway and within some political parties. It has, also, led to joint protests involving Lutheran traditionalists, Roman Catholics and Muslims (Bergland, 2008).

2. Child abuse by clergy

In relation to responses to the abuse of children by clergy in many countries and, most notably in Anglophone countries such as the US, Canada, Ireland, the UK and Australia, professional social workers, often with strong religious faiths, have been recruited by churches in significant numbers to develop and improve safeguarding procedures, only, in some cases, to experience professional frustration in the face of ongoing institutional resistance to what, in mainstream Western social work, would be seen as standard practice. Cumberlege (Cumberlege Commission Report, 2007), while reporting generally positive progress in the Catholic Church in England and Wales, notes:

> We are concerned that five years after Lord Nolan reported Bishops and Congregational Leaders may be minimising the distressing consequences, the harmful impact and the anguish that follows in the wake of child abuse. This ... has impeded the delivery of consistently good – let alone excellent – safeguarding arrangements. (2.21: 22)

Thomas Plante (2002) suggests that the Catholic Church in North America has had a history of 'acting in a highly defensive manner and circling the wagons on this topic'. He concludes that one factor underpinning the problems experienced is that Catholic priests answer to only one superior, usually a bishop, making the effectiveness of safeguards too dependent on the response of that particular individual (see also Plante, 2004). Meanwhile, in Ireland, Goode, McGee, & O'Boyle's (2003) conclusion that the Church's response has been seriously inadequate is reinforced by the report of the Commission to Inquire into Child Abuse published in May 2009 (www.childabusecommission.com/rpt/). In its recommendations, the report emphasizes the importance of rules and regulations being enforced, breaches being reported and sanctions being applied (7.10), and of services being inspected by those independent of the Church (7.12). At the same time, in England and Wales, there remains a clear discrepancy between the number of Catholic priests known to have been convicted of criminal offences against children and sentenced to serve a term of imprisonment of 12 months or more and the number reported by the Catholic Office for the Protection of Children and Vulnerable Adults (COPCA) as laicized, in line with Recommendation 78 of Nolan (2001) (COPCA, 2002–7; see also Armstrong, 1991; Carlson Brown & Parker, 1989; COPCA, 2006; Farrell, 2004, 2009; Furness & Gilligan, 2009; Gamble, 2002; Kennedy, 2000, 2003; Kennison, 2008).

3. *Spirit possession*

Controversies over appropriate responses to beliefs in spirit possession illustrate, perhaps in an even clearer way, the potential difficulties involved when practitioners or policy makers hold particular beliefs (see Gilligan, 2008). In the UK, for example, Eleanor Stobart (2006) suggests that what is needed is 'child protection procedures ... together with information about good practice in "praying for", "delivering" or "exorcising" children' (p. 30). However, David Pearson (2007) argues that even this 'may inadvertently end up alienating those faith communities who already feel marginalised' (p. 1), while Africans Unite against Child Abuse (AFRUCA, 2006) ask Parliament to 'make it an offence for anyone to ... describe a child as possessed by the devil' (p. 2).

In the examples above, one of the key differences evident between professional ethical standards and faith-based practice is that, for the practitioner or the client, we are dealing with voluntary submission based on membership consent to a religious or spiritual authority. For the secular social worker or service user we are often dealing with formal and normative mandates that are written into state law.

Faith-based organizations and social welfare

Faith-based organizations play a significant role in social welfare beyond the day-to-day practice of social work. Their role is politically controversial and their influence is vehemently opposed by some. Terry Sanderson (2007) asserts that 'Faith-based welfare is a dangerous concept that should be stamped on.' Similar views are expressed by the British Humanist Association (BHA, 2007), which suggests that the British government's plans to expand the role of religious organizations within public services involves dangers of discrimination against staff and potential barriers to accessing services for the public.

The BHA (2007) suggests that some of the organizations being encouraged by the government to take on public service delivery are 'religious with a deeper hue' (p. 6) than traditional providers and that the British government has been influenced by the policies of countries such as the US and Australia, where religious organizations, such as the Catholic Church, Salvation Army and Mission Australia, have considerable involvement in public services, e.g. Mission Australia (2007), as an equal opportunity employer, requires employees to adhere to Christian values, while 'standing up and advocating for the most disadvantaged people in Australian communities' (p. 2). Mel Gray (2008b) notes that Australian community service organizations are often staffed by volunteers and employ relatively few qualified social workers and that their rise has paralleled government cutbacks in the direct provision of services.

In the US, the Welfare Reform Act (1996) requires states to give faith-based providers equal consideration with secular, non-profit non-government organizations when bidding for social service contracts. The trend since at least 1999 has been for religious groups to accept and compete for public money (see Chambré, 2001; Wuthnow, 2004). Alexander-Kenneth Nagel (2006) suggests that 'Charitable Choice' and 'Faith-Based-Initiative' are expressions of a political ideology advocated by successive administrations, which seek to include religious organizations in public welfare. Faith-based organizations receiving federal funds cannot make services conditional on participation in religious activities and cannot use funds to support 'inherently religious activities' (p. 2). However, Ram Cnaan (1999) reports that they are allowed to control the lifestyles of employees outside of the work environment and that many social services are becoming more openly religious. Meanwhile, in the Republic of Korea, by 2003, 53.4 percent of social welfare agencies were run by religious organizations (Koh, 2006) and this is a common pattern in postcolonial contexts (see Ling, 2008).

Conclusion

The faith-based approach to social work inevitably raises questions about the relationship between religion and professional ethics, the latter of which have tended to be secular. Secular ethics have persistently engaged in criticism of particular religious practices, just as religions criticize secular practices. In Margaret Battin's (1992) influential book, *Ethics in the Sanctuary*, a model is developed for the application of principles from contemporary professional ethics to faith-based practices. As an example, Battin applies the principle of confidentiality to the practice of religious confession and the principle of informed consent to high-risk religious practices, such as going to a Christian Scientist who uses a version of faith healing rather than a physician for medical care. By using a professional ethics framework for faith-based practice, Battin provides clarity around some of the dilemmas and tensions that were raised in the above discussion. This kind of modelling can provide for a positive relationship between secular professional standards and faith-based religious practices.

There are several faith-based approaches to social work. All, perhaps, share strong religious motivations, values and beliefs as defining characteristics, which have a powerful impact on the practice of social welfare agencies and social work practitioners, and cannot be ignored. They also give rise to perplexing dilemmas and heated controversy, especially when it comes to moral matters. The impact of faith-based approaches may be to extend, enhance and enrich the services available to vulnerable individuals and groups, but it may also serve to restrict access to them. Some faith-based approaches challenge oppressive practices by the state, while some may promote what are seen by others as equally oppressive views and practices. Any faith-based approach needs to be analysed and evaluated, not only by those responsible for the regulation of social work, but, perhaps more especially, by those adopting it and those on the receiving end of its services. It may provide exactly what is needed in particular circumstances, either because of or despite its faith characteristics, but, at the same time, it may fail to do so, for the same reasons.

Study Questions

1. Should social workers practising from a faith-based perspective make this known to their agencies and clients? What might the implications be were they to do so?
2. How might connections with faith be beneficial or detrimental to service users?
3. How do your personal beliefs and connections, if any, with a faith impact on your social work practice?

Part II
Moral Perspectives

Moving on from professional value perspectives, in Part II we examine the core moral perspectives that have developed beyond deontology, consequentialism and utilitarianism discussed in Chapter 1. Moral perspectives attempt to articulate a normative way of thinking about morality by arriving at moral 'gold standards' that regulate right and wrong conduct. A moral perspective will formulate fundamental principles for the guidance and evaluation of human conduct. Sometimes such perspectives are very general and abstract in nature. Therefore, recognizing that social workers do not receive a strong grounding in moral philosophy as part of their training, Part II will enable you to begin to engage with key foundational concepts and debates. Given that social workers constantly make moral judgements when they discern whether something is morally right or wrong, social work writers on ethics have argued for the importance of moral philosophy. Goldstein (1987) referred to this as the 'neglected moral link' in social work practice. An understanding of moral philosophy provides a depth of understanding about moral issues and ethical practice which is essential to the critically reflective approach in social work.

In Chapter 7, Brid Featherstone discusses the 'ethic of care', which many social work writers attribute to a feminist value perspective. These writers tend to draw heavily on feminist moral theory and the interdisciplinary work of political scientists, such as Sevenhuijsen and Tronto. However, Featherstone notes that they stray into a wide range of ethical theories in the development of their approach and raise many issues that lie at the heart of social work concerns. She proposes that the feminist ethic of care might not help with some of the things social workers urgently need help with, such as how people, including social workers, in a range of complex situations and managerial environments develop and maintain the capacity to care.

In Chapter 8, Sonia Tascón examines the 'ethics of responsibility', drawing on the phenomenological philosophy of Levinas. She argues for an ethics of responsibility that is beyond borders of clearly defined rules, duties and roles and instead relies on compassion for the 'Other'. It commands social workers to respond beyond the demands of their organizations to be accountable to prescribed rules and roles, and reach out in a human-to-human gesture because, ultimately, Levinas's ethics of responsibility are not about making 'moral life easier [but] ... making it a bit more moral' (Bauman, 1993, p. 15).

In Chapter 9, Stan Houston discusses Habermas's 'discourse ethics', where Habermas puts forward the Kantian view that moral agents should treat each other as 'ends' in their own right and never as a 'means' to an end. For Habermas, ethics are a matter of communication, for it is in the implicit nature of face-to-face talk, rather than in detached, complex, solitary thought that the question of 'what is to be done' is answered from an ethical standpoint. Habermas believes in the value of communication as a process in which people develop well-reasoned arguments about the merit of one value position over another. He values a rational approach to decision making and his discourse ethics is consistent with much contemporary thinking on ethics in social work as presented in Part I.

In Chapter 10, Stephen Webb examines virtue ethics, which has often been linked to the phrase 'doing the right thing', as an approach that relies on a 'call to conscience' in the social worker, and is a function of critical reflection and self-understanding. Virtue calls upon the inner sense of the rightness of one's ethical stance commensurate with the situation and the determinations of a moral dialogue with the rest of society. It moves ethics beyond the call of duty to the organization or client or profession or society and brings back to the centre of debate the importance of the individual worker, not in terms of his or her role, but in terms of character, of human *being,* of intellect and agency. Modern virtue ethics has always emphasized the importance of moral education, not as the inculcation of rules but as the training of character. For social workers to become more fully virtuous requires that they think about themselves, hard and critically, about the moral concepts that relate to practice, and those virtues that surround the agency context of their work.

In Chapter 11, Mel Gray discusses postmodern ethics, drawing on the seminal work of Zygmunt Bauman. She notes that the 'post' in postmodern ethics does not herald the 'end of ethics' but rather the attempt to deal with the limitations of modern ethics typified in the philosophy of Jürgen Habermas. For Bauman (1993), there *are* 'principled positions', and following Levinas, he bases them on an 'ethic of *individual* responsibility'. Bauman is critical of modern ethics – as are many modern ethicists, who have subjected philosophical ethics to critical scrutiny and acknowledged its limitations. Gray argues that social work has much to learn from Bauman's version of postmodern ethics and, as a consequence, would revive human traditions when the importance of a deep understanding of morality was recognized. She believes that too much emphasis has been placed on ethical rules and procedural decision-making frameworks and too little on a deep understanding of what it means to be moral.

7
Ethic of Care

Brid Featherstone

Key Concepts

Caring is a social and moral practice that involves not only dealing with feelings of love, compassion, empathy, and involvement but also of grief, anger and rejection. As a foundational element in social relationships, caring allows for an engaged and intimate space for the articulation of values associated with trust, respect for differences, and mutual recognition.

The **ethic of care** is concerned with understanding the moral frameworks which people use to make judgements about their actions. While consequentialist and deontological theories emphasize universal standards of impartiality, the ethic of care emphasizes the importance of relationships and, particularly, the interdependence between individuals in achieving mutually beneficial outcomes.

Feminist writings have highlighted the importance of the gendered division of caretaking in understanding how selves are formed and develop. It has been argued that situated judgements need to be understood as located judgements and that gendered practices are central in such processes. The insistence by feminism on rendering visible inequalities in relation to the giving and receiving of care, and on challenging binaries such as dependence/independence and public/private, has contributed to an extensive scholarship as well as political campaigning in the last decades.

Introduction

This chapter explores the work of key thinkers within the wide-ranging and influential scholarship on the ethic of care. It traces the journey from its origins within feminist psychology through its contributions to moral theory, political science and social policy. This is, therefore, a very specific and selective reading of the literature informed by the author's own location within feminist scholarship. Writings on the ethic of care focus on concerns of central significance to social work. However, this chapter argues that there are compelling reasons for resisting the seductive wiles of an ethic which promises a great deal, delivers quite a lot, but just not some of the key things social work needs.

Key ideas

Gendered moral frameworks

Carol Gilligan's book *In a Different Voice*, published in 1982, revolutionized discussions in moral theory, feminism and theories of the subject and was one of the most influential books of the 1980s. It has led to a vast and continuing scholarship (see Hekman, 1995 for a sympathetic account, particularly of the contribution to moral theory). Gilligan was to become one of the most influential US feminists of the 1980s and was named *Ms* magazine's Woman of the Year in 1984. She published an empirical and interpretive analysis of the decision-making process of a sample of girls confronted with a range of dilemmas. She challenged the then influential approach of Kohlberg, her teacher, a Harvard psychologist, specializing in moral development. His studies had concluded that women stayed at an inferior stage of moral development, with few attaining the highest stages of moral reasoning. Indeed, in order to avoid the 'distortions' that female subjects created, he went on to study male subjects only. Gilligan argued that there are gender differences in the moral frameworks within which men and women operate. Men operate within an ethic of justice, whereas women operate within an ethic of care. The ethic of care revolves around relationships and responsibilities, in contrast to an ethic of justice, which stresses rights and rules.

The morality associated with an ethic of care is tied to concrete circumstances rather than being an abstract philosophical concept. Moreover, the morality is best expressed not as a set of principles but as an activity – the activity of care. Different conceptions of selfhood underpin the differing frameworks. To understand these differing conceptions of selfhood, Gilligan relied on object relations theory and, in particular, the work of Nancy Chodorow. In *The Reproduction of Mothering*, Chodorow (1978) argued that the gendered division of caretaking had consequences for boys' and girls' development. In a society where women are devalued, mothers' relations with their sons and daughters cannot but develop in contrasting ways. Mothers experience their daughters as less separate from themselves and girls, in turn, retain their early and intense identification and attachment to their mothers. Moreover, they grow up with a weaker sense of boundaries and with a greater capacity for empathy and sensitivity towards others.

Boys, by contrast, are pushed to disrupt their primary identification with their mother. They must repress and deny the intimacy, tenderness and dependence of the early bond if they are to assume a masculine identity. Thus they do not define themselves in relational terms but rather in terms of independence and autonomy. As indicated, Gilligan tied morality to self-hood and Chodorow's analysis was very influential in this.

Gilligan was hailed as both the harbinger of a new moral theory and as the final blow to the exhausted masculinist tradition of moral philosophy. However, her work has also been condemned as methodologically unsound, theoretically confused and even antifeminist (Hekman, 1995). In relation to the latter points, her exclusive research focus on women has been criticized. Her findings have been disputed as well as her emphasis on the importance of gender as the basis of the ethic of care, for example, Tronto (1993) notes that Patricia Hill Collins characterized the ethic of care as an African American rather than a gendered phenomenon. Moreover, she also notes that Carol Stack's research with African American men and women found no gendered differences. Overall, critics argue that Gilligan contributed to essentialist thinking about women and problematic assumptions about women's moral superiority to men and failed to deconstruct the category of woman (Segal, 1987). However, Hekman (1995) argues that Gilligan's work was both an indication of, and a major contributor to, a sea change that was under way in late twentieth-century intellectual thought. There was an already existing move away from the universalism and absolutism of modernist epistemology towards conceptions that emphasized particularity and concreteness. The linchpin was the attack on the centre piece of moral philosophy and modernist Enlightenment epistemology: man as the rational, abstract autonomous constitutor of knowledge. Gilligan identified the ethical code of Western societies as based upon universalizable concepts, such as objectivity and partiality, which reflected a partial and masculine world-view. Hekman (1995) argues that she has made a major contribution to moral philosophy, although she was not a moral philosopher and her work was empirically based. As Hekman (1995) notes, this may bear out the truth of Foucault's observation that challenges to established disciplines often come from outside or the margins.

A key issue which emerged from Gilligan's work, and is the subject of a comprehensive scholarship, concerns the relationship between the ethic of care and the ethic of justice. Are they complementary or hierarchical? While she has continued to maintain their equality, some followers have used her work to assert the superiority of the care voice. Williams (2001), whose own influential work applied the ethic of care to social policy concerns, explored in a later section, locates Gilligan within the first wave of feminist research on care. She notes that Gilligan, among others, signalled a shift away from the emphasis in second-wave feminism on equating care with oppression and exploitation. She notes that Gilligan, alongside Finch (1989), from a more sociological perspective, moved away from the exploitation paradigm into the territory of social obligations to study the normative structures that influence caring activities.

A second development in the scholarship on the ethics of care is represented in the work of the political scientists Joan Tronto (1993) and Selma Sevenhuijsen (1998). Both have tried to resolve the tensions between an ethic of care and an ethic of justice in wide-ranging attempts to broaden the scope of applicability of a reformulated ethics. Because of space constraints it is the work of Tronto that I will now consider in detail.

Care as a moral and political practice

For Tronto (1993), what distinguished her approach from that of Gilligan's and others is her insistence that we cannot understand an ethic of care unless we place it in its moral and political context. It is only if we see care as a political idea that we will be able to challenge its status and the status of those who do caring. Care should not be reduced to a narrow psychological concern or a kind of practice that is corrupted by broader social and political concerns. Her definition of care, developed with Berenice Fisher, is as follows:

> On the most general level, we suggest that caring be viewed as a species activity that includes everything we do to maintain, continue and repair our 'world' so that we can live in it as well as possible. That world includes our bodies, our selves and our environment, all of which we seek to interweave in a complex life-sustaining web. (Tronto, 1993, p. 103)

She suggests the importance of the following underpinnings for such a definition. Care is not restricted to human interactions. Her definition does not presume that it is dyadic or individualistic. The activity of caring is largely defined culturally and will vary. It is ongoing and both a practice and a disposition. She notes that although care consumes much of human activity, not all human activity is care. One way that we can begin to understand the limits of care is by noting what care is not, such as the pursuit of pleasure, creative activity, production and destruction. What is definitive about care seems to be a perspective of taking the other's needs as the starting point for what must be done. Tronto excludes ideas about protection from the main parts of care, although she recognizes that some aspects of protection are within the realms of care. This is returned to when discussing social work in a later section. In a formulation which continues to be highly influential, Tronto argues that, as an ongoing process, care consists of four analytically separate but interconnected phases: caring about, taking care of, care giving and care receiving. From these four elements arise four ethical elements of care: attentiveness, responsibility, competence and responsiveness. Thus care as a practice requires more than good intentions. It requires both thought and action, which are interrelated and directed towards an end. The emphasis on practice is important: care is neither a principle nor an emotion. This signals her location within a concern to tackle the power inequities often involved in care. For example, she argues that, in the US, caring about and taking care of are often the duties of the powerful, and care giving and care receiving are left to the least powerful.

In an example which is left tantalizingly underdeveloped, she notes that men can see themselves as taking care of their families by working at their jobs. Equally doctors see themselves as taking care of their patients, although it is nurses who do the hands-on care. To operate within an ethic of care would seem to have to involve all of the four elements identified above: caring about, taking care of, care giving and care receiving. But there are a range of issues left unclear here. Contemporary theorists of fathering have noted how often psychological and policy discourses of the 'good father' leave out breadwinning as an aspect of good fatherhood to the detriment of some men, in particularly those in marginalized circumstances. For example, some non-resident fathers may see it as both central to emphasize in the context of societal discourses about feckless non-resident fathers, and as a concrete way in which they can demonstrate care. Other men may have to live and work continents apart from their families in order to provide for them economically (Featherstone, forthcoming).

Tronto is surely correct in stressing that if care were seen solely in dispositional terms, it would be sentimentalized and romanticized, and in seeking to link activity and disposition, but it is important to continue to explore the complexities of context in relation to who does what, why, where and when (see Williams, 2001 and discussion in a subsequent section). As a political scientist, Tronto introduced important concerns in relation to care into the scholarship. We need, she argues, strong conceptions of rights and must not separate care and justice. Care as a practice can inform the practices of democratic citizenship:

> If through the practices of giving and receiving care we were to become adept at caring, I suggest that not only would we have become more caring and moral people, but we would also have become better citizens in a democracy. (Tronto, 1993, p. 167)

Her book is called *Moral Boundaries* and she argues for the redrawing of three boundaries in order to understand how care might inform political and social practices. The boundaries are: the separation between public and private life, between morality and politics and the abstract account of morality:

> Care is not a parochial concern of women, a type of secondary moral question, or the work of the least well off in society. Care is a central concern of human life. It is time that we began to change our political and social institutions to reflect this truth. (Tronto, 1993, p. 180)

Sevenhuijsen (1998) follows Tronto's lead in exploring how care can be placed within the conceptions of democratic citizenship. She argues against some of the feminist tendencies to locate it within a mothering paradigm, as care can be seen in all settings. We should not counterpoise care to justice, but see it as a social process engendering important aspects of citizenship. The process of caring for or being cared for make one aware of diversity, of interdependence and of the need for acceptance of difference, which form an important basis to citizenship and are as likely, or more likely to be learned through care than through paid work practices.

Sevenhuijsen (2000) deconstructs the policy prescriptions and underlying normative framework espoused by Anthony Giddens in his book *The Third Way* (1998). What is key here is that care should be seen as a democratic practice and democratic citizenship should guarantee everyone equal access to the giving and receiving of care. An important point here, which is also made by Tronto, is the distancing of a care approach from the Third Way emphasis on responsibilities:

> We need to reframe norms of equality and access to public provisions in such a way that they meet the basis standards of social justice. This is also important in order to counter the deeply entrenched tendency towards thinking in terms of an opposition between an ethics of care and an ethics of justice. (Sevenhuijsen, 1998, p. 142)

I will now move onto exploring the highly influential work of Fiona Williams, which builds on that of Tronto and Sevenhuijsen and explores contemporary social policy concerns.

Care, power and diversity

Williams (2001) argues that care as a practice involves different experiences, meanings, contexts and multiple relations of power. She calls for a 'political ethics' of care in order to engage with the challenges and differences posed by disability, 'race' and migration. She locates her analysis within the political moment of the New Labour project intent on promoting paid work as the pathway to social inclusion, cohesion and citizenship. She also locates her call within a theoretically sophisticated and substantial feminist social policy scholarship in which care has become a central analytic concept in the comparative study of welfare regimes. For example, Daly and Lewis (2000) have argued that policies associated with the giving and receiving of care provide a unique lens with which to view what is changing in the unfolding of new welfare settlements in European welfare states. Throughout the decade, such policies have continued to be interrogated particularly within analyses seeking to explore the construction of social investment states (Featherstone, 2004).

Daly and Lewis (2000) identified the following changes: there have been shifts in demographic relations, employment patterns, relations between carer and cared for, cash and services and between family, state, market and voluntary and community sectors as providers of care (see Williams, 2001, p. 469). They suggest that without an understanding of the ways in which different welfare states are responding to these changing boundaries of welfare provision, the picture of changing welfare trajectories is incomplete. Williams (2001) agrees and reinforces their argument through the development of the political ethics of care. She locates herself within the second wave of care scholarship as highlighted above. She suggests that, while writers such as Gilligan were important, they had limitations. They were almost entirely gender-focused, with tendencies towards an undifferentiated category of womanhood, underpinned by essentialism around gender differences. There was also an assumption that the site of care was the heterosexual family and 'the focus on the carer and care as either work or ethic ignored care as a set of relations involving power and featuring both carers and cared-for' (Williams, 2001, p. 476).

Williams (2001) argues that care literature needs to engage with the critiques from the disability movement. (The debates in relation to care and disability have spawned a large and ongoing literature). Moreover, she argues for the importance of asking how the ethics of care might be applied in a racialized and global context. The following summarizes what she considers to be the key issues for a political ethics of care with which to engage (Williams, 2001, p. 486–8).

The starting point is a recognition that care of the self and care of others are meaningful activities in their own right and they involve us all, men and women, old and young, able-bodied and disabled. We are neither just givers nor receivers of care. Care is an activity that binds us all. In giving and receiving care, we can, in the right conditions of mutual respect and material support, learn the civic responsibilities of responsibility, trust, tolerance for human limitation and frailties and acceptance of diversity. Care is part of citizenship. Interdependence is the basis of human interaction and autonomy and independence are about the capacity for self-determination rather than self-sufficiency. Vulnerability is a human condition and the experience of vulnerability varies contextually and temporally. Moral worth is attributed to key dimensions of caring relationships, such as dignity and the quality of human interaction, whether based upon blood, kinship, sexual intimacy, friendship, collegiality, contract or service. Moreover, diversity and plurality in the social process of care are respected and recognized.

Inequalities in care giving and care receiving are exposed through questioning who is and is not benefiting from existing policies. Inequalities may be constituted through different relations, particularly gender, but also disability, class and occupational status, age, ethnicity, 'race', nationality, religion, sexuality and marital status. Care requires time, financial and practical support and the recognition of choice. Quality, affordability, accessibility, flexibility, choice and control are the key to service provision. The importance of an inclusive citizenship, where all those involved in the processes of care have a voice, is stressed. Care is not only personal, it is an issue of public and political concern whose social dynamics operate at local, national and transnational levels:

> The reprivatisation of care services, in conditions of women's increased participation in paid work, has intensified national and international forms of gendered exploitation constituted especially through class, 'race'/ethnicity and migrant status. (Williams, 2001, p. 488)

While the above might seem a rather programmatic wish list (akin to motherhood and apple pie), Williams (2001) does recognize and, indeed, advance concrete strategies in concrete political conjunctures. What is less well addressed in this or contemporary scholarship is whether there is a continued need for an explicit adherence to an ethic of care when many of the issues above are accepted by a wide range of scholars in social policy. Does the language of care act as a way of advancing causes or is it a barrier either for particular groups (for example, those with a disability have argued so at various points)? How does it engage with important debates around a reformulated notion of human rights?

In the next section I signpost a more recent critique of the literature around the ethic of care, which I consider not only has resonance for a general audience but certainly acts as a useful bridge to addressing social work concerns.

Overview of the Social Work Literature

Developing the capacity to care: what counts?

Wendy Hollway (2006) locates her concern within a psychosocial perspective. This perspective has a long history in social work but it is important to note here that Hollway's work comes from her critical engagement with psychology and she is part of a more recent interdisciplinary group of scholars from sociology, social policy and psychology. Frogget (2002) has located this 'new' take on psychosocial perspectives within an analysis of differing welfare projects historically, thus offering the opportunity to assess how psychosocial perspectives today differ from those advanced in previous decades. Hollway's interest is the psychological capacities involved in care, which remains unexamined in the literature outlined above. She wants to problematize assumptions either that the capacity to care is natural, which has led to it being taken for granted, or that it is simply social, the result of habit, training or practice:

> Babies are not born with capacities to care and the acquisition of the morality that underpins good caring is a complex and conflictual process that is an integral part of psychological development. Boys and girls experience the development of identity in very different ways because of the deeply entrenched meanings of gender everywhere round them. The meanings of care are gendered too and so the acquisition of the capacities associated with caring is never a gender-neutral process. (Hollway, 2006, p. 5)

Hollway (2006) asks what understanding of subjectivity underpins Tronto's analysis. She suggests that in her model of care, Tronto never engages with the question of how people might be able to care. It is only towards the end of *Moral Boundaries* that she suggests that it is practices that teach them and reinforce their sense of moral concern about caring for those around them or in society. According to Hollway (2006), Tronto draws implicitly on a simplistic model of social learning to account for moral conduct, reinforced with the idea that practice is a sufficient conveyor of moral values. In this, like many other theorists, she reduces subjectivity to an empty category filled by social products. Often Tronto implies that if the political barriers to a care ethic were removed by shifting existing moral boundaries then people would naturally care. According to Hollway (2006), Sevenhuijsen takes us a little further, arguing that the practice of care can lead to the disposition to care but leaves it unclear if, when and how such a process takes place.

Overall, most of the influential contributions to debates about care lack a psychology, notably a full, critically based theorization of the self and its relational development, on which the capacity to care is founded. For Hollway (2006), it is developmental psychoanalysts (in which she includes the work of attachment theorists) who have provided the most theoretically fertile insights for understanding the relational acquisition of capacities to care and who have theorized the effects of sexual and gender difference in the development of care.

It is beyond the scope of this chapter to explore Hollway's analysis in any depth. The following is offered to signpost themes in the subsequent discussion on social work. Hollway (2006) points to a transdisciplinary paradigm shift from a model of the mind, which is intrapsychic (populated by inner drives) to an emphasis on intersubjectivity. The literatures from phenomenology, psychoanalysis and developmental psychology draw attention to the importance of relationships in understanding care in the sense that the caring and careless subject is constituted relationally, right through to the deepest, most hidden parts of their subjectivity. Hollway (2006) notes the work of Levinas (1999), for example, who attempted to found philosophy on an ethics based not on the cogito but on the relation to the Other, and situates this within the paradigm shift outlined above (see Chapter 8).

She argues that not only do the theorists within the ethic of care scholarship need to engage with the capacity to care but the stakes are much higher than merely at the level of the academic. The capacity to care needs to be protected. It cannot be taken for granted. It is crucial to what kind of society is developed and sustained. While she does not offer policy prescriptions, it is clear that she sees early care-taking experiences as crucial. People are products of their pasts and these cannot be left behind in a voluntaristic project. In what she calls a critical-realist approach to infant and child development, she cautions against a relativism that flows from treating theories of child development simply as stories or discourses. The Kleinian emphasis on phantasy and the internal mother and internal father is also influential in her work, which means she cannot be placed within an attachment paradigm. This paradigm focuses on the role of the real mother or father, although, as indicated above, she sees attachment theory as of value:

> I am trying to theorise the effects of real circumstances and real relationships through the grid of how these achieve meaning. And meaning is not just achieved through the availability of certain discourses rather than others, but through the mediations of psychic processes, themselves inextricably captured by language, but also by phantasy, anxiety and desire. (Hollway, 2006, p. 132)

To conclude this section, I think Hollway is correct to question problematic assumptions about subjectivity and she has made an important critique of ethic of care literature. However, I would suggest that her analysis, as the quote above illustrates, is reductive, not only in relation to the importance of early care-taking dynamics, but also in terms of integrating the complexities of the interplay between social and psychic forces. There is little or no social in her psychosocial. This weakens her usefulness for social work and suggests to me that we need to continue to work on theorizing subjectivity. However, it is beyond the scope of this chapter to discuss this further (see Frogget, 2002). In this next section, I offer some tentative observations on the dangers for social work of being seduced by the ethic of care.

Application to Social Work Practice

Helping people?

Social work academics will probably recognize the following scenario only too well:

The scene: An office in a university with a university lecturer, a social worker and a candidate seeking admission to study social work.

Interviewer: So can you tell me why you want to become a social worker?

Interviewee: Because I want to help people who need help, and I've always been told I'm good with people.

Usually part of the interviewer's decision making is linked to what else happens in the interview and, crucially, their assessment of whether the candidate is aware of the control aspect of the job and the need to take very difficult and often painful decisions which may not be perceived as helpful at all by service users. The point I want to make here is perhaps a very obvious one. While many other students may wish to study the social sciences because of a concern to understand what makes people 'tick', understand society, and so on, social workers, alongside those in other applied disciplines, are distinguished from the onset by their orientation towards engaging in interactions with others. This is the very 'bread and butter' of the ethic of care. The 'ethics of care posits the image of a "relational self", a moral agent who is embedded in concrete relationships with others and who acquires a moral identity through interactive patterns of behaviour, perceptions and interpretations' (Parton, 2003, p. 10). So far so good; our mythical interviewee equates beautifully with the moral agents required to implement the ethic of care. Except ... they won't be allowed to in Parton's analysis. They will be corrupted by the increasingly bureaucratized, rational procedural demands of their organizations and by the dominant model of professionalism. Thus in this version of events, it is hardly surprising, perhaps, that Parton (2003) sees writings within the ethics of care as directly applicable to rethinking professionalism in social work, but does not offer concrete pointers for how that might happen.

Moreover, there are a number of other possible outcomes from the scenario above which suggest fault lines in the dominant assumptions behind much of the ethic of care scholarship. It may become apparent, for example, that though the interviewee says she is good with people, she is actually not able to manage the interview encounter at all, which leads the interviewer to question whether she is, in fact, good with people or, indeed, knows herself very well. Or the interviewee may want to be good with people, may desire it desperately, and see social work as a way of repairing old wounds, but it may be very apparent in the interview or later that her attempts are doomed at this point in time anyway. As Hollway (2006) notes, much of the ethic of care literature has little to say on this. Indeed, the social work literature often has little to say about this either, as it retreats into 'fitness to practice' procedures, which deal only with the correctness or otherwise of the student's 'attitudes'. What about the social control aspect of the job? While there is some attention paid in the literature to the conflicts that arise, for example, between cared for and carer, the theorization of power is, overall, quite poor. In particular, there is little attention paid to the complexities of using power on behalf of the state to safeguard those who are vulnerable. Indeed, Tronto (1993) is rather doubtful about whether protection as an activity can embody the ethic of care. In Williams's (2001) analysis there is a recognition of competing needs and interests, and her emphasis on the importance of 'voice' is a vital antidote to the paternalism and authoritarianism which can characterize safeguarding activities (see Featherstone & Evans, 2004, for example, on the views of children about child protection systems).

Conclusion

A very important literature spanning a range of disciplines has emerged from within the ethic of care. At its heart are concerns that are central to social work. However, this chapter suggests that that all that glitters is not gold and that it may not help us with some of things we urgently need help with. How do people, including social workers, in a range of complex situations develop and maintain the capacity to care? What models of subjectivity do we need that can understand the dynamic and ongoing interplay between the social and the psychological? While these are age-old questions in social work, the answers are only fitfully apparent within the ethic of care literature.

Study Questions

1. The ethic of care literature covers so many diverse and conflicting perspectives that it can no longer be understood as having an essential coherence. Discuss.
2. How can the capacity to care be sustained and developed?
3. Is it helpful to continue to develop scholarship from within an ethic of care perspective?

8
Ethics of Responsibility

Sonia Tascón

Key Concepts

Responsibility to the Other: In Levinas's terms this is a primordial relationship of responsibility that arises from being in the world with others; we are commanded to react to other human beings by virtue of our human relations and being a part of a social world.

Interhuman is a foundational aspect of all human ethical relations. It refers to the phenomenological nature of Levinasian ethics, where responsibility occurs prior to rules of conduct or ontologically defined roles as a 'first philosophy'.

Encounter with the Other: Levinas derives the primacy of his ethics from the experience of the encounter with the Other. This irreducible relation, the epiphany, of the face-to-face, the encounter with another, is a privileged phenomenon in which the other person's proximity and distance are strongly felt.

Introduction

One of the characteristics of modernity is the dominance of binary divisions. This applies not only to our ways of categorizing the world, but also to the way in which we characterize ourselves and our relationships with others. This creates a boundary, a barrier, between our self and the other. We are separate, isolated individuals, living in different worlds of constructed 'identities', and to cross that barrier, to inhabit the world of the other, becomes problematic, rather than natural. By creating this self/other binary, by emphasizing individual identity, and because we tend to see binary categories as necessarily in opposition, we have, in turn, created a certain kind of ethics, deeply rooted in Western modernity.

Ethical responsibility, in this description of the world, is difficult other than to those who exist on our side of the ocean or fence. This chapter takes up and discusses this very notion of ethical responsibility and the ways in which it has been traditionally conceived and applied in social work, and then considers (an)other way that might extend the current discourse of ethics within social work towards one that can encompass those beyond that boundary. In so doing, it draws largely upon the work of Emmanuel Levinas, a philosopher whose project of developing an ethics of responsibility towards others beyond our self-contained borders of identity – whether they be national, ethnic, gendered, classed, professional or any other form of subject position we adopt throughout our lives – have been seminal in many fields of enquiry and practice, but mostly in those that may be loosely termed 'cultural'. That is, in the fields of enquiry and practice defined as 'cultural', questions about the ways in which we make meaning, and hence construct relationships accordingly, and the ways in which fields of representation develop not only our subjectivities but also our intersubjectivities, are of central importance. Levinas has engaged with these questions from the perspective of *difference* and how it acts to define both our subjectivities and intersubjectivities in a cultural moment loosely defined as modernity, and the relationships of obligation these result in. He does this to address the possibilities of an ethics of responsibility that do not rely on *sameness* or on cultural or group homogeneity, nor on the *assimilatory* urge inherent in many traditional approaches to ethics, but allows a response of compassion towards (an)other across difference in a stance of human-to-human.

In social work, responsibility has been a discourse framed largely around accountability and duty, and, indeed, little attention has been given specifically to ethics as responsibility in the professional literature. This may have much to do with an ideological avoidance of notions of 'responsibility' and the questions of self-determination they raise. It may also, more significantly, however, be related to the fact that responsibility has been articulated within a fairly defined and rule-bound field of activity that refers its members, if not instantly, then eventually, to the discourse of *professionalism* (see Webb & McBeath, 1989). Thus responsibility in this restricted landscape becomes the direct lines of responsibility to specific groups or roles, within the bounds of a specific group or role. *Professionalism* is, after all, a subset of modernist methodologies that demand clearly articulated roles and rules of evidence, while the ethics of responsibility posed by Levinas instruct responses that transcend roles and enter into engagement at the human-to-human rather than the human-to-professional. We therefore need to explore how social work engages or attempts to engage with these ethics. It is at the point where social work gives entry to what some might call the virtues of compassion – largely defined as empathy within social work – that responsibility can be given acknowledgement in the shape suggested by Levinas (see also Chapters 10 and 11). There is already some work being carried out towards this widening of the scope of ethics within the profession, but perhaps considering how Levinas shapes our thinking about responsibility, as compassion, may further advance this movement.

Key Ideas

Traditional frameworks and moving beyond them

The philosophical debates in the area of the ethics of responsibility occur largely within discussions around *freedom of the will* vs. *determinism* (Ayer, 1969; Honderich, 2004; Taylor, 1979; Waller, 1991). The concern is whether we are free to act and whether our wills are formulated by nothing outside ourselves so that we may be said to be inherently and ultimately responsible for our actions. Because, as the debates note, unless we can be said to hold a level of absolute agency over our actions influenced by nothing but a freestanding will, then our actions are invalidated by interference by others or, at the very least, contaminated by others' influence. Related but separate are also discussions of *causality* (Klein, 1995) and *ends and means,* as in Max Weber's well-known lecture on *Politics as a Vocation* (1918), differentiating between the 'ethics of ultimate ends' (intentions) and the 'ethics of responsibility' (consequences). Responsibility under this latter set of discussions refers us to a person who might only experience or be held responsible if her or his actions had negative effects on another. Responsibility in the earlier set is premised on a person who is autonomous, atomistic and uncontaminated by a world that necessarily remains outside, in order for the will to be free and, in the latter, it is only effective according to the consequences (consequentialism; see Chapter 1). Moral responsibility exists if each autonomous subject can be said to be totally and ultimately free to choose and, therefore, responsible for those choices, devoid of external (or internal, in the case of some mental processes that compel an individual to certain actions) influences that may be said to act as direct manipulations on his or her freedom to choose or, if in that freedom, their actions result in some detriment for another individual. Responsibility in these views can only be apportioned if we command a human subject who is fully free from all influences and bounded by plans of actions that prescribe, predict and prevent clear lines of accountability for any possible harmful effects.

Responsibility, however, is not a technical enterprise, best suited to the drafting of clear and detached programmes of behaviour, nor is it a rule-bound enterprise. It is one of the most deeply fundamental aspects of the human condition. It goes to the very heart of ethics. That is, if we see ethics as 'a process of formulation and self-questioning that continually rearticulates boundaries, norms, selves, and "others"' (Garber, Hanssen, &

Walkowitz, 2000, p. viii), or as 'the set of values which underwrite a cultural order, where official and everyday decisions are made about how we will relate to others, to whom we owe what, and to whom we owe nothing' (Tascón, 2009), then ethics is about a process. This process is bound to a set of obligations dynamically and fluidly engaging our intersubjective life-world, that is, ethics and obligations to others become wedded to each other because there is a relational framework in the way we perform ethics. While both of these definitions refer us to a pervasiveness of ethics to everyday aspects of our lives that might seem to dilute ethics to everything and nothing, it also does not allow us to 'escape' its presence and promise in our lives. Furthermore, and more important for this chapter, inscribed within the very notion of ethics is a relational assumption, an assumption that is indeed primary and prior to any formulaic or philosophical discussion about ethics itself. In this sense, ethics *arises* from this reality, as does the command to respond, as an engagement, with it that we cannot escape. It is by virtue of being born into the world, to a world of others, whatever their shape and colour, whatever their world-views, that ethics takes on meaning.

Modern subjectivity: The autonomous subject

Ethics has traditionally, in the Western tradition at least, focused on the autonomous, atomistic and independent subject. This understanding of the human subject is not new, nor is it universal. Binary constructions that begin to imagine the human subject in this way do not become an important concept until modern times. In previous times, most important were the similarities between subjects, or what Michel Foucault (1970) calls *similitudes*. In modern times, *the border* – as segregated division – acquires dimensions of precise and radical differentiation between things in ways that had not been present before. That is, until approximately the eighteenth century – the time of the Enlightenment – much of our existence, at least in the Western world, had been experienced in the subject–object relationship of undifferentiation, including the human subject. These were deep epistemological and ontological shifts, which had dramatic cultural consequences. No longer 'drawing things together' but 'discriminating' (Foucault, 1970) meant that objects were no longer seen as part of each other, and that the human subject no longer saw him or herself that way either. The rational human, in his/her autonomous state of knowing, separated from all other life, was given shape at this time (Kelly & Popkin, 1991; Taylor, 1989). That is, *the border* not only confines objects and subjects to eternal separation from each other, but also delineates a clear 'inside' – organized by the logic of identity or 'the same' – from an 'outside' – defined by its radical differences to the 'inside' (Taylor, 1989). As Charles Taylor (1989) discusses, notions of 'insides' and 'outsides' – in such radical separateness – did not become the dominant way of thinking about ethics until after the Enlightenment. We can see how the birth of the modern self emerged out of this Enlightenment thinking and later came to influence social work.

Responsibility across modernist borders: Being ethical

As already mentioned, this way of seeing the human subject is not universal, so it is not necessary for us to consider responsibility in terms of the free-floating, unattached mobile subjects whose ability to be responsible is measured according to how uncontaminated by their environment they are. In a different take on responsibility as ethics, Levinas instead poses for us a subject who is encompassed in ethics as a primary encounter in a world of Others. That is, immersed in ethical responsibility as something inescapable from being born into a world of Others. He calls it a *first philosophy*, which is not formulated by rule-bound schedules of behaviour, but arises more primarily as foundational.

> [N]ot as abstract systems of obligation ... rather, ethics is born and maintained through the necessity of performative response to the other person, and such a responsiveness (which he calls 'responsibility') comes necessarily before the solidification of any theoretical rules or political norms of ethical conduct. (Nealon, 1998, p. 34)

It is not 'universal rule-dictated duties, but moral responsibility ... [that] resists codification, formalization, socialization, universalization' (Bauman, 1993, p. 54). It is an ethics that involves the self in an eternal response to the Other, that which is outside the self, in an asymmetrical relationship of responsibility to the Other without an expectation of return. This is a Levinasian view of intersubjectivity based on a relationship between the self and Other that places the self in a constant state of response to the Other, thus removing the autonomous individual from centre stage, without effacing her or him. Contrary to the dominant modernist world-view, this is because the two are not separate in that dominant mode. They are not distinct entities, although at the same time they simultaneously are. In that vein, Judith Butler (2000) argues that while Levinas's ideas may be regarded as tantamount to 'slave morality', this is because the relationship between self and Other has been constructed as dualistic and oppositional in modernist terms. By contrast, we need to view these ideas as leading us to think that the relationship is primordial. It is always with us and is what defines our own subjectivity:

> there is no self prior to its persecution by the Other. It is that persecution that establishes the Other at the heart of the self, and establishes that 'heart' as an

> ethical relation of responsibility. To claim the self-identity of the subject is thus an act of irresponsibility, an effort to close off one's fundamental vulnerability to the Other, the primary accusation that the Other bears. (Butler, 2000, p. 25)

The idea of persecution being used here is not the same as in traditional political discourse. The concept here is that originary and inescapable relationship created between the self and that world of Others that calls us forth. It does not allow us to remain sheltered within self-enclosed boundaries – with Others who are the same (identity, role, and so on) – away from the risks that the world beyond calls for us to do, a world entwined with differences and diverseness not encased in distinct roles and schedules of behaviours. That relationship is originary. It is primordial and exists by virtue of being human and being born into a world of Others. We cannot escape it, nor should we resist its call to respond to and be with, and act with and for those Others. It does not allow me to hide behind a fence with Others like me, and draw a distinct line between 'us' and 'them'. It is a world of Others, furthermore, that cannot be responded to after a process of assimilation. Assimilation returns the Other to the same in order to be responded to. It makes that Other palatable for the self to enable a response. The possibility of assimilation as 'devouring' of the Other (Bauman, 1995) is one that is ever present when ethical response is reliant on a clear schedule of activities and accountabilities that require the Other to be 'something' specific before responsibility can be engaged – in the role of victim, or some other bureaucratically-prescribed role, such as low-income or unemployed.

Levinas's ethics of responsibility, however, poses for us a response that relies on being human, in the human-to-human or interhuman. The interhuman is the response to (an)Other, to a world of Others that occurs prior to any set of 'impersonal laws' but is, rather, one that erupts as a primary response to the other because that other's presence demands my recognition, reaction and action. It is, thus, an 'ethics of the welcome' of the stranger, of 'hospitality' (Levinas, 1998) that does not consume or subsume the other to one's own frames of reference or requirements, but provides support in their difference. This is a difficult notion for social work, its practice occurring within the context of highly prescribed activities and organizations. Is it possible to apply here, then?

Overview of the Social Work Literature

> The interhuman is also in the recourse that people have to one another for help, before the astonishing alterity of the other has been banalized or dimmed down to a simple exchange of courtesies that has become established as an 'interpersonal commerce' of customs. (Levinas, 1998, p. 100)

> In the encounters between social workers and their clients, social workers are confronted with the dependency and vulnerability of human beings. (Kjørstad, 2005, p. 394)

Much of the ethics literature in social work makes little direct reference to responsibility as a basis for ethics other than in terms of divided loyalties (Kjorstad, 2005) or in terms of professional ethics and responsibilities arising from these (Bisman, 2004; Meacham, 2007; Skehill, 1999), whether it be to question them or to engender new thinking in this arena (Banks, 2006; Briskman & Noble, 1999; Fraser & Briskman, 2005). The distinct silence in this area may have something to do with an ideological trepidation to speak of responsibility in normative terms other than the professional due to an ideological association with discourses of the political or religious right (Ife, 2005). The application of rights, however, has found fertile ground in this profession and numerous writers now canvass human rights as a valid and justifiable discourse to apply to social work (Ife, 2008; Mapp, 2008; Reichert, 2003, 2007; see Chapter 13). What can justifiably be said in defence of responsibility for social work that will not invoke these ideological incantations?

The profession has already begun to forge discussions of ethics that are beyond the professional sphere (Banks, 1998, 2008a), the implications of ethics in the challenges posed by the ambivalences, uncertainties and ironies of 'the postmodern turn' (Hugman, 2003; see also Gray & Lovat, 2006 and Chapter 11), or towards ethics that emerge out of compassion (Bilson, 2007) and are beyond rule-bound, procedural and institutionalized decision-making (Clark, 2006; Gray & Lovat, 2007; Houston, 2003; McBeath & Webb, 2002). This distinct shift suggests that the brand of ethics Levinas brings to us (and which has been highly influential for social theorists such as Bauman (1989, 1993, 1999) and Burke (2001, 2002), as well as for philosophers such as Derrida, Blanchot, Baudrillard, Irigaray and Lyotard) is already implicit as a possibility within social work theorizing, although not strictly speaking attributed to Levinas. Indeed, even within more practice-based research, (ethical) decision-making is being articulated as a messy, contradictory and ambiguous process (Bennett & Zubrzycki, 2003; Kjørstad, 2005), unable to be clearly bounded and captured by 'roles' and a distinct separation between private and public definitions of subject positions, in other words, by the attempts to institutionalize or control ethical decision-making (see Chapters 4 and 5).

The vision of responsibility that has been described above is consonant with many of the values in social work. This allows responsibility to be imagined as a radical gesture of welcoming, particularly of strangers, such as those who are distinctly different to the 'ideal' human – the disabled, the poor, the uneducated, non-whites, the migrant, and the refugee (Tascón,

2002), in other words, those disenfranchized and marginalized by sociocultural forces. This vision of responsibility, therefore, compels, but in a way that all of us are compelled, by virtue of being human in a world of other beings.

Application to Social Work Practice

Turning to Levinas can show how these ideas may have relevance for social work as a human service profession. Social work has the potential to enact Levinas's welcome of the stranger in a gesture devoid of pity, devoid of self-serving interest and devoid of narcissism. Social work's central tenet of respect and empathy for the Other carries this implicitly. Most codes of ethics embody this in one way or another in the centrality provided to the needs of clients over the practitioner's. Indeed, in a recent study carried out in Norway exploring ethical decision making by social work practitioners applying the new policies of 'workfare' (unemployment benefits), this demand becomes a central tenet for their decision making. As one respondent said:

> I hope that my primary loyalties are to my clients. I believe they are. Occasionally, I should probably be more loyal to my employers ... I have to do what I think is right. That means that I have to act in the best interests of my clients. If that were not the case, I would quit my job. (Kjørstad, 2005, p. 393)

The welcoming gesture expressed by this practitioner, while articulated as 'loyalty' towards that vulnerable Other, is apparent. This is not pity, as this becomes an act of the self's narcissism to enclose [an]Other's needs within the self's needs. Pity is the self's need for self-absolution through another's suffering. Pity is not wholesale compassion for the humanity of the Other, in all her or his situated complexity, in their terms and for them. Pity holds the self in her or his self-interested core, venturing only so far towards the Other as is safe for the self, withdrawing swiftly behind borders that protect the self from any perceived threat from the Other. Pity takes us only so far towards the Other. Zygmunt Bauman (1993), following Levinas's notion of 'proximity', mentions this distance as 'cruelty': 'Humanity turns into cruelty because of the temptation to close the openness, to recoil from stretching out towards the Other' (p. 89). Pity is always remaining safe on the self's terms. Pity only gives up what is exuberant, what is excess to the self. Quoting another participant in the above-mentioned Norwegian study, this move towards [an]Other from their framework of meaning is again apparent:

> The usual approach is to point out that when people don't work they get sick, physically and mentally. However, reality is not that simple. Some people get sick

> because of their employment. Unskilled jobs often have such poor working conditions that employees get sick at work. Most of our clients have little formal education and low self-esteem. Many of our clients do get work, but their employment ends rather quickly. When they return here, I ask them why they aren't working anymore. I often hear them respond by saying that they had a terrible pain in their stomach, while at work, or that there was so much noise at their place of work that they just couldn't handle it. As a social worker, I am unable to identify with the blatant idea that employment for our clients will lead to their salvation. I let my clients receive social assistance and I don't make any demands upon them whenever I don't have anything better to offer them. Sometimes it's best to wait and see. (Kjørstad, 2005, p. 391)

The demands of this Other, unable to be captured by instrumental policy requirements or rule-bound ethical decision-making, is circumscribed by the practitioner. But she responds to that Other in their complex, ambiguous situations, from their 'difference', i.e. from within the bounds of that Other's experiences. This is not pity. A call for pity, indeed, 'the emphasis on the "height" of the other is intended to prevent me from exercising my responsibility "as pity" for the other' (Ferreira, 2001, p. 460). Levinas instead recalls us to compassion at a time when suffering globally and historically has seen no precedent in sheer numbers of people involved. It is a globe that:

> in thirty years has known two world wars, the totalitarianism of right and left, Hitlerism and Stalinism, Hiroshima, the Gulag, and the genocides of Auschwitz and Cambodia. This is ... suffering and evil inflicted deliberately, but in a manner no reason set limits to, in the exasperation of a reason become political and detached from all ethics. (Levinas, 1998, p. 97)

This modern suffering was perpetrated because of the modernist cultural impulse to control, classify and apply detached schedules of behaviour that could dehumanize each human being to technocratic roles. Responding entirely from a role can dehumanize, directing action that only goes so far, allowing us only so much scope before the boundedness of the role limits us. As I also teach media studies in another life, a recurring question faced in this profession is 'To what extent would a journalist feel compelled to assist a victim of a tragedy, after interviewing them for a story?' Some would say that the journalist's role ends with the interview; others reply differently. Many of the answers rely on the limits of the role where the common reply might be 'We're not there to make their life better; we're there to show how it is', and walk away. Relying on roles and rules is tantamount to seeing suffering and only going as far as the role allows. This cannot be a position for social workers because we *are* 'there to make their life better'. Can we walk away when we are given the task to assess a refugee in detention from within the role of a mental health social worker and notice all the inmates are suffering similarly? Did we walk away when the images of ejected and dejected refugees hit television screens in Australia, made to endure dehumanizing conditions in detention centres? Many in the Australian community did not (Tascón, 2006).

Conclusion

In conclusion, enabling the translation into the profession of an ethics of responsibility that is beyond borders of clearly defined rules and roles and that instead relies on a response from human-to-human, allows social workers to respond beyond their organizationally defined roles, and commands compassion for refugees (as one example) and the marginalized when their difference invites fear in others. It commands social workers to respond beyond the demands of their organizations to be accountable to the rules and prescribed roles, and reach out in a gesture of human-to-human because, ultimately, Levinas's ethics of responsibility are not about making 'moral life easier [but] ... making it a bit more moral' (Bauman, 1993, p. 15).

Study Questions

1. Researching further this approach in ethics, consider more fully what 'the interhuman' and Levinas's notion of 'the Face' demands of us as human beings.
2. This approach guides us to consider ourselves as human first and then 'in role'. Is it possible to consider this approach as useful in its application to a professional endeavour such as social work?

9
Discourse Ethics

Stan Houston

Key Concepts

Lifeworld is the reservoir of meaning that human subjects draw on in order to make sense of their world, to negotiate and to create and maintain relationships with others.

Discourse ethics refers to Habermas's normative theory which sees ethical formulations arising from the rules of communication. These rules insist that it is only through the force of better argument that we can arrive at ethical decisions. It is only truly open and rational debate that counts.

Commodification is the attempt to recast human subjectivity as a commodity of the market, to be purchased, sold or manipulated for economic ends. Commodification violates the ethic of respect that is fundamental to social relationships.

Introduction

It is a popular misconception to think of a philosophical approach to ethical problem-solving as a lofty exercise, one elevated to the heights of arcane contemplation, conducted in a rarefied atmosphere, way above the practical everyday world of the mere mortal by the lone thinker cogitating and wrestling with the ills of the day. This misconception comes into sharp focus when we consider the work of the philosopher, critical theorist and social commentator, Jürgen Habermas. For Habermas, ethics are a matter of communication, for it is in the implicit nature of our face-to-face talk, rather than in detached, complex, solitary thought that the question of what is to be done is answered from an ethical standpoint. Habermas's ideas on the subject are set out in his theory of discourse ethics.

Before exploring the content of this theory in detail, it is important to understand what he has to say, in a more general vein, concerning the nature of everyday communication as it takes place in real life settings, such as the shop floor, the classroom and in family interactions. For Habermas the *sine qua non* of communication is reasoned argument. It expresses claims to validity in three ways. First, it is truthful (it must concur with the facts based on empirical investigation). Secondly, it is sincere, hence it proceeds from genuine feelings and the absence of deceit. Thirdly, it is appropriate. For this to be the case communication must be comprehensible and meaningful, coherent and justifiable in the context in which it is uttered. In expressing any one of these three claims the speaker is acting on a number of assumptions about the nature of the world around him or her. However, these are assumptions that can be contested by others. Essentially, they can be challenged legitimately using reasoned argumentation that is truthful, sincere or appropriate.

According to Habermas (1971), this inbuilt tendency to validate what has been said derives from an ineluctable quest for understanding and agreement in social life. 'Our first sentence expresses unequivocally the intention of universal and unconstrained consensus' (p. 314), writes Habermas. He goes on to state that 'the goal of coming to an understanding is to bring about an agreement that terminates in the intersubjective mutuality of reciprocal understanding, shared knowledge, mutual trust, and accord with one another' (in Outhwaite, 1996, p. 119). Mutuality, in this formulation, becomes the inherent 'telos' of communication, its veritable end point.

Validity claims and mutuality form the supportive pillars for Habermas's chief construct: *communicative action*. This occurs when individuals reach a consensual understanding on goals and actions. It is used tacitly in everyday life to establish social relationships with others, convey information and express opinion. It acts as a coordinating mechanism for social endeavours. Denoting accountability, communicative action invokes my responsibility to you to make claims that are truthful, sincere and morally appropriate and to expect a reciprocal response. Importantly, when routinized, consensual agreement forges social integration and solidarity and, in so doing, adumbrates social order.

For Habermas, communicative action reaches its apogee in the 'ideal speech situation'. This sets the conditions for free and transparent communication. It occurs in the context of:

- Agreement that is forged on the force of the better argument.
- Open participation.
- Freedom to question any assertion.
- Rightful interjection.
- Full expression of attitudes.

These strict criteria can be used as a counterfactual measure to identify 'disorders of discourse', for example mendacious comments or manipulative inveiglement. Taking up this theme of disordered discourse, Habermas directs our attention to an aberrant derivate of communicative action which he terms 'strategic action'. This occurs when speakers treat each others as objects rather than fellow human beings with needs and aspirations. Adopting strategic action, I treat you in a purely instrumental manner. I am concerned with my own success and, in certain circumstances, will engage in disputation to achieve it. There is no shared understanding here: 'in strategic action one actor seeks to influence the behaviour of another by means of the threat of sanctions or the prospect of gratification in order to cause the interaction to continue as the first actor desires' (Habermas, 1990, p. 58).

According to Habermas, strategic action morphs into a number of offshoots. I can be openly strategic, making it overtly clear that I have instrumental goals in mind, with no pretence, and even with the threat of violence, or I can deceive my audience through subtle rhetoric and emotive posturing or by presenting a veneer of reasonableness and pseudo-consensual bonhomie. More insidiously, I can engage in systematically distorted communication (here, there is no coherence whatsoever in the linguistic exchange). Alternatively, I may use strategic action to reach objectives that are purely innocuous, as in attempting to win a game of chess.

What concerns Habermas is the predominance of strategic action in the modern world: how it continues to eclipse communicative action. This has resulted in alienation, mental breakdown and the disruption of social norms. According to Habermas, we need to recapture the illocutionary force of reasoned argumentation, that is, the power of the ethical utterance to forge social relationship and meaningful engagement between the speaker and listener. The next section takes up this theme.

Key Ideas

Habermas on ethical decision-making

In his path-breaking works, *Moral Consciousness and Communicative Action* (1990) and *Justification and Application* (1991), Habermas develops his ideas on the 'ideal speech situation' to evince a procedure for ethical decision-making with communicative action at its heart. The procedure comprises three main elements: the conditions of moral discourse, the principles of moral discourse and the rules of moral discourse. Let us take each of these elements in turn.

The conditions of moral discourse

The conditions indicate that those taking part in an ethical discussion must be free to raise any topic or to accept any proposition without being coerced; they must also be equal in the sense that they have the same rights as everyone else, that is, to be listened to, to make a case for something and to be treated with respect. For example, in an important child welfare decision, such as whether to remove a young person into residential care, all the relevant information would have to be shared with the decision takers. Moreover, no one should be forced into a decision or silenced or prevented from raising alternative courses of action. Habermas (1990) then goes on to outline two principles of moral discourse. The first states that:

> Every valid norm has to fulfil the following condition. All affected can accept the consequences and side effects its general observance can be anticipated to have for the satisfaction of everyone's interests (and these consequences are preferred to those of known alternative possibilities of regulation). (p. 65)

This is the universalization principle and is denoted as (U) in the remaining text. To render the meaning slightly more accessible, I have paraphrased it in lay terms as follows: 'A valid moral decision is reached when those affected by it endorse it as the preferred way forward. In reaching this agreement, participants must accept the consequences of the decision for all concerned and its impact on everyone's interests.'

The principles of moral discourse

From a close inspection of the wording in (U) a number of crucial, interrelated premises are revealed. First of all, the principle suggests that universality, or what is best for all, cannot be achieved by the lone individual reflecting on whether the decision under question is right for everyone else. Instead, we are required to take the perspective of the other, to see the world from her viewpoint. Such reciprocity creates empathy for other positions that may not concur with our own. Without this empathy it is doubtful whether we can ever achieve a moral position. McCarthy (in the Introduction to Habermas, 1990) neatly encapsulates this aspect of Habermas's thinking:

> Habermas' discourse model, by requiring that perspective-taking be general and reciprocal, builds the moment of empathy into the procedure of coming to a reasoned agreement: each must put him or herself into the place of everyone else in discussing whether a proposed norm is fair to all. And this must be done publicly; arguments played out in the individual consciousness or in the theoretician's mind are no substitute for real discourse. (p. 8)

It can also been seen that (U) requires decision makers to be impartial. What Habermas is saying here is that it is important to balance the interests and needs of all the stakeholders when reaching an ethical decision. But this necessitates contributors having an accurate understanding of their own, and other's interests and needs. Impartiality rests, therefore, on clear communication and awareness.

Finally, it is important to highlight that (U) does not provide a pre-cast, substantive morality applying to all situations at all times, much like the 'ten commandments'. Instead, it offers a formal procedure for resolving contentious issues in an uncertain, pluralistic social world.

From (U) Habermas (1990) develops a second principle (denoted as (D) in the remaining text). He writes: 'Only those norms can claim to be valid that meet (or could meet) with the approval of all affected in their capacity as participants in a practical discourse' (p. 66). Through (D) Habermas reiterates the point that communication is the only medium through which actors can reach morally binding decisions.

The rules of moral discourse

With the conditions and principles of moral discourse in place, Habermas (1990) sets out a set of accompanying rules:

> 3.1 Every subject with the competence to speak and act is allowed to take part in a discourse.
>
> 3.2a Everyone is allowed to question any assertion whatever.
> 3.2b Everyone is allowed to introduce any assertion whatever into the discourse.
> 3.2c Everyone is allowed to express his attitudes, desires, and needs.
>
> 3.3 No speaker may be prevented, by internal or external coercion, from exercising his right as laid down in 3.1 and 3.2. (p. 89)

Habermas (1990) goes on to explain the meaning of these rules:

> Rule 3.1 defines the set of potential participants. It includes all subjects without exception who have the capacity to take part in argumentation. Rule 3.2 guarantees all participants equal opportunity to contribute to the argumentation and to put forth their own arguments. Rule 3.3 sets down conditions under which the rights to universal access and to equal participation can be enjoyed equally by all, that is, without the possibility of repression, be it ever so subtle or covert. (p. 89)

Participants should use the rules to plan how meetings are chaired, to decide who will be invited to attend, to select the setting in which discussions will take place and to direct how the discussion will unfold. If we do not operate a policy of inclusive dialogue, there may be a danger of rubber-stamping preordained views that are contaminated by prejudice, cognitive distortion or psychological counter-transference. If the agenda was not open to modification or development, then the breadth of debate would be curtailed. If modes of engagement misuse power, perhaps through an over-reliance on professional jargon, then role-taking will be thwarted.

To conclude this section, it is important to say that Habermas attacks sceptics who argue that all moral statements have equal worth. He rejects the relativism inherent within this position by arguing that through reasoned argument we can reach a position of saying that one moral view is justified over all others.

Overview of the Social Work Literature

Habermas's normative theory has received increasing interest in the social work literature where he is seen as a champion of individual empowerment. I will start this overview with my first attempt to extrapolate his ethical ideas to social work. Taking a cue from Graham McBeath and Stephen Webb (2002), Houston (2003) argued that professional virtue was nourished when instantiated in the kind of ethical deliberation promulgated by Habermas:

> Virtue is linked to the empirical world of interacting subjects. It arises from ethical deliberations on tangible moral dilemmas ... (it) is a product of the social act regulated by conditions, principles and rules. Institutionalising the latter within our daily decision-making activities over time and in different contexts is ... the main way of enhancing moral awareness and virtue in social work. (p. 823)

Staying on a synthetic quest and still on the theme of virtue, Houston (2008) subsequently attempted to align Habermas's discourse ethics with Axel Honneth's (1995) theory of recognition. The argument proceeded by identifying a crucial weakness in discourse ethics: its lack of emotional content. By concentrating on a procedural, cognitive approach, Habermas, it was argued, had strayed from grounded experiences of heartfelt pain to an abstracted preoccupation with universal justification. Such experience, and the selves that endured it, could be understood more compassionately by adopting Honneth's three limbs of interpersonal recognition, namely, his pathbreaking recognition through loving relationships, accorded rights and respect, and validation of a person's contribution to social life. This alignment, which I described as 'complementary, mutually rectifying and concordant at the meta-ethical of analysis', was offered as a wellspring for virtuous social work practice.

Terry Lovat and Mel Gray (2007) picked up on these themes of virtue and communication in their adoption of a 'proportionist stance'. Integrating Aristotelian, Thomist and Habermasian epistemologies, they attempted to transcend utilitarian and deontological ethics. For them, what was important was ethical balance. Interestingly, Habermas's ethical project was cast as one that mediated between the extremes of universalism and cultural contingency; but more than that, it moved on to source virtuous deliberation in social work. In this formulation, discourse ethics equipped social workers to navigate their way through the Scylla of unbending codes of practice and the Charybdis of ethical relativism.

Building on this contribution, Gray and Lovat (2008) connected Habermas's early ideas on emancipatory knowledge and his later work on discourse ethics. Such knowledge and ethics were relevant for today's social work with its hegemonic, technocratic mindset. Unafraid to extol the necessity of compassionate practice, the authors opined that pluralistic conceptions of virtue ethics gave added lustre to the Habermasian project. Ethical perspicacity could be enhanced through virtue applied discursively. The authors cited Mattias Iser's (2003) work to support their thesis. For Iser, it was axiomatic that ethical discourse sprang from the virtuous character. Communication reflecting sensitivity, empathy and compassion was to be seen as consonant with the virtuous attitude. A fortified virtue ethics emerged from this scholarship – one that provided an alternative approach to the sterility of deontological and consequentialist positions in social work (see Chapter 10).

Richard Hugman's (2005) view on the potential of discourse ethics resonates with the previous authors' ideas. For him, Habermas's contribution could be used to overcome the fissure between universalistic and particularistic approaches to ethical quandaries in social work. The former was exemplified in Kantian-inspired codes of practice and exalted value statements. The latter was grounded in the specific, the relational and the contextual realities of lived encounters in social work. Consensual dialogue, apropos discourse ethics, was the means through which abstract ethical criteria and situational exigencies could be apprehended in a blended way to source the virtuous response.

These contributions are interesting in that they attempt to reach for alignment, integration and connection between different, but contiguous, philosophical positions. This is justifiable in order to avoid the cardinal sins of essentialism, reductionism, reification and functional teleology that permeate sociological and explanatory failures (Sibeon, 2004). There is 'no God's eye view' on matters of ontology, says Nietzsche. Plurality, diversity and complexity in social life require theoretical erudition and synthesis if the Platonic cave were to be illuminated. What marks the foregoing contributions is their attempt to justify conceptual integration by examining congruence at the meta-ethical level of analysis.

Other scholarly contributions to the area can be summarized briefly as follows. In a recent paper, David Hayes and Stan Houston (2007) argued that the family group conference was emblematic of Habermas's plea for structures that mediated between the 'lifeworld' and 'system'. They went on to say that the decision-making phase of the conference had not been scrutinized from the viewpoint of ethical standards of communication. The contention was that discourse ethics, when aligned to Honneth's recognition-theoretic, could fill this gap.

Staying within the field of child and social work, Houston (2005[not in refs: please give details]) also looked at the potential for discourse ethics to illuminate ethical decision-making when it came to decisions regarding children in state care. He highlighted the problem of those subjects who may be communicatively ill-equipped to contribute to discourse, thereby excluding them from idealized speech. The example of the young child was presented. To remedy this stumbling block, a model of reflective examination was introduced for appointed advocates. This was to enable them to role-take and convey the views of the excluded child through accurate, empathetic representations that held ideological bias in check.

I will finish this section by acknowledging a seminal paper by Ricardo Blaug (1995). This paper never ceases to inspire and to read it is to build the kind of virtue extolled by Lovat and Gray. It is a 'moral must'. In the text, the author presented a myriad of applications of the ideal speech situation, citing its role in user involvement, case conferences, community work and advocacy. In a somewhat evocative turn, he stated that the central conclusion of the theory of discourse ethics was the prosaic act of drinking copious amounts of tea with service recipients. Tea drinking, it was argued, engendered human interaction – the basis for caring. Simply put, it gave rise to ethically intelligent social work.

Application to Social Work Practice

Let us now consider a case study from the perspective of Habermas's discourse ethics. It concerns the separation of a young child from his parents. Such a move raises enormous issues, not least those pertaining to human rights legislation. More specifically, social workers involved in decisions of this kind need to balance the rights of the biological parents to bring up their child without disproportionate interference, the rights of the child to have his or her needs met, and the rights of alternative carers to be treated with respect, taking into account their emotions, needs and sentiments. However, we know from research that the rights of these different parties are sometimes thwarted or jeopardized by delays in decision making, drift within the care system, and contested perspectives on what is best for the child (Ward, Munro, & Dearden, 2006). It is argued below that Habermas's ideas concerning moral communication have a direct bearing on cases of this kind, providing a compass for social workers and other professionals to navigate their way through a sea of complex and competing ethical issues.

The case concerns John, a 4-month-old boy, and although some details have been changed, is based on actual events that came before the Court of Appeal in Northern Ireland (*AR* v *Homefirst Community Trust*, 2005). John is the third child in the family. His two older siblings were adopted at an early age due to parental neglect. They had also witnessed domestic violence. Both of these siblings were placed together and bonded well with their adoptive parents.

John's biological parents have a long history of abusing alcohol. Mary, his mother, began drinking when she was a teenager. Apart from a number of brief periods of abstinence in the past, her drinking has been a persistent problem. Over the years, John's father, Robert, has indulged in a similar pattern of alcohol abuse. Six months before John's birth, the couple separated owing to long-standing domestic violence. Support from the extended family has been sporadic and inconsistent.

When it came to the attention of social services that Mary was pregnant with John, a multidisciplinary case conference was held. The conference decided that the baby's name would be placed on the child protection register, under the category of 'potential neglect', following his birth. For Robert and Mary, this decision was grossly unjust. From their perspective the decision did not take account of their recent sobriety and attendance at counselling sessions with a community psychiatric nurse. Feeling angry and fearful, they withdrew from any contact with social services.

On the day of John's birth social services were granted an 'emergency protection order', allowing them to remove the baby into care. Weighing up all the evidence, they decided not to pursue a residential assessment of Mary's parenting and to limit contact to John. A consultant psychiatrist's report indicated, at this time, that Mary showed little insight into the triggers leading to her past abuse of alcohol. Previous history, he suggested, was 'the best guide to the future'. Mary's recent abstinence was seen to be linked to her pregnancy which, having come full-term, was no longer a protective factor. Supporting his prognosis, the psychiatrist made reference to previous pregnancies where a similar pattern of abstinence, followed by resumption of alcohol abuse, had taken place. The prognosis would worsen, it was opined, should Mary reunite with Robert – a distinct possibility, it was felt, given the couple's history.

Because of John's 'tender' years, and the view that rehabilitation was ill-advised, social services reached the conclusion that adoption, with or without parental consent, was in his best interests. The plan was to place him with the couple who had previously adopted his two older siblings, thus helping to bolster his biological identity. For social services delay was to be avoided at all costs if an optimal psychological attachment was to form between John and his carers. This notion was supported by a specialist social worker for adoption appointed by the agency to make a recommendation concerning John's future placement.

Mary, however, had maintained her abstinence from alcohol throughout all of this. This had been aided by the counselling received from the psychiatric nurse. In fact, it was the latter's view that Mary had made sufficient progress – 12 months' abstinence in all – to warrant a residential assessment of her parenting capacity. Disputing the view of the two social workers, she indicated that Mary had shown 'good insight' into her problems, including the need to remain separated from Robert if a residential assessment was to take place and form a positive conclusion.

Given that an application for a care order had been made to the court by social services, an independent guardian, June, was appointed to investigate the matter and make recommendations. June had been qualified for t13 years. The early part of her career had been spent in child and family social work, mostly carrying out child protection duties. She had moved to the Guardian-ad-Litem agency when it had first been set up three years prior to receiving this case. In her qualifying training she had completed a dissertation on the link between moral philosophy and social work. It was in carrying out a literature review for this piece of work that she had first encountered Habermas's ideas on discourse ethics. What immediately appealed to her was the notion that it was through democratic forms of communication that ethical quandaries were best approached. From June's perspective, discourse ethics offered a means for highlighting key ethical standards to guide social work practice or to identify breaches of such standards when critically reflecting on a piece of work that had taken place.

When June read the case file and reports to the court a number of concerns struck her. Drawing on Habermas's thoughts, it seemed, primarily, that the views adopted rested on a series of 'untested' *validity claims*. The first of these referred to the social worker's opinion that an urgent decision had to be taken on John's future before he attained the age of 6 months. According to the social worker this was to ensure that the baby was given the best opportunity to form an attachment with a main care-giver. June was aware of the research evidence showing that it was desirable that permanent arrangements be made for an infant expeditiously. Quite clearly, an early attachment could easily form with a temporary foster carer, only to be disrupted later on, to the detriment of the child. While the social worker might be sincere in her view on this matter (meeting one of Habermas's claims to validity), it did not follow for June that this view was *justified*. Others matters needed to be factored into a *rational* debate about what was best for John. It was important to recognize that the long-term welfare of a child could also be adversely hampered by the knowledge that he had been forcibly removed from his mother's care. Furthermore, while expeditious planning was required in most cases, there might be situations when 'appropriate' or 'purposeful' delay was warranted – particularly in a case such as this where an informed assessment was required to ascertain parental insight.

A second validity claim centred on the idea that the past was the best prognosticator of the future. This claim had originated from the consultant psychiatrist on the basis of only one interview with Mary. June reflected on its merit. Certainly, it would be foolhardy, even dangerous, for social workers to neglect historical factors in risk assessment. However, human beings, she surmised, also showed a great capacity to adapt and change. They were not simply cogs in a machine fated to replicate 'time past'. Previous behaviour was never an infallible guide for predicting future action. What is more, for June there was a danger of labelling Mary, thereby creating a self-fulfilling prophesy.

Of course, the community psychiatric nurse and Mary herself had also made a series of validity claims painting a different picture of events; however, these seemed to be more justified from a *reasoned* point of view. The nurse had *only* said that there was enough evidence of sustained sobriety to warrant a residential assessment; she had made no comment on parenting capacity *per se*. Mary, too, on the basis of a year's abstinence, was only asking to have her parenting assessed. These claims appeared to June to be sincerely struck and appropriate, particularly when one considered that Mary had not relapsed after giving birth (as predicted by social services). Blanket phrases such as 'Mary lacks insight and refuses to take responsibility for her past' were not necessarily true or appropriate. Drawing on Habermas's ideas on *strategic action*, June felt that such comments had the ring of 'wanting to argue a predetermined case' rather than make a *balanced* judgement. Validity in argument was more a matter of weighing up all the evidence, thinking through all the options impartially, considering all of the different perspectives using reason as the sole arbiter of truth.

A second concern, for June, was the lack of real communication between the parties. The two social workers had made no attempt to speak in person to the psychiatric nurse, nor had they reflected her view in their court reports. It was only in the context of unfettered communication that validity claims could be fully tested. Barriers to open communication had also been erected through the use of social work jargon. In the court reports, the social worker had referred to Mary's children as having being 'parentified'. Such ambiguous and invidious remarks as these would only militate against understanding, agreement and consensus, the three pillars of Habermas's *communicative action*.

For June, the principle of 'U' necessitated a close attention to John's interests and needs but also those of Mary's. It required that all the parties reflect on the consequences of proposed courses of action. For June, social services had not factored Mary's interests into their thinking. They had focused exclusively on John, and while there were good grounds for viewing his needs as the first and paramount consideration, this did not mean that they should have neglected Mary's interests and rights. Indeed, social services had not taken account of the European Convention on Human Rights which, under Article 8, states that everyone has the right to respect for their private and family life. Balance, impartiality and proportionality had to be factored into decision-making and open communication. It was not only that the social workers had to engage more fully in perspective taking, empathy and reasoned argumentation with Mary, but she too had to consider the concerns expressed about her history and its serious implications for John.

In constructing her report to the court, June felt it was overly precipitate to recommend adoption. While conscious of John's young age, there needed to be more attempts at *communicative action*. Within this context, June would be required to act as an independent advocate representing the 'voice of the child'. However, for communicative action to be achieved, social services would need to consider closely the power differentials involved in such a process. Position power, status power, the use of jargon, the bureaucratic ambience within meetings, power dressing and adversarial dispositions would militate against genuine understanding, agreement and consensus. Purposeful delay to explore the options further, communicatively, in an impartial manner with power held in check, seemed to June to be the best, interim recommendation to the court.

Conclusion

In the case described, Habermas's model of discourse ethics will not tell the parties what the right decision is, but it does offer a procedure and a set of constructs for examining very contentious, ethically fraught areas in order to reach a consensual position. Centrally, we can only justify a decision if it arrives from reasoned, explicit argumentation based on validity claims that are true, sincere and appropriate. The use of communication is pivotal. It must avoid strategic, 'winner-takes-all' approaches. Instead, participants in dialogue must think of the common good – the rights and interests of all, particularly in a case where adoption is being mooted and human rights are to the fore. In 'face-to-face' encounters, Habermas reminds us that we should strive to take the perspective of the 'Other'. We must adopt a post-conventional morality that goes beyond narrow institutional objectives and consider what is universally applicable. In the struggle to apply discourse ethics to their practice in a concerted way, social workers build up inner virtue. It is from this inner wellspring that moral inspiration flourishes.

Study Questions

1. To what extent is discourse ethics compromised by subjects who may be communicatively hampered by disability, age or mental health circumstances?
2. Do individuals naturally incline towards attaining consensus in communication as Habermas suggests, particularly in situations where social control is to the fore?
3. What is the contribution of discourse ethics to social work as practised under a neoliberal framework?

10
Virtue Ethics

Stephen A. Webb

Key Concepts

Communitarianism emphasizes the need to balance individual rights and interests with that of the community as a whole. It is opposed to individualism and libertarian political perspectives. Unlike liberalism, which construes communities as originating in the voluntary acts of individuals, it emphasizes the role of the community in defining a shared civic engagement. Communitarians argue that values and moral beliefs exist in public space, in which dialogue and criticism take place.

Virtue ethics is not a theory which tells us what to do. In social work we should neither have nor want such a thing. Rather virtue ethics guides us by improving the practical reasoning with which social workers act. It directs us, as we are judging what to do, towards emulating practitioners who are more compassionate and caring and generally better than we are. Virtue ethics has a built-in recognition that the moral life is not static, but dynamic and situational.

Introduction

Consider the ways in which you might describe individuals to other people. It is likely that you will use a range of evaluative terms, perhaps in common parlance, referring to someone as a 'nice person' or even a 'horrid person'. What does it mean to be a 'nice person'? Is being a nice person the same as being a good person or a decent person? Can a person be good but not nice, or nice but not good? These kinds of question sit at the heart of moral considerations in virtue ethics. Social workers in their day-to-day talk similarly use a person's characteristics and dispositions to describe clients as well as other professionals. Everyday talk in social work is often based on a series of moral evaluations that are inferred about other people. If someone is described as a nice person this can imply a set of moral dispositions or demonstrable behaviours. Now imagine what you might think if someone viciously blasphemed about another person you knew by either falsely demeaning that person or telling lies about them. What would you feel like if a close friend deliberately betrayed you? Do you think it is the right thing to do to lie about someone or betray a close friend? Less obviously, but just as controversially, perhaps, do you believe that uploading adult porn from the internet is the right thing to do? Is it the kind of thing a virtuous person would do? Taken together, each of these examples is illustrative of the contours that reflect on key considerations in virtue ethics and the way it explores the relationship between virtues and vice. Virtue ethics is about the evaluation of individuals in relation to their acts and whether the combination of virtuous acts contributes to human flourishing. It is my contention that this sort of focus is necessarily one of the virtues of virtue ethics in its relevance for social work. By focusing on virtue, we get to the very core of the moral stuff of social work. Indeed, some writers have maintained that many leading ethical theories are incomplete because they fail to account for *both* right *and* wrong (Moore, 2007).

In this chapter, I suggest that many of the moral judgements that social workers make are based, at least implicitly, on presuppositions of virtue or vice, even though the two terms are not commonly used in social work discourse. Virtue is about *how we evaluate* certain things when we make moral judgements about ourselves or other people and *what we decide to do* that is considered to be right in moral situations. As Rosalind Hursthouse (1999) writes, 'An action is right if it is what a virtuous agent would characteristically (i.e. acting in character) do in the circumstances' (p. 28). Being virtuous is about doing the right thing and, in order to do the right thing, you need to be a particular sort of moral person. This begs the question of whether you need to be a virtuous person to be able to make right moral judgements. But what guidance does all this give us in social work when we must decide what we should do in certain circumstances? I discuss this central question below, and especially in relation to whether virtue ethics requires us to follow moral rules. For now an introduction to virtue ethics will be offered to map some of the main features and background understandings associated with this ethical theory.

Key ideas

Unlike many other perspectives discussed in this book, virtue ethics is rooted in a particular philosophical school of thought that originated in the writings of Aristotle. Historically, virtue ethics is grounded in an account of how a Greek citizen was positioned in relation to the Greek city-state and was a theory of the relation between individual character, morality and public life. The relevance of this approach in today's society rests with considerations of how right moral relations can exist between state agencies, such as social workers and clients in terms of the character and 'excellences' of the practitioner, the nature of the social care agency and the response of the client.

Since the late 1970s there has been a significant shift in the concerns of moral philosophy. However, in the area of moral theory two dominant frameworks still prevail, that of Kantian or deontological ethics, which is concerned with duty and respect, and utilitarianism, which is concerned with the value of ends for the greater good. Until the mid-1980s, there was no third way. As Angela Everitt and Pauline Hardiker (1996) noted, in the mid-1980s one or two writers began to consider whether an Aristotelian notion of 'the good', defined in terms of the virtues, might be helpful as a source of ethics in social work. That an 'Aristotelian' perspective in social work ethics has not been taken up, but merely mentioned, is perhaps, in part, testimony to the persistent preoccupations with Kantianism and utilitarianism or a mix of the two (in the UK, BASW, 1979; Central Council for Training and Education in Social Work, 1976). Equally the routine teaching of values in social work encompassed other value bases, such as anti-oppressive notions in regard to inequalities of gender, race and social power, which, though pitched at a lower level of abstraction, nonetheless were seen to be given equal status to the higher-order theories. Social work professional training has dictated the relevance of some value bases over others, and the absence of virtue theory from social work's ethical framework or cognate knowledge base in part explains its continuing absence.

Unlike its Kantian and utilitarian competitors, which rely upon the mechanical application of rights claims, moral rules and adherence to duties (the General Social Care Council 'Code of Conduct' is a good example of this; see Chapter 5) or upon the comparison of anticipated outcomes, virtue ethics makes foundational the qualities of one's character, which are manifest in one's actions. Taking this with a claim that virtue is a cultural product, we may see that a virtue ethics is the formation of a way of being developed through practice inside a culture of experience, reflection, understanding and judgement which brings its (virtuous) self into contact with others.

We may ask, how might a virtue ethics be cashed out in social work terms? To connect a virtue ethics to a dimension crucial to social work one might put the question thus: what is the relation of morality to experience? Could the latter, in some way, produce the former? To fashion an answer to these questions involves making links between virtue, its cultivation, judgement, and professional social work. Given that some accounts of virtue ethics make virtues, as intrinsic qualities, logically prior to moral outcomes, I shall use the links just mentioned to defend virtue ethics against those who argue that virtues are pointless without a prior determination of the goals of human flourishing, i.e. prior value commitments.

Aristotelian virtue ethics

For virtue ethics, a good act is good because it results from a good character that is intrinsically going to deploy action in line with one or more virtues. Thus the goodness of the act is not a result of the outcome or of the indexing of one's moral actions by their universal standard and the duty entailed always to act similarly in similar cases. The connection between the actor and the acted upon, whether in terms of respect or advantage given to the latter by the former, is not of primary concern. It is not that the ends do not matter but that the intended result does not make the actor moral. It is rather peculiar to want to suggest that an action or its result, in and of itself, can be good. The goodness of an action lies in persons *and* their motivations and dispositions in the execution and aims of *their* actions. To account for the structure of this process is, in effect, to understand the thick stuff of moral action, and this requires scrutiny of the making of the inner self not merely through a psychology, but through the identification of social and cultural factors, which shape how the components of the inner life are woven in the project of being human in the world. And this question exploring the meaning of the good life – the question of 'the best way to live' – was central to Plato and Aristotle and the Hellenic world-view.

Aristotle's notion of the good life placed greater importance upon the collective of the city-state than it did upon the good of the individual. For even if the good of the community coincides with that of the individual, it is clearly a greater and more perfect thing to achieve and preserve than of a community, for while it is desirable to secure what is good in the case of an individual, to do so in the case of a people or a state is something finer and more sublime (Aristotle, 1976). Ultimately, the interests of the state coincide with the interests of the individual – the well-being of the state is the *summum bonum* because it promotes the good of the individual and is the entity which the individual thus aspires to promote and for which he does his best. The reciprocal nature of the relation between the state and the individual requires that good as happiness is a function of the disposition towards certain ways of individual conduct, i.e. the virtues which are acquired through training and example. To be happy is not only to act in accordance with virtue – to live virtuously – but also to have material goods 'throughout a complete life' (ibid., p. 84). Human kind is, therefore, primarily active and practical, and secondarily contemplative.

The good life, which all want in their various ways, can only be achieved through participation in the political culture which individuals develop by debating well and acting justly. These are precisely the means by which to improve the structural conditions which, in turn, improve the conditions of the individual. So the conception of a good life is bound to the practices of the virtuous citizen and the state. At root then, is the good will – the totality of virtuous dispositions the individual brings into his social and political activity. These, as we have seen, are matured by forms of education. Here we may quickly note that a good will – the impetus to act well towards an object or goal – is the concept Kant appealed to as irreducibly good when he opened the *Groundwork* ([1785] 1948). Identifying the good with a disposition to be good, not surprisingly, has led many to see that there is more than a whiff of virtue ethics about Kant, despite it being widely held that he provided a form of ethical reasoning opposed to that of Aristotle (Baron, 1997; Sherman, 1997).

Aristotle distinguishes between two classes of virtue: *intellectual* and *moral*. Under the former fall wisdom, prudence and understanding, which are acquired by instruction, and need time and experience. Under the latter are liberality and temperance, which are chiefly acquired by habit and the example of others. However, a virtue can become a vice where there is either a surfeit or deficit of it. Another way in which one can easily fall short of full virtue is through lacking *phronesis* – moral or practical wisdom. With this idea in mind, Aristotle elaborates his doctrine of the 'golden mean' which has come to be captured in English phrases such as 'you can have too much of a good thing' or 'don't go overboard'. He sets out a table of virtues and vices where, in the sphere of social conduct, the virtuous mean would be friendliness, in deficient form would be cantankerousness, and in excessive form would be obsequiousness. Thus in Aristotle's ethics, to be virtuous is a practice of life which, if done well, is the process of producing the good life. To be virtuous contributes to the good life. This links to the concept of *eudaimonia*, a key term in ancient Greek moral philosophy, which standardly translates as 'happiness' or 'flourishing' and occasionally as 'well-being'. Virtue ethicists argue that a human life devoted to physical pleasure, personal fame or the acquisition of wealth is not *eudaimon*, but a wasted life, and also accept that they cannot produce a knock-down argument for this claim proceeding from premises that the happy hedonist would acknowledge. The good life requires judgement of what is a just measure of action commensurable with the situation obtaining, for this is implied by the doctrine of the mean. How such judgement is acquired is itself a sociocultural product. The relation between the good of the individual and that of the community is bi-conditional.

Having discussed the context and terms of Aristotle's virtue ethics, I shall now turn to exploring how post-Aristotelian versions have found their way into the social work literature. For the purpose of this chapter, I will only consider work since the later 1980s inasmuch as they are responding to developments in moral philosophy, which have set the parameters of argument in applied ethics for social work. What is important in this respect is for readers to understand the difference between a virtue ethics approach to social work and other dominant perspectives that currently weigh down various professional codes of ethics in social work. The dominance of other moral theories in social work has meant that virtue ethics is rarely discussed or focused upon in professional social work training courses.

Overview of the Social Work Literature

Except for the recent work of Banks (2003a), Banks and Gallagher (2009), McBeath and Webb (2002), Clark (2006), Gray (2009) and Gray and Lovat (2007), the social work literature is dominated by Kantian and utilitarian versions of professional ethics, and usually a combination of the two (see also van den Bersselaar, 2005). Most professional codes of ethics are dressed up in the language of these two 'deontological' perspectives. Unlike its Kantian and utilitarian competitors, which also rely upon the mechanical application of rights claims and adherence to duties and moral procedures, virtue ethics makes foundational the qualities of one's character which are manifest in one's actions. Taking this along with a claim that virtue is a cultural product, we may see that a virtue ethics is the formation of a way of well-being inside a culture of experience, reflection, understanding and judgement, which brings the virtuous self into contact with others.

The practice of virtue is developed through experience, reflection and circumspection, which are the very stuff of good social work. They provide criteria for a profoundly human moral theory, which is not perfectionist in its ambition, but rather is defensible in terms of the 'good enough'. This is precisely because the structure of human relationships and moral evaluations are variable and dynamic. Only in a static world is perfection possible and, of all worlds, the social work world is no utopia. Thus virtue ethics fit well with a field of activity, such as social work, which is subject to change, accident and flexibility. The criticism that virtue ethics cannot adequately be applied to moral problems of the 'what ought I to do in this case?' is a strength in that, at a time when social work aims to become more prescriptive and criteria led, a theory of moral action rooted in the development of persons-as-subjective-agents is, perhaps, to be welcomed (Louden, 1997). In this sense, virtue ethics may be seen as partial but revitalizing in its focus upon the virtues of the social worker and not just of the work done. Doing a task well is not merely a matter of rule-following. Expressed in it are the skills and virtues of persons. Virtue ethics, then, may not tell us what must be done in this or that case to satisfy an image of social work as a moral enterprise. Rather, virtue ethics can be used to offer an account of the modes of moral *existence,* which can shape the activity of *being* a good social worker. More simply, then, the basic question is not what is good social work, but rather what is a good social worker?

Virtue ethics, then, is a reaction to the predominance of Kantian and utilitarian ethical theories which concern either giving ethical directives to specific moral problems or to defining the meaning of the predicate 'good'. Virtue ethics tends to dispense with criteria, such as duty, responsibility and ends, deemed essential to justifying actions. Michael Stocker (1997) gives the example of telling someone that one has visited them in hospital because it was one's duty. This carries the implication that one did not visit them because one wanted to. In this sense, acting from duty is of lesser moral worth than an act done because one *purely* wanted to. One is neither doing the act for oneself or for the other. Michael Slote (1997) also runs the argument that if duties have a reference point, it is that of the person for whom a duty is performed and not for the performer. Slote identifies this as a 'self-other asymmetry', which implies that the moral agent (performer) lacks positive moral worth, and that 'agents are viewed as mere tools for helping others' (1997, p. 5). He discusses well-being rather than eudaimonia, and maintains that this consists in certain 'objective' goods. He argues that virtuous motives are not only necessary but also sufficient for well-being. These points go to the heart of becoming a social worker. Why would one become a social worker today? At one time, it was common to appeal to political or religious motivations. People committed to doing the right thing in relation to a socialized conception of the good life. Today, the motivations are not so clear. Many perhaps enter the profession in pursuit of a public-sector job that is relatively secure, but it is also dictated by the consequent set of duties which prioritize social work as a *task*. This brings into play the self–other asymmetry and thus undermines the celebrated Kantian criterion of treating people as ends and not as means. The social worker who does the task because she or he is obliged – or duty bound – to do it once employed, lacks moral commitment as a self-responsible being pursuing the good life. Supplication to duty leaves social workers without moral identity because they are acting for the sake of others, i.e. the social work agency or the client. If social worker does not recognize her moral identity and calling, then one may wonder whether such a person ought to do social work at all. We may see here that the Stocker and Slote criticisms of Kantian ethics can be brought to bear upon current concerns about the future of social work as a profession.

A third point about deontology is what Bernard Williams (1985) has called the problem of moral luck. This points out that our duties are limited by our abilities such that contingency does not enter into duty-based accounts of morality. However, the fact is that our lives are filled with the unpredictable, and affairs over which we have no or little control. Given the latter, we cannot in most situations act morally. In other words, much of life is a matter of luck, and traditional moral frameworks exclude this property as they view morality as only a matter of that for which we are entirely responsible. Again, if we relate these arguments to social work, they require us to accommodate complexity and risk (Webb, 2006). It is false to pretend, as casework managers and evidence-based advocates tend to do, that each case is essentially controllable and predictable. Positivist methodologies have taught us to believe that this is the case, but experience tells us it is not. The complex character of each case calls upon us to do our best, using our judgement and situational understanding to adapt to changing circumstances. Here lies the skill of the social worker giving concrete expression to Aristotle's intellectual virtues of wisdom in relation to prudence.

Against utilitarian theories which aim to maximize the welfare of persons and society, one powerful argument virtue ethics runs is that it would be virtuous to do less than the optimizing action welfare-wise if the minimizing action entailed transgressing virtue. Christine Swanton (1997) gives the example of someone refusing to betray a friend for the sake of optimizing the welfare of themselves or someone else. To keep faith with friends is an act which shows that one possesses the virtue of friendship. This is the way one best performs friendship. One does not keep faith simply because of abstract rules of duty. Once more, relating arguments to social work, we can argue that if defensive social work were a primary consideration so as to maximize the interests of social care agency and elected members not to suffer public embarrassment, it might be that necessary and expensive but unpopular services to, say, a drug user or a paedophile would be refused. The political discomfort caused by the *News of the World* exposé of 'paedophiles in your neighbourhood' was threatening to overturn virtuous public policy for the sake of maximizing the welfare of the government. The social worker would surely endorse virtue against the cruder instincts of a utilitarian pay-off. The contours of a virtue ethics are laid out precisely by the application of good judgement leading to right action in the face of the complexity of the world, and by actions rooted in concrete qualities of the agent's character. Such an ethics escapes the problems of duty-based accounts.

Application to Social Work Practice

Virtue ethics is distinct in pointing the ethical way back to the need for the cultivation of character, and thus to the precedence of the quality of the actor over that of the action. To this end, I have reviewed some of the arguments which virtue ethicists have deployed against more established positions. This section now turns to considerations of how virtue ethics can be applied in social work practice.

Doing the right thing in social work is not a matter of applying a moral rule. It is not the work-as-activity that is morally right, but rather the worker-as-agent expressed in the range and subtlety of use of the virtues. In this sense, the virtues are not specific moral concepts, but generalizable capacities of self, the application of which are acquired, *pace* Aristotle, via training and experience. The morality of the agent emanates from his disposition to do the best he can in the circumstances conjoined to good judgement and perception. We must not forget that judgement itself has a moral character in that it requires mental effort, commitment to thinking and deliberation. Morality under virtue ethics has an intellectual and motivational content which culminates in practical action.

If we want to find ethical constants in a dynamic context, then perhaps we have to look to the reflected-upon character of the ethical agent in terms of his dispositions, and not the actions he actually does or that he will always do in similar cases (under his terms of recognition of what is similar). The individual's character is the stable reference point, not the actions. In the case of the actions he actually does, these could be spontaneous and coincidentally fit the circumstances, i.e. they would be pure luck and thus have no ethical value whatsoever and further, contain little possibility of being repeated in some way. When we try to abide by the virtues, as we noted above, we try to act as best as we can in a manner and to a degree appropriate to the situation. We judge the situation and what is needed and this takes the successful action beyond mere serendipity. In social work one tries to work with the grain of the sociocultural situations of a family, and not impose an abstract moral solution. In a virtue ethics for social work we emphasize exactly this, the role of perception, judgement and flexibility.

The virtuous social worker is the person who strives to do her best granted that the world is in flux. Doing well is not purely tied to 'moral' matters, but to a broad conception of human flourishing or successful way of life. Happiness for Aristotle does not consist of a specific set of 'moral' goods which we must attain to be truly good. Happiness for him is the end(s) for which we strive and which is chosen for its own sake. We are most happy when we realize it best. Thus we realize happiness when it is in accord with excellence where the latter is expressed through virtue (Clark, 2006). In this idea, then, is contained the suggestion that social workers should be striving to reach goals which are done for their own sake, that is, due to conscious commitment and not only because someone said so. Further, we want to do that task well because it will be best fitted to doing good social work for the client. Such dispositions of virtues carry the agent of social work forth to realize best practice.

To the degree that we accept that any application of virtue ethics to social work may reflect Aristotelian strictures, we are obliged to come to the question of human flourishing as a community enterprise. Since Alasdair

MacIntyre's *After Virtue* (1981) and Michael Sandel's *Liberalism and the Limits of Justice* (1982), the primacy of community as a basis for political societies over that of the individual, the latter being set out in the work of John Rawls (1971) and Robert Nozick (1974), has become well established in the literature. In this the appeal to Aristotle's virtue is evident. Indeed, MacIntyre argued that any account of the virtues must indeed be generated out of the community in which those virtues are to be practised: the very word 'ethics' implies 'ethos'. The basic idea is that the structure of the community, which presumably wishes to realize its *telos* best, shapes and socializes the individual citizen towards that end. The evaluation of virtue is thus linked to the conception the community holds of its own flourishing. So while the virtues themselves as abstracts remain, their concrete application in terms of how much of a virtue one uses is relative to the aims of any particular society or organization, such as social care agencies. The good life is thereby not a subjective account of the individual who makes it up as he goes along, however virtuous his intentions. It is a reflection of, and practice internal to, the civic culture or a part of it in which the person is brought up. For example, in most societies not telling the truth or deliberately misleading is not acceptable as a principle. We do not have that much flexibility of judgement. Equally, we do not consider that lying is proper when it suits for some kind of activities and not others within a whole society. A conscience against lying is good. At the level of social worker–client relations, the client would not want to engage with the worker who lied for advantage because, although it may be to the advantage of a client one day, it may be to her disadvantage the next. The client would never quite be at ease once she realized that the worker lied strategically. Further, if a worker lies, then the client may think that he can do the same, which would tend to undermine effective work since neither side would be in possession of the correct facts or understandings for good decisions. Virtue itself is pointless if it cannot be brought into a proper relation with the world because of misperception or misrepresentation.

The virtues, as the ground for modes of moral evaluation that help reproduce society, act as society's conscience. Having been educated to be virtuous, we would not feel easy about abandoning them. It does not feel right to do things without reference to a system of virtues which help to ethically calibrate how we go about practices. Virtue ethics draws upon skills of self, of perception, judgement and measure, and not just automated response. It envisages a set of human qualities which, by their nature, tend to promote the social good, but which can be used variably according to the situation arising. The possibility of the virtuous self is primordially a question of what it is to be human, and not a function of moments in our lives determined by pure self-interest. To be virtuous is prior to any particular configuration of life. Using one's virtuous capacities effectively is a skill of being human, and not just, in this example, a social worker. The development of the virtues is rather like the development of the use of the senses. We have an inborn capacity to use our senses, but we can still be trained to use them effectively. We can be given guidance as to how we might see things better if we stand here rather than there, and so on. We can be shown how to judge, and we come to realize that this basic skill can be used in any number of cases, not just in the one or two we were shown in training. This, indeed, would suggest that the education of the social worker does not just consist in practice placements plus formal teaching of law, values and techniques, but should demand deep engagement and analysis with case studies, examining them in all their dimensions. This is a dialogical enterprise with peers and tutors alike, not to find out how the case should have been handled, but to explore how one might go about thinking, judging, reasoning, reflecting, imagining and feeling about the aspects of a case, opening up its possibilities for human action. This is to get a sense of what is possible as a social worker in various situations and settings.

Social exclusion and deprivation create a range of negative emotions in clients including anxiety, powerlessness and vulnerability. A virtue ethics approach to the client–social worker relationship focuses on personal sensibilities and character traits rather than just on moral actions. Social work practitioners are often torn between acting from virtue and acting from duty. A strong version of virtue ethics provide a plausible and viable alternative for social work practice based on three features: (1) exercising the moral virtues such as compassion and kindness; (2) using moral judgement based on a sense of fairness and justice; and (3) using ethical wisdom to a develop a more nuanced set of moral perceptions, sensitivities, and imagination in the case situation.

Conclusion

A virtue ethics approach relies on a call to conscience in the social worker, and is a function of reflection and self-understanding. As Timms (1983) notes, 'Conscience refers to moral feelings and reflection as well as the decision about what one ought to do in a particular situation' (p. 37). Resistance to the idea of virtue is to escape from a bad conscience. As we saw above, virtue ethics has often been linked to the phrase 'doing the right thing', and with social work, as with other welfare services, we have a conscience about what we ought to do when constraints imposed by weaker moral, though stronger political reasons do not permit the action informed by virtue. We might call this bad conscience the inconvenience of supererogation. That is, virtue demands as a matter of course that one do more than one's duty. Indeed, duty is not a moral factor. Virtue calls upon the inner sense of the essential rightness of one's stance commensurate with the situation and the determinations of a moral dialogue with the rest of society. It should not consist merely of duty to the organization or client or profession or society.

A virtue ethics for social work would bring back to the centre of debate the importance of the individual worker, not in terms of his or her role, but in terms of character, of human *being,* of intellect and as an agent of subtle judgement and sensibilities. Modern virtue ethics has always emphasized the importance of moral education, not as the inculcation of rules but as the training of character. The virtuous social worker must learn to bring together strength of mind, judgement, perception of situation, and action in a highly analytical way, sorting through alternative courses of action as competing expressions of the good life – of *eudaimonia* – and these are capacities which have been much discounted by the dilution of the demands of social work training in the UK, with the new three-year degree in social work. Virtue ethics is not prescriptive and rests on developmental learning in attaining the virtues. For social workers to become more fully virtuous requires that they think about themselves, hard and critically, about the moral concepts that relate to practice, and those virtues that surround the agency context of their work. As the social worker progresses in virtue, her practice becomes more virtuous, with understanding, and she also gets better at doing the right thing. She acts compassionately and with caring with a greater understanding of what compassion means and does the right thing as a truly compassionate person would do it, from the right reasons and as a result of having the right dispositions.

Study Questions

1. Critically comment on how a virtue ethics appraisal might assist your personal and professional development.
2. Describe the relationship between virtue ethics and social well-being.
3. Do virtue ethics provide a more appropriate framework for professional social work ethics than deontological approaches?

11
Postmodern Ethics

Mel Gray

Key Concepts

Ethics and morality: In postmodern ethics, a distinction is drawn between ethics as a normative domain and morality as a descriptive one. Ethics is associated with the modernist search for 'golden rules' of conduct and morality with the postmodern acceptance of the individual impulses of the here and now. Individuals are first moral then social. In other words, ethics follows morality.

Moral responsibility is where morality begins. It begins when the other becomes the self's responsibility. It is rooted in my encounter with the other. Being for the other is the cornerstone of morality, which is primarily a personal pursuit, but implies taking responsibility for the other. It presupposes safeguarding the uniqueness of the other.

Moral ambivalence is the term used to describe what postmodern ethics emphasize as the uncertainty and unpredictability of moral choice. It believes that moral decisions and actions have more to do with passion, sentiment and emotion than with reason.

The 'Other' is opposite to the self, often constructed as an alterity. In postmodern ethics the cardinal sin is to 'totalize' the Other, to speak on behalf of the Other in a reductive, essentializing way that makes it 'the Other' of the same (see also Chapter 8).

Introduction

In Chapter 9 we saw how Jürgen Habermas's ethical theory epitomizes social work's modern ethical tradition, not least his distinction between values, ethics and morals. For Habermas (1990), since all societies and cultures have *values*, they assume the character of *objective* facts that are distinguishable from ethics, the *socially* agreed-upon normative requirements of a particular group or society about what can rightfully be expected from people in that society or group. And ethics are distinguishable from *morals*, our beliefs about right and wrong. For Habermas morality is personal and Bauman (1998, 1995, 1993), the major proponent of a postmodern ethics, agrees, but for different reasons. For Bauman (1993),

> [while rules can be universal and] one may legislate rule-dictated *duties*, moral *responsibility* exists solely in interpellating the individual and being carried individually. Duties tend to make individuals alike; responsibility is what makes them into individuals ... the moral is what *resists* codification, formalization, socialization, universalization. The moral is what remains when the job of ethics ... has been done. (p. 54)

For Bauman (1998), 'to be moral is to face the choice between good and evil, and to know that there is such a choice ... [it is] a cruel predicament ... [a] *drama of choice*' (p. 13). Hence moral responsibility (see Key Concepts) carries with it an existential angst:

> solitude marks the beginning of the moral act ... We are not moral thanks to society (we are only ethical or law-abiding thanks to it); we live in society, we *are* society, thanks to being moral. At the heart of sociality is the loneliness of the moral person. Before society, its law-makers and its philosophers come down to spelling out its ethical principles, there are beings who have been moral without the constraint (or luxury?) of codified goodness. (Bauman, 1993, p. 61; original emphasis)

For Habermas, morals are personal in the sense that only individuals can know in the depths of their being whether or not they are behaving morally, in keeping with their values or, in the case of the professions, with their codes of ethical conduct. In true Enlightenment tradition, Habermas (1971) believes in the search for truth and in the emancipatory power of knowledge. He believes that we need to differentiate between valid and invalid knowledge and that we should not abandon the search for standards to determine whether a belief or knowledge claim is or is not valid or justified. For a profession like social work, with its strong claims to social justice, beliefs determine the tenor of the social order, and there are limits to the kind of beliefs that underlie a just social order. For social workers that is one based on democracy and human rights.

Habermas's ethical theory – and his discourse ethics discussed in Chapter 9 – typify social work's modern view of values as foundational and universal, of the propensity to reach agreement on ethical codes, to make rational decisions and to adhere to a set of values that are non-negotiable. Like

Habermas, social work believes in rational argumentation, in the justification of some values over others and in the expectation that society and the profession ought to promote these agreed-upon values. Social work presents a rather orderly picture of its values and ethics and their rational moral foundation. It is this view of ethics that a postmodern ethics overturns.

Key Ideas

There are many misconceptions about a postmodern ethics which arise from those theorists who extrapolate ideas from postmodern thinking more generally, such as the obsessive emphasis on difference, the narrative construction of self, the celebration of diversity and the social construction of knowledge, and attempt to apply them to an ethical theory (Webb, 2009). This is unfortunate because the moral theory presented by Zygmunt Bauman (1993) in his seminal study of *Postmodern Ethics*, as well as his other work (Bauman, 1998, 1995), involves a complete rethinking of morality which is something social work would do well to do. As Douglas Kellner (1998) notes, 'it is arguably in ethical analysis that Bauman excels and his admirable work in this field is deserving of a study that focuses exclusively on his conceptions of postmodern ethics and his critique of modern ethics' (p. 81). Kellner (1998) sees Bauman as 'a distinguished moralist, attacking the ills and evils of the age, while sketching out more humane and sane moral perspectives' (p. 81).

Rather than the constant focus on externally driven moral criteria, Bauman (1998, 1995, 1993) brings us back to rethinking what it means to be moral, not in an interpretive sense, but in trying to discern a deeper understanding of morality. However, before we can begin a positive examination of his key moral concepts, we need to dispel some negative thinking attributed to a postmodern ethics relating to moral relativism and the discursiveness of morality.

Moral relativism?

Bauman (1993) would have us believe that postmodern ethics do not herald the end of ethics or the advent of an 'anything-goes' relativism. This is an important point because the main criticism of postmodernism by its detractors is its relativism and eschewing of universal moral values. For example, Chantal Mouffe (in Squires, 1993) believes that what is at stake in postmodern ethics 'is not a rejection of universalism in favour of particularism, but the need for a new type of articulation between the universal and particular' (p. 6) or, as Harvey (in Squires, 1993) expresses it, for a 'dialectical relation to particularity, positionality and group difference' (p. 108). For Jeffrey

Weeks (in Squires, 1993), the 'key issue is whether it is possible to find a common normative standard by which we can come to terms with different ways of life, whether we can balance relativism with some sense of minimum universal values' (p. 6). This aspect of postmodernism is taken up most often by social work writers who see the postmodern emphasis on *difference* as either illuminating (Fook, 2002) or problematic in today's pluralistic, multicultural societies (Gray & Lovat, 2006).

The discursiveness of morality?

This claim to relativism is bolstered by postmodernists who spend a great deal of time discerning the meaning of the language we use and the way in which it is tied to culture and context. For Connor (in Squires, 1993), questions of judgement and value important in modern conceptions of ethics have been superseded in postmodernism by questions of meaning and interpretation Thus concepts like 'positionality' assume significance implying that we can only understand and interpret reality from within our own discursive position, since our conceptual understanding is constructed by the discourses of our culture, class, gender, race, and so on, which all comprise our 'position' in society. Hence our constant need for hyper-self-reflexivity. For them, concepts like social justice have no universal, objective meaning. They can, indeed, have no meaning outside socially situated discourses and, by implication, mean whatever some individuals or groups at some particular moment find it useful to mean (Flax, in Squires, 1993). These postmodernists, following Foucault, focus on the power of discourse or language, on the propensity of certain discourses, such as the discourse of science, to dominate and silence others. Significantly, in relation to values, postmodernism, especially as embraced by postcolonial theory, points to the way in which Western values trump traditional or Indigenous values (see Gray et al., 2008). But this is not a feature of Bauman's (1998, 1995, 1993) postmodern ethics; for him, morality precedes thought and knowledge and cannot be discursively redeemed or defended, for this implies a rationally defensible kind of morality – a mentalistic view of morality – which follows some hard and fast universalizable principles (like positionality). For Bauman morality is non-rational. It does not arise in an orderly, cause-and-effect manner as concepts like positionality imply. He says:

> This cannot be done ... and there is very little one can do about it, however strongly the modern, logical mind, or postmodern, aesthetic spirit rebel. The ambivalence of the moral condition and insecurity of the moral probing that follow are here to stay. This is, perhaps, the curse of the moral person – but it is certainly the moral person's greatest chance. (Bauman, 1993, p. 185)

His is a creative view of morality, one which sees the birth of the moral self through an encounter with the Other, and not as a product of social engineering. Let us now turn to the central concepts in Bauman's postmodern ethical theory: moral uncertainty, moral ambivalence and moral responsibility.

Moral uncertainty

For Bauman (1998, 1995, 1993), these misreadings of the relativism and discursiveness of a postmodern ethics detract from its main aim: to encourage critical examination which is all too easily lost in modern ethics. Hence he wants to lift the veil of illusion created by the sought-for *certainties* of modern ethics – the type to which social workers subscribe as typified in Habermas's ethical theory discussed above. Bauman (1993) is at pains to point out that the business of ethics is transacted on murky grounds; life is messy; human behaviour is not orderly or predictable in the way of rational decision-making, generating options and anticipating consequences. Evil is often difficult to discern. It masquerades as principled concern and all too often matters of belief and value – issues of morality – are fraught with emotion, not reason. More often than not it is not the facts that prompt us to act but belief or opinion; 'ought' does not follow from 'is'.

Hence 'post' does not signal a chronological passing of the modern. It acknowledges that the 'modern' is still with us but takes a critical stance to its orderliness and its predilection towards moral utopia or perfection. The starting point of postmodern ethics is the recognition of the ever-present uncertainty when it comes to issues of morality, of the ongoing tensions in matters to do with values, ethics and morals. We have to learn to deal with these tensions, to muddle through, to be morally responsible for others, to care for others unselfishly in situations we might not understand and for which there are no knowable solutions. Bauman's postmodern ethics is not about rational judgements, decisions and choices. It does not involve a weighing of all the factors involved. It is a responsive form of ethics evoked by what is needed and called forth by my responsibility for the other.

Moral ambivalence

This does not mean that I always respond and do the right thing. Bauman's postmodern ethics points to the *moral ambivalence* of the human subject. It makes no sense, then, to say that all humans are essentially good, though some are bad. We are all both and one or the other at certain times in our face-to-face dealings with one another. Each of us is equally capable of doing good or bad:

> being cast in a moral situation, in the situation of choice between good and evil, does not necessarily mean being good! To be a moral person is one thing ... to be good, is another. Being in a moral situation means no more than a *possibility* of being good (or of being evil for that matter). (Bauman, 1998, p. 17; original emphasis)

For Bauman (1993), the emphasis placed on moral rules is deeply distrustful of the individual moral self's propensity to do or be good. Jeremy Bentham's (1748–1832) utilitarianism, so influential in modern society – and in professions like social work – takes its inspiration from Thomas Hobbes (1588–1769) in believing that individuals are inherently deficient in goodness or altruism – and over-supplied with self-interest – and thus need to be coerced into looking after the interests of the majority. Moral intentions and acts could thus only result from social engineering; they did not spring from a moral self. Thus it was important to look for foundational moral rules to ensure that people would look after the interests of the majority. But this was a futile undertaking, says Bauman, because moral phenomena are inherently *non-rational*. They are not 'regular, repetitive, monotonous and predictable in a way that would allow them to be represented [as in social work] as *rule-guided*' (p. 11; original emphasis). Instead morality is incurably *aporetic*, that is, it is fraught with uncertainty, and seldom involves unambiguous rational choice or decision. It is *not universalizable* but, as already mentioned, for Bauman (1993) this does not mean it is relative. His intention is to undercut concrete universals to highlight the tendency of modern ethics to smooth over difference by appeals to sameness. On the surface we may share some common values, but when their meaning is interrogated we find that we disagree on their application in particular circumstances. So Bauman (1993) eschews ethical relativism and the nothing-to-be-done-about-it immobility highlighted by critics of postmodern ethics:

> By exposing the essential incongruity between any power-assisted ethical code on the one hand and the infinitely complex condition of the moral self on the other, and by exposing the falseness of society's pretence to be the ultimate author and the sole guardian of morality, the postmodern perspective shows the relativity of ethical codes and of moral practices they recommend or support to be the outcome of *politically* promoted parochiality of *ethical codes* that pretend to be universal ... it is the ethical codes that are plagued with relativism. (p. 14; original emphasis)

Moral responsibility

Central to Bauman's ethical theory – following the philosophy of Levinas ([1974] 1991), whom Bauman regards as the first postmodern ethicist – is the notion of moral responsibility (see Chapter 8). For him 'responsibility' is the direct antithesis to the externally imposed deontological notion of 'duty' prominent in Kantian modern ethics. To understand what he means by moral responsibility, one has to understand that for Bauman, morality precedes or transcends *being*. There can be no *being* without morality; there can be no *being for* or *being with* the other – the pillars of his notion of moral responsibility – without it: 'Morality is *before* ontology; *for* is before *with* ... Moral relationship comes *before* being' (Bauman, 1993, p. 71). By the same token *being for* the other, i.e. having a moral attitude or moral regard for the other, precedes *being with* the other, i.e. showing the other love and care, bringing comfort to others, and so on. Importantly for Bauman, morality comes from an internal wellspring. It cannot be socially engineered or externally imposed, as modern ethics has made us believe.

Being* for *the irreplaceable other precedes *being with the* other, not in a chronological before and after sense, or in any foundational sense, but ontologically: *Being for the other* is the act of *self*-constitution; the realisation not that 'I am I' but 'I am for' (Bauman, 1993, p. 76). The self becomes present in the absence of self-interest, in a regard for the other: 'Awakening to being for the Other is the awakening of the self, which is the *birth* of the self' (Bauman, 1993, p. 77). Conversely, 'losing the chance of morality is also losing the chance of self' (ibid.) found in union with the other. Moral responsibility involves being for the other whether or not the other is for me. It is unselfish. It includes respect for the other's autonomy which means not interfering in any way with the other's freedom. There is no demand for repayment or mutuality or expectation of reciprocation, no owing-me-anything, no dues to be paid. Responsibility loses its moral content 'the moment I try to turn it around to bind the Other' (Bauman, 1993, p. 50). It is a concern for the other entirely for the other's sake. Morality thus begets an essentially unequal relationship, and it is this which makes the encounter *with the other* a moral event. To remember the distinction it is best to think of *being for the other's sake*, not mine.

Being* with *the irreplaceable other is the 'first reality of the self, a starting point rather than a product of society. It precedes all engagement with the Other ... It has ... no "foundation" – no cause, no determining factor' (Bauman, 1993, p. 13) as modern ethics would have us believe. It just is: 'Ontologically, we are at best *with* each other ... two separate and self-enclosed beings' (Bauman, 1993, p. 70), paradoxically *with* but *apart* from the other. *Being with the other* happens daily and repeatedly 'each time that people care, love, and bring succour to those who need it' (Bauman, 1993, p. 185). The first step, then, is 'to listen to the unspoken demand, to *take responsibility for one's responsibility*' (ibid.; original emphasis):

> [T]he Calvary of the moral person starts ... at this point. From now on, there is but sailing between the reefs which punctuate the risky voyage of the moral self. On one side ... lies the Scylla of indifference and the washing of one's hands, masked as unqualified respect for the Other's freedom ... On the other side there waits for the unwary moral sailor the Charybdis of oppression: I know what is good for her ... having her best interest in mind. (Bauman, 1998, p. 18)

What emerges out of the acceptance of one's unconditional responsibility is 'being for the Other' but this is not merely about moral obligation and

> has nothing to do with the Other's ability to extract services from me ... *moral responsibility tends to grow in such situations in which contractual obligation tends to shrink and vice versa.* Moral responsibility is all the greater the weaker and more helpless the Other ... *It is the weakness of the Other which makes me responsible. It is the strength of the Other that makes me obliged ... The weakness of the Other makes me powerful.* (Bauman, 1998, p. 19; original emphasis)

From Levinas, Bauman (1998) learns that

> in admitting the Other's right to live, I give her the chance of confronting me as a Face ... of another subject, endowed with needs and the ability to command. I award her the right to resist me by her opposition, her difference, her separateness as another subject. I then engage in conversation; we talk *with each other* ... we come to respect each other. (pp. 19–20; original emphasis)

And so we reach the cornerstone of social work ethics.

Overview of the Social Work Literature

Charles Atherton and Kathleen Bolland (2003), Jan Fook (2002), Richard Hugman (2003), Nigel Parton (1994) and Steven Walker (2001), among others, have written about postmodernism in social work while Gray (1995), Gray and Terry Lovat (2006), Dorothee Hölscher (2005) and Hugman (2005) have critically examined the ethical implications of the so-called 'postmodern turn' in social work. For the most part, they have been negative about postmodern ethics. For example, Gray and Lovat (2006) question whether a postmodern ethics is possible, whether talk of a moral, ethical and values base in relation to postmodernism is not a contradiction in terms. They perceive an enigma and insidiousness in postmodernist ethics which has the effect of clouding the moral arena and watering down the ethical standards that often need to be applied to complex social situations, especially in troubled multicultural settings. They advance several philosophical arguments to support the search for moral universals, no matter how minimal they might be, and advocate the enduring utility of ethical codes, despite their limitations. They argue that, by its very nature, ethics has a transcendent quality and see Habermas's ethical schema as having an enduring fit with the Western philosophical tradition and social work's thinking on ethics.

In reviewing current debates on the role and function of ethical codes and standard setting in social work in postmodern conditions, Hölscher (2005) laments the loss of the 'ability of modern institutions to ensure the moral conduct of individuals' (p. 239) and appeals for a 'discursive and non-essentialist Code of Ethics' (Hölscher, 2005, p. 237). But for Gray and Lovat (2006), ethics as moral philosophy makes no pretence to prescribe or enforce standards of moral conduct but rather highlights the complexity of moral matters and the need for a deep understanding of morality so that individuals might choose or commit themselves to behave morally (Gray, 1993, 1995, 1996). They note that philosophically, the limitations of ethics have been well documented (Williams, 1985). They believe that the 'postmodern turn' in ethics comes not from philosophy but from social theory and the transforming of ethics into a social science which became evident in the 1960s when utilitarianism established its dominance as the most acceptable ethical method by which the complex issues of modern pluralist societies could be addressed. As a consequence, ethical decision-making became a calculative business in which committees used checklists and computed scores. In many instances, this made the power of such committees to rewrite the rights and wrongs of the past determinative. Regardless of traditional or philosophical sources, this social scientific method for attaining ethical agreement became one of rational investigation, logical deliberation and democratic resolution. With the right software on hand, the results of such a process could be fed into a computer and the final ethical decision produced electronically (see Reamer's *Ethics Audit* (2001b)).

Gray and Lovat (2006) believe that, in today's pluralist society, hardcore utilitarianism and its ethical methods require modification. Postmodern ethics might have something to offer. We might have to accept Bauman's (1993) *aporesis* – a contradiction that cannot be overcome or conflict that cannot be resolved – and live with the truth that some problems are insoluble; 'there is no salvation ... only questions, indications, possibilities' (Berman, 2000, p. 245) and paradox. While recognizing that codes of ethics in social work will not solve moral and ethical problems, nor will standards of education and practice, Gray and Lovat (2006) believe that, despite their imperfections, they nevertheless can assist in focusing on micro-ethics, in providing guidance to social workers on ethics in daily practice. But codes of ethics cannot solve problems or recognize contradictions; only social workers can do this. At best they are tools we can use, among others, to guide practice and they can be helpful tools if we use them well.

Application to Social Work Practice

Social work seeks to have universal values, to reach consensus, as Habermas would put it, through intersubjectively generated discursive agreement within the profession. There is a belief in the possibility of developing shared values across divergent contexts. But what happens if and when this does not pertain, as Michael Yellow Bird and Mel Gray (in Gray et al., 2008) argue is the case in relation to Indigenous social work, which requires a strong political commitment, a championing of the rights of Indigenous peoples for which a weak relativist stance will not suffice? For social work, the challenge is 'how to balance a theoretical rejection of essentialism, objectivism and universalism with a moral and political commitment to non-oppressive, democratic and pluralistic values' (Squires, 1993, p. 6). Is Bauman correct? Are social work's dominant ethical theories inadequate to the task of facing the important moral issues of our time and ethical quandaries of practice? Should we pay attention to Bauman's critique of deontological approaches which base moral responsibility solely on externally driven notions of duty? Are we well served by utilitarian approaches which decry the notion of the moral self and for whom moral rules are needed to ensure that self-interested individuals show concern for others? Utilitarian ethics, as conceived by Jeremy Bentham, whom Bauman (1993) regards as 'arguably more than any other thinker responsible for the agenda of modern ethical philosophy' (p. 64), presumes that moral discussion originates from the point of view of the individual (and for social constructionists, the group) and, consequently, construes all values as personal (or group – professional) possessions, i.e. they decide which values to espouse. Marxism, Christianity, Confucianism – and other similarly comprehensive perspectives (see Part IV) – believe that utilitarianism is mistaken in this and so thus social work should reassert value from personal or professional preference. Social work needs a coherent, well-thought-through moral theory (Gray, 1996), or perhaps a neo-Marxist perspective might be more compatible with social work's stance on human rights and social justice and herald a new-found recognition that, strictly speaking, individuals or groups do not exist atomistically but in the totality of social relations (Gray & Webb, 2009). Moral selves are not simply narratively constructed, nor can they be socially engineered through prescriptive rules. If values are social, as Habermas says they are, they cannot be adequately defined by an inventory of personal – or even professional – possessions. Somehow the public dimension – Habermas's ethical realm – must also be assessed, not as utilitarians would do – to reduce obstacles to private projects and make individuals moral – but in the sense of measuring dedication to a goal, something that can be said to be objectively worth pursuing. It is in this sense that social work pursues social justice. It is 'concerned with concrete structures of power and normative expressions of value' (Squires, 1993, p. 12). Seeing too much in the moral realm as a matter of personal – or professional – choice detracts from our search for truth and justice which are not so much 'self' as social creation. By opening up a values-as-social dimension, a postmodern ethics redefines the ethical outlook as incommensurate with the utilitarianism and deontological ethics much favoured in social work, and thus individualizes morality by making it personal in a different – morally meaningful – sense. As Bauman (1993) notes: '[The] Utilitarian recipe for universal happiness differs from loving care the way the latest tariff of welfare handouts differs from sharing a meal. In the ascent to the standards of routinised care, love is the first ballast to be thrown overboard' (p. 103).

Love as 'care for the other', 'doing it for the sake of the other', 'doing what is best for the other' and similar – love – motives, says Bauman (1993), 'are now the legitimising form of domination. Most of the time, they accompany bureaucratically simplified routines of conscience-clearing' (p. 103). They are a variant of what Foucault calls 'pastoral power', 'one of the most insidious of the many shapes of domination, as it blackmails its objects into obedience and lulls its agents into self-righteousness'. Doing something, however minimal, to assuage one's conscience is deemed better than doing nothing. A postmodern ethics would hold that it is better to do nothing unless moral responsibility springs from within a genuine desire to be with the other, not for any pay-off but in the sense that Iris Murdoch (1970) meant it: it is good to be good simply because it is good to be good. As Bauman (1993) puts it, moral practices 'do not serve any purpose other than being mysteriously satisfying in themselves' (p. 184).

Conclusion

For Bauman (1993), there *are* 'principled positions'. He does not eschew morality but bases it on an 'ethic of *individual* responsibility'. He is naturally critical of modern ethics – as are many modern ethicists who have subjected philosophical ethics to critical scrutiny and acknowledged its limitations (Williams, 1985). Social work has much to learn from this version of postmodern ethics and, as a consequence, would return to a previous time when the importance of a deep understanding of morality was recognized (Goldstein, 1987; Gray, 1995, 1996; Siporin, 1983). Too much emphasis has been placed on ethical rules and codes and decision-making frameworks and too little on a deep understanding of what it means to be moral. The motivation for – and merit of – individual moral or ethical behaviour cannot be found in external sanction. It is internally located and evoked by the face of the other. It is because we are human that we are moral. It is because we are moral that social life is possible, not the other way round.

Study Questions

1. Examine the value perspectives presented in Chapters 7–11 and reflect on their compatibility with postmodern ethics. What key features would a postmodern ethics put under critical scrutiny?
2. Choose what you regard as the most pressing moral issue of our time and consider your ethical stance. How might the postmodern ethical perspective alter your view of this issue?
3. Using Bauman's perspective, how might social work learn from rethinking its view on morality?

PART III

Social Perspectives

The 'social question' has figured centrally in social work, at least since the end of the nineteenth century. In her diaries, Beatrice Webb (1926) wrote that 'social questions are the vital questions of today: they take the place of religion' (p. 164). Thus in early social work interventions morality was pursued through social reform and the machinery of charity (see MacKenzie & MacKenzie, 1982). In Part III we examine social perspectives where issues of social injustice, exclusion and inequality figure prominently in our thinking about value perspectives in social work.

In keeping with the international orientation of this book, Chapter 12 focuses on race as an issue about which there is a large literature in social work, since race enters into most discussions on discrimination, exclusion and intolerance. Most distinctively social work has evolved a particular form of practice – anti-racist practice – to deal with racial discrimination, which is related in several important respects to anti-oppressive practice, discussed in Chapter 14, which is a more generic attempt to address forms of discrimination. In contemporary social policy, single-issue approaches, such as anti-racist practice, have been overtaken by the broader 'compound' process of social exclusion where race and ethnicity form part of a network of factors with no clear cause and effect between a single variable. Exclusion in one area of life leads to exclusion in another. This broader notion has led to multi-effect modelling as the preferred methodological strategy for social-exclusion research and to 'joined-up practices' as holistic solutions for social intervention strategies. Clearly, diversity is an area where scholars have divergent views, and it is rife with controversies, often based largely on people's strong beliefs rather than empirical evidence, as Haluk Soydan notes in Chapter 12.

In Chapter 13 on human rights and social justice, Jim Ife shows that there are no easy answers, or clear practice prescriptions, for rights-based social work. Rather, an understanding of human rights and social justice leads social workers to engage in, and indeed relish, moral struggle. This requires that social workers address major questions about the human condition while at the same time helping people to cope with the challenges of daily living, crisis, loss, change, and the structures and discourses of oppression. Rights-based social work asks confronting and difficult questions, realizing that the answers to those questions are not always – or even usually – clear or 'achievable' in terms of 'outcomes'. Rather, it is in the struggle to answer them that our humanity is affirmed.

In Chapter 14, Lena Dominelli reviews anti-oppressive practice, which emerged in the 1980s as an approach which sought to deal with structural inequalities in social work relationships and broader society. Driven by the values of social equality, egalitarian power relations, social justice, empowerment, and rights-based citizenship, it sought to remove discrimination that marginalized and oppressed people in society based on the socially constructed categories of class, ethnicity and gender. It held that existing power relations should be transformed to allow people to control their own lives and to give service users a say in the services offered to them. Above all, advocates of anti-oppressive practice, like Dominelli, see the elimination of discrimination, oppression, injustice and inequality as a moral imperative.

In Chapter 15, Aila-Leena Matthies examines the important concept of citizenship and its relation to participation as a key value and ethical issue in social work. She reviews contemporary debates on citizen participation and how social work directs the focus to values beyond contemporary 'welfare-state' welfare politics. She highlights the challenges and successes of citizen participation and user involvement in social work practice and makes a plea for a return to the values of social work relating to the rights of service users to self-determination and participation as full citizens with social rights.

The significance of the adjective 'social' in social work underlines the importance of social perspectives in guiding ethical considerations and the construction of value perspectives. The verb 'work' to which the social is applied signifies that it incorporates communicative, co-operative and inclusive elements. As the chapters that follow will demonstrate for you, such social perspectives are also keenly concerned with issues of power, stratification and domination as they are mobilized in the development of exclusionary regimes. In some important respects, social work was historically formed as a reaction and struggle against some of the more perverse manifestations of social exclusion.

12
Anti-racist Practice

Haluk Soydan

Key Concepts

Racism: The belief that a certain 'race' is superior to another or all other races and thus has inherent right to dominate the members of other races. Biologically there are no discreet and scientifically measurable races among human beings. Race is a social construct and its purpose is to set social boundaries that can be used for dominance by power.

Responsibility to fight racism: The International Federation of Social Workers stipulates that 'social workers have a responsibility to challenge negative discrimination on the basis of characteristics such as ability, age, culture, gender or sex, marital status, socio-economic status, political opinions, skin colour, racial or other physical characteristics, sexual orientation, or spiritual beliefs'.

Cultural competence is the ability to work effectively with culturally diverse client populations in agencies and social work institutions in which ethnic sensitive behaviour patterns, attitudes and policies are prevalent.

Introduction

Anti-racist practice as a social work activity is generated, developed and employed in a context of diversity: diversity of values and diversity of identities, which is simply what human beings are about. Diversity of human values and identities is the social and political platform on which group boundaries are generated and maintained. Historically, in many societies, race has probably been the most powerful social construction in generating and maintaining social boundaries. Initially, we may define racism as the belief that a certain 'race' is superior to another or all other races and thus has an inherent right to dominate the members of other races. The belief in the supremacy of one race over other races has been and remains a central component of the political morality in many societies, which translates into the beliefs and values that people adhere to.

Intimately related to the concept of value is the concept of morality, which refers to what human beings believe is 'good and bad', 'right and wrong' or 'just and unjust'. Values and morals are generated by human interaction in social and political settings and, once institutionalized, impact and sustain beliefs, actions, intentions and decisions, as well as social institutions. In racist societies, groups of one race attribute negative characteristics to the members of another race and qualify them as 'bad', 'wrong' and 'unjust', a process of re-victimizing the victim.

The chapter begins with a discussion of race and racism, and goes on to explore the complex issue of social work's role and mission in relation to racism at an individual, collective or institutional level. Thereafter, social work practice with ethnic and cultural minorities is examined. Given the history and scope of racism as a worldwide phenomenon, the historical and contemporary dimensions of racism are explored from a global perspective. For the most part, the literature on social work with culturally diverse clients comes from the US and UK and deals with anti-racist (Dominelli, 1996, 2008) or anti-discriminatory (Graham, 2007; Thompson, 2006) and ethnic or culturally sensitive (Devore & Schlesinger, [1981] 2006) social work practice, respectively. As such, it has a distinctly Western bias (Gray et al., 2008). One serious problem related to these treaties is the lack of robust and high quality empirical evidence supporting the social work practice approaches advocated by the researchers. Most anti-racist approaches tend to be value-driven and ideological, and others, such as 'culturally sensitive' approaches (see below) tend, at times, to be supported by anecdotal 'evidence' only, and to lack high-quality evidence on effectiveness.

Key Ideas

Racism in action

It seems that no country around the world is immune to acts defined as racist or as expressions of racism. Let's begin with a few examples of racism:

> In Europe, Nazi Germany is a notorious case of destructive racism which resulted in a systematic extermination of the Continent's Jewish population and other 'inferior' races such as gypsies. The extermination of over six million people during the first half of the twentieth century is probably the most brutal case of race-based atrocities in modern times.

> Elsewhere in Europe today, racism is developed and sustained using other racial divides. In south-western Europe, racial riots and clashes between Spanish and North Africans have become a common occurrence; this includes mutual offences such as the burning down of Moroccans' housing facilities in the Spanish region of Almería and stabbings, such as the case of a Spanish woman by a Moroccan (http://news.bbc.co.uk/2/hi/europe/635092.stm).
>
> In south-eastern Europe, tensions between the Greek population and the Albanians take many forms, such as discrimination of the Albanian minority in the labor market, justice system and education, as well as in the hijacking of buses and hostage-taking by Albanian protesters (http://news.bbc.co.uk/2/hi/europe/4101469.stm).

Racism in Europe is present in most countries, including Denmark, France, Germany, Hungary, Italy, Turkey, the UK and former Communist bloc countries. It has vehement outcomes in the Balkan nations, such as Croatia, Kosovo and Serbia. In the Pacific, Australia is known to have a racist past, discriminating and harassing Indigenous populations. The term Stolen Generations refers to Indigenous children who were removed from their families and communities between the 1860s and early 1970s for reasons that still are contested. There is, however, no doubt that disrespect and disgust among some Australian groups for Indigenous value systems and life patterns and racist motives form the backdrop to the Stolen Generations. As recently as the 2000 Sydney Olympics, Cathy Freeman, an Indigenous athlete, became the object of racist attacks because she had wrapped herself in the Indigenous rather than the Australian flag during her lap of honour at the 1994 Canadian Commonwealth games (http://www.democracynow.org/shows/2000/09/15).

In this age of accelerating globalization, racism has become a growing concern among citizens, politicians and others in many parts of the world. Racism is a major item on the human rights agenda as emerged at the World Conference against Racism in 2001, for instance. In the US, the indicators of racial discrimination include the overrepresentation of African American children in the child welfare system (Derezotes, Poertner & Testa, 2005) and the disproportionate incarceration of African Americans, police violence against African Americans and poverty among African American populations (Gordon, 2000; Stafford, 1996). In the UK, rates of race-associated crime number more than 140,000 a year (Jepson, 2000). Racism is a plague in modern societies. So, what is the essence of race? Why is race the primary divider generating racism in all times and places?

Race as a biological term

It might be that categorizing human beings in terms of race is as old as human history. The original idea of the existence of different races was based on the assumption that there were distinct genetic differences between groups of human beings and that all members of a certain race shared the same biological and physiological traits. However, race groups have always been inconsistent, and therefore very difficult to capture. Obviously, certain physiological differences such as skin colour and facial features do exist, but the distribution of physiological traits among human beings is highly irregular. Genetic variations among individuals of one and the same race group may exceed the variations found between the racial groups. In general, race groups are not genetically discrete and, consequently, they are not scientifically meaningful. Hence, it is not meaningful to categorize individuals in race groups based on biological and genetic characteristics (Diamond, 1999; Graves, 2004; Helms, Jernigan, & Mascher, 2005; Smedley & Smedley, 2005; Sternberg, Grigorenko, & Kidd, 2005).

Race as a social construction

It is, then, chilling that race has been and remains a powerful social category in spite of the fact that there is no biological ground to identify any discrete and measurable biological races. Race is quite simply a social construction. Race is always defined by a group itself or others as a distinct social category based on perceived inherent biological characteristics. In the US, for example, race ideology began to develop during the late seventeenth century with slavery based on the black and white divide. During the eighteenth century, European whites, Native Americans and 'negroes' from Africa were the three major race categories. When by the mid-nineteenth century Asians started immigrating to the US, 'Asian' as a racial category was introduced. Even Irish populations that immigrated by the mid-nineteenth century were perceived as a distinct race by the English and northern Europeans, and 'Irish' as a racial category was introduced. Audrey Smedley and Brian Smedley (2005) argue that in the US, the single most important racial distinction is between black and white, even if Latinos would contest this (Rodriguez, 2007).

Based on a review of literature on race and racism, Smedley and Smedley (2005) identified the following characteristics of race and racism, alluding to the values with which they were associated:

- Race-based societies define racial groups as biologically discrete and exclusive groups based on markers such as skin color and physiological features.

- It is assumed that different racial groups are perceived as inherently unequal and ranked hierarchically.
- It is assumed that distinctive cultural behaviour patterns are always linked to their biology.
- It is assumed that physical features and behaviour are innate and inherited.
- It is assumed that differences between races are profound and, therefore, that racial segregation is justified.
- In race-based societies, racial classifications are stipulated in the legal and social system (institutionalized racism).

Power and domination is the core of racialization and racialized societies. The history of the Spanish conquest of Mexican territories and the high level of miscegenation between Spaniards and Indigenous peoples of these territories provides an illustrative example of the social construction of races. Widespread miscegenation made it clear that boundaries between the groups involved were porous and, ultimately, this would threaten the Spanish domination of Mexico (Rodriguez, 2007).

Given the background of race issues, racism and racial discrimination, it can be concluded that racism is a major factor in our societies. Its roots are old. Its main purpose is to create social boundaries and use these as an instrument of dominance and discrimination. Racism takes diverse forms in space and time, and continues to haunt our societies.

Ethnicity

A concept related to race is ethnicity. Ethnic identity is often defined by common descent with claims of shared history and characteristics, such as language, religion, nationality, and other markers. Although race and ethnicity may intersect in the sense that a specific group may be an ethnic and racial group at times, in most cases race and ethnic groups are separate instances. While ethnic groups may or may not involve power relations and ideas of inherent worth, racial groups are typically power relations and involve dominance, oppression and differences in worth. Consequently, while most societies are subject to ethnic divides, not all societies are plagued by racial divides. However, ethnicity remains a category that may potentially be racialized, depending on the dynamics of value systems and politics of a given society at a given historical period. The same might be said of culture (Park, 2005).

Overview of the Social Work Literature

Human rights and anti-racist social work

What are some of the important approaches associated with social work practice in encountering and combating racism and racial discrimination, supporting individual clients and communities who are victims of racism, and in more general terms, making cultural differences an integrated frame of reference of social work practice? During the period after the Second World War, the United Nations and its various branches, as well other international, regional and national organizations, affected by the wrongdoings of Nazi Germany against Jewish and other minority populations, has championed a series of charters to combat and eradicate racism, and social boundaries constructed on the basis of cultural and ethnic differences around the world. The most important documents directly pertaining to anti-racist policies and practices include the International Declaration of Human Rights (1948), the Convention on the Rights of the Child (1989), the UNESCO Convention Against Discrimination in Education (1960), the International Conventions on the Elimination of All Forms of Racial Discrimination (1965), the International Covenants on Economic, Social and Cultural Rights, and on Civil and Political Rights (1966) and the International Convention on the Suppression and Punishment of the Crime of Apartheid (1973). Some important regional anti-racist documents include the European Convention on Human Rights (1950), the European Social Charter (1961), the American Convention on Human Rights (1969), the Helsinki Final Act (1975) and the African Charter on Human and People's Rights (1981) (see Chapter 13). The UK Race Relations Act of 1976 makes it unlawful to discriminate on racial grounds in housing, employment, training, education, the provision of goods, facilities and services and other specified activities. 'Racial grounds' includes colour, race, nationality (including citizenship) or ethnic or national origins. The Race Relations (Amendment) Act 2000 extends coverage of the 1976 Act to all public authority functions and imposes a statutory duty on public authorities in carrying out their functions to have due regard to the need to eliminate unlawful racial discrimination and to promote equality of opportunity and good relations between persons of different racial groups. As one of several professional communities, in the mid-1990s the social work profession followed up the intentions of fundamental international anti-racist policy documents. Commissioned by the United Nation's Centre for Human Rights (1994), a group of social work leaders, under the auspices of the International Federation of Social Workers (IFSW), prepared *Human Rights and Social Work: A Manual for Schools of Social Work and the Social Work Professions* (http://www.ifsw.org/en/p38000019.html). The manual includes a brief section on anti-racist social work practice. The IFSW frames anti-racist policies and practices within a broader perspective of social justice. Hence the IFSW's (2004) Ethical Statement of Principles reads:

> Social workers have a responsibility to challenge negative discrimination on the basis of characteristics such as ability, age, culture, gender or sex, marital status, socio-economic status, political opinions, skin color, racial or other physical characteristics, sexual orientation, or spiritual beliefs.
>
> Social workers should recognize and respect the ethnic and cultural diversity of the societies in which they practice, taking account of individual, family, group and community differences.
>
> Social workers have a duty to bring to the attention of their employers, policy makers, politicians and the general public situations where resources are inadequate or where distribution of resources, policies and practices are oppressive, unfair or harmful.

Codes of ethics and anti-racist social work

Similarly, the Code of Ethics of the US National Association of Social Workers (NASW, 2008), like that of many other national professional associations around the world (see Chapter 1), sets high standards in this area. It reads:

> Social workers should obtain education about and seek to understand the nature of social diversity and oppression with respect to race, ethnicity, national origin, color, sex, sexual orientation, age, marital status, political belief, religion, and mental or physical disability.

Social work education and anti-racist practice

As a reflection of high standards set by various international and national organizations, schools of social work integrate these standards into their social work education programmes. For instance, on an operational level, the intention of promoting anti-racist practices is reflected in the Mission Statement of my own school at the University of Southern California as to what the graduates of the MSW programme will accomplish:

> Demonstrate the ability to understand diversity in complex urban environments and to practice effectively with a broad range of individuals, families and groups;

> Demonstrate willingness and interest in working with a board range of clients, and work non-judgmentally and effectively;
> Apply key concepts related to cultural competence and strengths-based practice to work effectively with clients, community residents and colleagues of diverse backgrounds and characteristics, i.e. differences of class, disability, gender, age, sexual orientation, race, religion, and national origin. (University of Southern California School of Social Work, n.d.)

It goes without saying that every single one of these goals has to be reflected in the social work curriculum, as well as in the skills developed by the students. Failure to reach these goals would potentially lead to deaccreditation of the programme by the Council on Social Work Education (CSWE).

Attitudes of social workers: A challenge

Most social work literature describing anti-racist or culturally sensitive social work indicates that social workers' positive attitudes to clients whose race and ethnicity differs from theirs and avoidance of stereotypical thinking are necessary components of ethical social work practice. An important issue is whether these high professional standards of anti-racist social work are reflected in the attitudes of social workers. Though such studies are rare, an empirical study of a sample of non-retired members of the NASW probed white social workers' attitudes about people of colour (Green, Kiernan-Stern, & Baskind, 2005). Members of the NASW were randomly selected from a state chapter and from the national membership from all other states. The sample comprised 157 subjects from the state and 135 subjects from the nation. The demographic and professional characteristics of the respondents were strikingly consistent with the membership characteristics reported in 2002 by NASW. In the sample, 87 percent of the membership reported their racial/ethnic background as 'white/Caucasian', 4 percent as African American, 2.4 percent as Latin American/Hispanic, less than 2 percent as Asian/Pacific Islander, 1 percent as Native American, and less than 1 percent as Mexican American (Green et al., 2005). The empirical data indicated that the vast majority of respondents had positive attitudes about ethnic and racial diversity. Social workers' attitudes were found to be far more positive when compared with those of the general population and other human services professionals, such as psychologists. Additionally, the attitudes of respondents were consistent with professional ethical codes as described above. The authors concluded that '"social workers'" own ambivalences about race, intimacy, and social distance are strikingly similar to racial attitudes reported by national polls of the U.S. citizenry' (Green et al., 2005, pp. 64–5). My own conclusion is that:

- The black and white divide and its racist expressions are strikingly strong in many countries, especially in countries of European heritage.
- Racist behaviour can also be based on other characteristics, such as ethnicity, culture and religion, and generate similar kinds of sentiments and hardship.
- International and national laws, and professional codes of ethics and conduct are necessary but not sufficient to educate against, limit, combat and avoid racist practices.
- Although it might be the case that social workers of the 2000s in many countries have positive attitudes towards peoples of colour and take anti-racist stands, probably much more has to be done to tame racist sentiments and educate social workers to appreciate the diversity of value perspectives in social work, and to adopt an anti-racist stance.

Application to Social Work Practice

Prior to the 1980s, there was very little literature on culturally sensitive and anti-racist practice in social work. What was available drew strongly on the pathology of people of colour and made no constructive contribution to social work practice (Schlesinger & Devore, 1979). In the aftermath of the publication of international and national conventions and documents emphasizing human rights, social justice and diversity, as well as growing cultural awareness among social work professionals, a number of handbooks on ethnic-sensitive social work practice began to appear during the early 1980s. Two pioneers, Wynetta Devore and Elfriede Schlesinger, tell the story of the original galley proofs of their 1981 book *Ethnic Sensitive Social Work Practice* – now in its fifth edition – being displayed at the annual programme meeting of the CSWE in Louisville, Kentucky in 1981, and the approval and support they received by teaching faculty who viewed the display (Schlesinger & Devore, 2007). In the UK, Juliet Cheetham published *Social Work and Ethnicity* in 1982. She has worked tirelessly with the UK government to develop anti-discriminatory standards.

Besides Devore and Schlesinger ([1981] 2006) and Cheetham (1982), three other handbooks of ethnic-sensitive social work practice have dominated teaching in the US and elsewhere: Eleanor Lynch and Marci Hanson's (1992) *Developing Cross-cultural Competence*; James Green's (1995) *Cultural Awareness in the Human Services*, first published in 1982; and Doman Lum's *Social Work Practice and People of Color* (1996). These widely used handbooks are generally very similar in their approach, and are intended for generalist social work practice. Culturally sensitive social work practice builds on the general principles and ethical standards of social work. The core of the model is to recognize and respect clients' ethnic, cultural and race-based values, characteristics, traditions and behaviour, and to integrate these characteristics successfully into social work practice. Culturally sensitive social work practice requires that social workers are aware of their cultural values and perceptions and how these impact upon their work with clients. It aims to make clients comfortable and gain their acceptance and compliance with the interventions used by social workers.

Monica McGoldrick, Joe Giordano and John Pearce (1996) offer family therapy interventions in a large number of diverse ethnic, national and language populations. For UK readers, Mekada Graham (2007) discusses anti-discriminatory practice pertinent to diverse fields of social work practice, such as children and families, mental health, older adults and clients with disabilities. Also developed in the UK, Colin Lago and Joyce Thomson (1996) provide instrumental advice to social workers and other professionals who work with ethnic and racial minority clients.

One of the concomitants of culturally sensitive social work practice is cultural competence. It may be defined as 'a set of behaviors, attitudes, and policies that come together in a system, agency, or among professionals that enables them to work effectively in cross-cultural situations' (Cross et al., 1989, p. 1). Unfortunately, there is a gap between the goal of educating culturally competent social workers and the measurement of cultural competence. There is also a gap between what is being taught as culturally sensitive social work practice and the availability of culturally sensitive services to clients owing to, among other things, broad and inconsistent terms used to define cultural competence, the slow evolution of measurement instruments and the lack of culture-specific training and measurement instruments (Boyle & Springer, 2001). However, the concept itself has been challenged. Yoosun Park (2005) views 'culture' in the social work discourse as a marker for difference and notes that 'difference' then becomes an indicator of deficit. Ruth Dean (2001) suggests that social workers cannot be culturally competent at something that is continually changing. In *Beyond Racial Divides*, Lena Dominelli, Walter Lorenz and Haluk Soydan (2001) elaborated on peoples' ability to exercise agency in the formation of racialized categories, and suggested that agency must become a central feature of any social work intervention. In a more recent book, *Indigenous Social Work around the World*, Gray et al. (2008) provide a strong critique of the way in which the social work profession has dealt with diversity. They point out that anti-oppressive practice preserves power inequities between oppressed and marginalized clients and the more powerful social workers who advocate on their behalf.

Mainstream versus ethnically tailored intervention methods

There is reason to question the degree to which social workers give particular attention to the ethnicity or race of the client and tailor their interventions accordingly. A five-country cross-cultural comparative study conducted by Soydan et al. showed that in child protection, given national variations in legislation and professional practice, the child's ethnic or racial affiliation evoked little significant response by social worker in the participating countries/states – Denmark, Germany, Sweden, Texas and Wales – confirming uniform social work intervention across these diverse contexts (Williams & Soydan, 2005).

One of the most controversial issues in social work practice concerns the ability of mainstream or generic social work practice methods and interventions to serve culturally diverse populations (de Anda, 1997). Controversies in this area include a broad array of issues, such as whether the therapeutic process would be more effective if the client and the helping professional were of the same ethnic or cultural group, whether ethnic agencies were able to offer effective services to culturally diverse populations, and so on. Unfortunately, there is very little scientific evidence to provide guidance on these issues.

The interest in the effectiveness of mainstream and culturally tailored social work intervention methods has increased with the growing interest in evidence-based practice. Given the lack of high-quality experimental studies on anti-racist and culturally sensitive practice in the human services, including social work, sceptics raise questions about their effectiveness with young people and families from diverse cultural backgrounds. This is a legitimate and healthy concern for the advancement of the profession. As we have seen, culture, race and ethnicity have a profound impact on the way in which people experience, perceive and interpret the world around them.

So, what is known about the effectiveness of mainstream social work interventions with minority populations? In terms of robust empirical studies, outcomes are limited. While many high-quality empirical studies are needed, two studies have shed some light on this. In the area of crime prevention among youth, Sandra Jo Wilson, Mark Lipsey and Haluk Soydan (2003) conducted a comprehensive systematic research review on the effectiveness of mainstream intervention methods among ethnically diverse and majority youth. The study was a meta-analysis of 305 evaluation studies of mainstream intervention methods not specifically tailored for minority youth. The ethnic and racial groups included in the studies were African American, Hispanic and white youth. Based on empirical material that included outcome measures on more than twelve different types of intervention methods, including counselling, vocational programmes and cognitive-behavioural intervention, and 11 outcome variables – delinquency, academic achievement, attitude change, behaviour problems, employment problems, family functioning, internalizing problems, peer relations, psychological adjustment, school participation and self-esteem – Wilson et al. (2003) concluded that mainstream interventions were not any more or less effective for culturally diverse youth than culturally sensitive programmes. When interventions were effective for white youth, they were also effective with minority youth. Likewise less effective or non-effective interventions with white youth produced similar outcomes for minority youth. In a review of mental health care, Miranda et al. (2005) concluded that they had found

> a growing literature that supports the effectiveness of this care for ethnic minorities. The largest and most rigorous literature available clearly demonstrates that evidence-based care for depression improves outcomes for African Americans and Latinos, and that results are equal to or greater than for white Americans. (p. 133)

They concluded that mainstream evidence-based interventions were more than likely appropriate for most individuals in ethnically diverse populations. Several studies suggest that some mainstream interventions may be effective with clients from diverse cultural and racial groups, especially if supported by manuals specifically adapted for their race, ethnicity or culture (Botvin et al., 1995; Cardemil, Reivich, & Seligman, 2002; Dumka, Lopez, & Carter, 2002; Kulis et al., 2005; Muñoz, Penilla, & Urizar, 2002). However, further empirical research is needed to establish the effectiveness of culturally tailored social work practice, including studies comparing mainstream and culturally sensitive practice methods.

Conclusion

Historically, the phenomenon of racism is based on the white race's claimed superiority and thereby domination and denigration of the black race. However, racism may be generated on the basis of other ethnic and cultural divides, which are all situated or culturally embedded social constructs. The social work profession has recently developed and implemented anti-racist practices. On a pragmatic level, the social work profession is now developing evidence-based practice promising to remedy social and psychosocial problems of clients, individuals and families. Although not entirely immune to racism, racist values and discriminatory practices, the social work profession strives to tame negative cultural sentiments within its own ranks and in society in general.

Seen from a professional perspective, the lack of robust, high-quality empirical evidence to demonstrate whether a specific practice works or is potentially harmful is one of the most serious problems the social work profession faces today. The implementation of social work interventions in general and anti-racist practice in particular continues without any solid empirical evidence of their effectiveness. For all we know, social workers might potentially be harming the client and thus practising unethically. This is unacceptable. Fostering good science in understanding what works and what is potentially harmful in anti-racist and anti-discriminatory practice may also help the profession to transcend traditional deficits generated by models of cultural sensitivity and cultural competence. Such a development would pave the way to a more effective and ethical understanding of practices by asking what practices work for what racial and ethnic groups, under what circumstances, thus supporting the profession to shake off its monochromatic mantle and its disinterest in practices supported by high-quality evidence.

Study Questions

1. Have you detected racism, cultural discrimination or racial exclusion in your organization or workplace? In what way was the racism and discrimination expressed and what should be done to combat it?
2. How would you reform the professional training curriculum in social work to ensure that education is based on culturally competent, anti-racist and anti-discriminatory principles?
3. Which types of social work intervention lend themselves most appropriately to an anti-racist perspective?

13
Human Rights and Social Justice

Jim Ife

Key Concepts

Human rights refer to the basic rights and freedoms to which all humans are entitled. They are socially sanctioned entitlements to the goods and services that are necessary to develop human potential and well-being.

Natural rights (also referred to as moral or inalienable rights) are rights which are not contingent upon the laws, customs or beliefs of a particular society. Unlike civil rights, which are culturally and politically relative, natural rights are necessarily universal.

Social justice refers to the concept of a society in which justice is achieved in every aspect of society, rather than merely through the administration of law. It is generally considered as a social world which affords individuals and groups fair treatment, equality and an impartial share of the benefits of membership of society.

Introduction

The idea of human rights, although often discussed as if its meaning were self-evident, is, in reality, a complex and contested field. The words 'human' and 'rights' have been the subject of significant inquiry and debate (Carroll, 2004; Herbert, 2003), so it is little wonder that when the two are brought together they produce a term that is highly problematic. Far from being self-evident, the idea of 'human rights' poses some very fundamental questions, about the nature of 'humanity', what it means to be 'human', about how we treat each other, and about what we can reasonably expect of our fellow humans. These are serious and profound questions, that defy simple answers, yet human rights discourse is often naively simplistic, as if these profound issues about human existence can be understood simply by referring to a human rights convention or a Bill of Rights. If only it were that simple. Readers who may have come to this chapter expecting human rights to provide a clear easy rationale to guide practice will be disappointed. A human rights approach does not provide easy answers. Instead, it asks profound questions of the practitioner.

Key Ideas

Some problematic issues in human rights

There is insufficient space in this chapter to discuss the problematic issues of human rights in anything like the detail they deserve. A number of such issues will be identified, and illustrated by simple questions which they pose. Thinking about these questions shows how complex and contested human rights can be, and for the reader seeking a more comprehensive treatment there is a vast literature on human rights where these issues, and more, are addressed (see, for example, Campbell, Ewing, & Tomkins, 2001; Douzinas, 2000, 2007; Dunne & Wheeler, 1999; Hayden, 2001; Meijer, 2001; Monshipouri et al., 2003; Orend, 2002; Pereira, 1997).

Universal, indivisible, inalienable and inabrogable

- How can we say that human rights are universal, when the world in which they operate is so diverse, and where concepts are given meaning in very different cultural contexts?
- How can we say human rights are indivisible, when there are often conflicting claims of rights, requiring one to be privileged over another?
- How can we say rights are inalienable, when we routinely remove rights from some people (e.g. prisoners and the right to freedom of movement) and deny them to others (e.g. children and the right to vote)?
- How can we say rights are inabrogable, when people are often asked to abrogate their rights, e.g. in employment confidentiality agreements?

Non-human rights

- Is the idea of *human* rights too anthropocentric at a time when we need to reconnect to the non-human world and understand rights and responsibilities in relation to the biosphere?

Universal human rights and cultural diversity

- How can we move beyond the simple binary of universalism/relativism in relation to human rights, and develop a perspective that sees human rights as both universal and contextual?

The Western tradition of human rights

- How can we move beyond the Western bias in human rights discourse, given the origins of the contemporary human rights movement in Western liberalism?

Individual and collective rights

- How can we recognize collective understandings of rights, when the traditional human rights discourse, and human rights instruments, have reflected a dominant individualism?

Gender

- How can we move beyond the patriarchal assumptions behind traditional human rights, and ensure that the rights of women are as adequately protected, promoted and realized as the rights of men?

The secular tradition of human rights

- Modern human rights, as defined within the environment of the UN, international law and international NGOs, and within the Western liberal tradition, have been inherently secular. How can these secular understandings be related to understandings of rights and duties derived from different spiritual traditions?

The Enlightenment

- Human rights, as commonly understood, arose from Enlightenment thinking, especially about 'the nature of man'. How can human rights be reconstructed in a world where the legacy of the Enlightenment is being increasingly questioned?

Rights and duties

- Rights and duties/obligations are clearly linked, but are often discussed in isolation. What are the implications of understanding rights and duties/responsibilities as one?

Conflicts of rights

- How do we deal with competing claims of rights?

Excessive exercise of rights

- Exercising a right to excess may impede the rights of others. What are the limits that need to be placed on the exercise of rights, and how might they be implemented?

Frivolous claims

- How do we deal with apparently frivolous claims of rights?
- What is necessary to make a rights claim legitimate?

The public and private domains

- Human rights have tended to operate more in the public domain than in the private domain. How can rights such as the right to be treated with dignity, the right to a share of resources and the right to free expression be realized in the family or household as well as in the public arena?

A few moments pondering these questions should be sufficient for the reader to realize that human rights are difficult, complex and contested, and that they cannot be taken for granted, or given uncritical acceptance as if their meaning, and indeed their worth, were self-evident. The human rights literature deals with these and other questions at considerable length, and if social work is to adopt a human rights perspective it needs to address these issues and dilemmas, and to be familiar with and critique that literature (Ife, 2008; Mapp, 2008; Reichert, 2007). For the rest of this chapter, however, we will not be concerned with these matters, but will look simply at *different ways of thinking about human rights*, and what this means for social work.

Ways of thinking about human rights

In 1948 the UN declared: 'All human beings are born free and equal in dignity and rights. They are endowed with reason and conscience and should act towards one another in a spirit of brotherhood.' However, many discussions of human rights define three 'generations' of rights. The first generation is known as civil and political rights, and the second generation is economic social and cultural rights. These are the two groups of rights defined in UN human rights conventions, and reflect the world in the period immediately after the Second World War when the United Nations, and its human rights regime, was born. This was the world of the Cold War, and these two groups of rights represent the ideological divide of the time. Civil and Political rights – rights of individual freedom and political participation – were embraced by the Western powers, while the Soviet bloc was more attracted to economic and social rights: rights to health, housing, income security, and so on. Subsequently, in response to the so-called 'Asian critique' of human rights which criticized Western human rights as individualist and so inapplicable in more collectivist Asian societies, a 'third generation' of collective rights was proposed, though these did not have the same recognition in UN conventions (Galtung, 1994). This three-way division of human rights, though intuitively appealing, and corresponding to the French Revolution slogan of 'Liberty, Equality, Fraternity', is conceptually inadequate, as it, by implication, defines first- and second-generation rights as purely individual, though they too can be understood collectively. And the second generation – economic, social and cultural rights – is effectively a grab-bag of post-war era rights that are excluded from the first generation, and are not conceptually coherent (Ife, 2006, 2008).

A further problem with the 'three generations' approach is that it assumes that rights somehow 'exist', and merely need to be classified, rather than questioning how they come into being, or how they are enacted. In this sense, it assumes the uncritical acceptance of things called 'rights', and does not interrogate their origins or the way in which they are understood. To reject this implicit positivism, an alternative approach is needed, which concentrates on *how rights are conceptualized*. For this perspective, we can identify three different traditions of thinking about human rights, which lead to three very different approaches to practice.

The first of these traditions is the *natural rights* approach. This sees rights as somehow inherent in the very nature of humanity. It assumes that we are born with our rights, they are 'God-given' or part of an essentialized humanity. If this were the case, then to understand human rights we would have to ask philosophical, biological or theological questions about the nature of humanity. This view is heavily influenced by Locke, who saw 'man' as born into a state of nature which carried with it ideas of our 'natural' rights (Locke, [1690] 1946; Hayden, 2001), and it is reflected in the famous words of the US Declaration of Independence: 'We hold these truths to be self-evident: that all men are created equal; that they are endowed by their Creator with certain unalienable rights; that among these are life, liberty and the pursuit of happiness.' If this were the approach taken to rights, they would 'exist' as part of a natural order, and our only task would be to uncover them, through processes of philosophical inquiry as to the nature of humanity, biological research about the human organism, or theological inquiry as to divine will. It is reflected in a different form in Rousseau's notion that we are born free (though 'everywhere in chains' as a result of the strictures of civilization), and that it is in the form of the 'noble savage' that we can see humanity at its truest and finest, and hence where our natural rights are to be found (Rousseau, [1762] 1913; Hayden, 2001).

The natural rights approach was influential in shaping the

Enlightenment view of human rights, as enshrined in the various declarations of 'the rights of man' that emerged at that time (Hunt, 2007; Lewis, 2003). However, this was overtaken by the second approach to human rights, which emerged not as an answer to the question, 'What are human rights?', but rather the question, 'How can they be guaranteed?' This led to a concern for laws, human rights conventions, and the whole range of human rights instruments and mechanisms that make up the modern human rights regime. The focus shifted from rights as inherent in 'the nature of man' to rights as claims we make on the state, and so rights become enshrined in constitutions, laws and human rights charters. This tradition of human rights can be called the *state obligations* approach. It sees rights as being defined by the obligations of the state to protect negative rights, and further to provide for positive rights. It is a natural progression from the natural rights perspective; Locke, and the US Declaration of Independence, both moved from the grandiose statements of natural rights to infer that states had a responsibility to uphold these natural rights, and indeed that the citizens had a right to overthrow a state that did not do so (hence the justification for the American Revolution). Thus human rights became in practice less a question for philosophy and theology, and more a question for law and politics.

That natural progression from grand declaration to legislation/charter/bill of rights, seen in the US example, is replicated in the human rights regime today. The UN typically develops a declaration, e.g. the Universal Declaration, the Declaration on the Rights of the Child, and so on, a visionary statement of rights to which states are asked to assent, and this is followed by conventions, giving specific legal guarantees and mechanisms, which states are asked to ratify. Visionary declaration is followed by legal agreement: the general is nailed down in specific articles which have legal validity, and the 'right' is seen as established. From this point, the right becomes almost sacrosanct, given its validity by the law of the land or of the international community. It is the law that defines the right, and the right becomes equated with the laws that define and protect it. This has echoes not of Locke, but of Hobbes, who argued that we need a strong sovereign (state, monarch, dictator or whatever) to maintain social order, and that authority has legitimacy simply out of its very existence (Hobbes, [1651] 1968; Hayden, 2001). Once human rights are enshrined in the regime of the state, they no longer need to be questioned, but must be accepted and implemented. They gain their status not as a natural attribute of humanity, but from their existence in law. Thus there was a significant shift in the way human rights were thought about: instead of rights residing in human beings, as natural attributes of some kind, they instead are seen as residing in laws, and it is these laws and conventions, rather than the human beings who claim the rights, that give those rights legitimacy and validity.

Equating human rights with laws in this way reinforces the positivist view of human rights, as law is at heart a positivist discipline, at least in its modern Western form. If human rights are equated with laws, they are to be respected and applied; they 'exist', and their existence is not to be questioned. The legislation may need to be improved, but only so that it allows for better protection of the right concerned; the right itself is not under question.

This approach is very evident in contemporary human rights, where legal discourse and legal practice hold a dominant position. Lawyers are regularly and unthinkingly called on as the human rights experts, and the assumption is made that human rights are primarily a matter for the law. Thus when human rights are talked about, it is often in a way that equates human rights with laws, charters and conventions. The assumption is that our rights reside in these various legal or quasi-legal documents, such as the Universal Declaration, Bills or Charters of rights, and UN conventions. Many programmes of human rights education, for example, start with such human rights documents and seek to apply them, and this also applies to the way in which human rights are thought about in professions such as social work. Human rights work becomes thus concerned with making sure people receive their entitlements as guaranteed in human rights instruments, and in finding ways those instruments can be improved and strengthened. In such work, lawyers will always hold the key professional role; they after all are the experts in the design and application of laws and conventions. And human rights will be accepted uncritically as 'a good thing', something worth fighting for, and as furthering the cause of human welfare and a just world.

While not wanting to devalue the important human rights work done within this paradigm, which has undoubtedly led to significant improvements in the way people are treated and respected, it is important also to understand its weaknesses, and to probe its blind spots. One of these, as already noted, is that it tends to treat rights as positivist and unproblematic. Rights 'exist', are by definition a 'good thing', and there is little more to be said. Interrogating those rights, their history, rationale, and the cultural and political contexts in which they were derived, may be an interesting sideline, but is not seen as central to the perceived main task of human rights work. It therefore fails to problematize rights, when as we saw earlier in the chapter, human rights are in reality highly problematic. Another problem is that this approach to rights devalues rights that are not readily justifiable, i.e. rights that do not lend themselves to legal definition, and to protection through the courts. This includes many cultural rights, for example. A law-based human rights regime may be effective in protecting some rights, especially negative rights, but can pay less attention to those rights that do not fit neat legal definitions. A further problem is that it can lead to a form of human rights fundamentalism. This is an approach where everything is seen only through the lens of human rights, where the holy texts of human rights – the Universal Declaration, UN covenants, bills of Rights, and so on – are seen as having infallible authority, and where there is an imperative to spread the gospel of human rights to the non-believers. Such fundamentalisms are dangerous and potentially totalitarian, in a world characterized by contradiction, complexity, messiness and uncertainty, and where more subtle and nuanced reasoning, and humility in the face of competing worldviews, are required; fundamentalist human rights has the potential to erode the very humanity which it claims to champion.

However, the major problem with this approach to rights, which is the main concern for this chapter, is that it is anti-democratic. The writing of the noble declaration, the drafting of the legislation, and the passing of that legislation by governments or the UN, is a very elitist exercise, involving only a very small number of people, who have taken on themselves the responsibility of defining the rights of the rest of the human race. The criticism used to be that it was mostly white men who were defining our rights, but this is less so in the contemporary world. Certainly the voices of women, and of people from non-Western cultural backgrounds, have become significant in human rights forums, and in the drafting of human rights declarations and conventions. But they are still voices of privilege. They are lawyers, politicians, academics, public intellectuals and a small number of activists from human rights NGOs. Although no longer exclusively white and male, they still come from privileged backgrounds, with their own experience of the world and of the human condition, and are hardly representative of the people of the world as a whole. There is an irony in that the definition of human rights is thus a process that excludes the overwhelming majority of the human population, who are reduced to the role of passive consumers. If human rights are to have significance for people, surely people should have the opportunity – or right – to be involved in the definition of those rights; the denial of people's right to define their own rights can itself be seen as an abuse of human rights. This irony is largely lost on those within the mainstream human rights movement. They are so embedded in the legal discourse of human rights that they happily accept this state of affairs, and even embark on 'human rights education' which is about teaching people their rights, as decreed by somebody else, without facing the uncomfortable question of whether this itself might constitute human rights abuse.

This brings us to the third approach to human rights, the *constructed rights* approach, which has the potential to move social workers out of the shadows of the lawyers in human rights practice, and to overcome the anti-democratic, and hence contradictory, tendencies of conventional human rights. This sees human rights not just as something handed down from above on tablets of stone, but as being constantly constructed, reconstructed and enacted in daily life. We all live our lives on the basis of assumptions about the rights and duties of both ourselves and others; such assumptions govern our behaviour in workplaces, shopping centres, recreational spaces, and indeed anywhere we may interact with others, especially with those we do not know, where our interactions are governed by some generalizable understandings of what our fellow humans can expect from us, and what we can expect from them. Indeed, how we treat other people in our daily lives, and even in our professional relationships, bears little immediate relationship to what may be stated in the Universal Declaration of Human Rights, but is much more determined by our own values, intuitions, socialization and experience. Certainly if human rights are seen as applying in the private or domestic sphere, where the law and the human rights discourse have little traction, commonly held values are far more significant than human rights instruments in determining whether people's rights, for example the right to be treated with dignity, are respected.

This suggests that it is in the day-to-day lived experience of people that human rights need to be situated, and the idea of human rights as constructed by the people concerned, or 'human rights from below', thus becomes critical (Goodale & Merry, 2007; Rajagopal, 2003). One way of understanding this is to run a workshop or focus group with a group of people asking them to define human rights as they see them, without reference to the Universal Declaration or any other document. The rights that they define will be different from the Universal Declaration, and even where they are similar, they will be expressed in different language. One can then start with these rights, as people understand them, and from there derive a declaration that people themselves can own. This 'charter of rights' is relevant within the context of that group, and in debating the rights among themselves, people will engage with the idea of human rights, in all its complexity, in a far more significant way than if they are confronted by the Universal Declaration and told to think about how it applies to them (for a matrix which can be used in such a workshop, see Ife, 2006).

Human rights from below is about participation, facilitating people to think about rights from within their own perspective, to generalize that to the rights they would wish for others, to debate that within their various communities of interest, and to develop a sense of ownership about rights. It can also extend to finding ways in which the construction of human rights instruments can be more participatory, allowing many more people to engage with the process than is currently the case. This is clearly a task for community development, which has a central concern with participation, and human rights and community development can come together, not merely to promote 'rights-based development' but also to allow community development processes to influence the construction of human rights.

Overview of the Social Work Literature

The common approach to human rights in the social work literature, as epitomized by the work of Elisabeth Reichert (2003, 2007), and also the various statements on human rights made by the International Federation of Social Workers (see the IFSW website, www.ifsw.org) is largely within the legal, 'state obligations' perspective, as described above. This is hardly surprising, given that this is the dominant human rights discourse, but it has led human rights to be seen by social workers as relatively unproblematic, and accepted as unquestionably a 'good thing'; the task of the social worker is therefore seen as to implement and protect these rights. Within this perspective, social workers have largely avoided having to address the questions posed at the beginning of this chapter, and have been caught up in simply implementing an apparently self-evident moral imperative. A constructed rights approach, however, promises both a more engaged and also a more problematic role for social work, but it is an area where social workers are able to use their expertise to make an important contribution to human rights, rather than merely making common cause with activist lawyers.

Application to Social Work Practice

This constructed rights approach represents the democratization of human rights, and can also form the basis of social work practice. This is practice that requires both the social worker and the people with whom he or she is working to engage with ideas of human rights and how they apply in a particular context: family, institution, community and nation. This is very different from the more common approach to social work and human rights, which elsewhere (Ife, 2008) I have described as the deductive approach, where human rights documents are taken as a given, and social work practice is deduced from them. Rather it is an inductive approach, where social work engages in identifying and enacting human rights.

For social work to move towards a human rights perspective 'from below' is to move beyond the top-down rationality of modernity towards a more organic form of practice. It is to recognize the Enlightenment origins of contemporary human rights ideas, and to engage with a project of the reconstruction of human rights and their integration with community development. In this way human rights become a project to be lived and realized, and defining and enacting that project locates human rights firmly within the lived experiences of people, and the choices they make each day, whether major 'life-changing' choices or relatively minor choices, which, of course, are also life-changing though in less immediately obvious ways.

These are the choices made by the people with whom social workers work, and the choices made by social workers themselves. A human rights approach to practice thus requires that social workers focus not only – or even primarily – on human rights conventions and treaties, but on understandings of human rights and responsibilities within the lived experience.

As indicated at the outset, the term 'human rights' comprises two words, each of which is problematic: Much of the human rights discourse has focused on *rights* and left the *human* relatively untouched and untroubled. However, the constructed rights approach, in practice, requires a focus on the idea of *human*, what that means in a particular context, and what the enhancement of humanity might involve in a specific social work practice event. This change in emphasis from the problematic of 'rights' to the problematic of 'human' moves human rights into a new arena, beyond the problematic issues identified earlier in this chapter, beyond the constraints of modernity and its rationality, and into a new realm, academically tied to the humanities rather than to law, accepting diversity as inevitable and valuable, without trying to impose 'human rights' as a universal system into which everyone, everywhere, is required to fit.

This requires that the central question for social work be one of humanity: what does it mean to be human, and how can humanity be enhanced, not as an abstract universal question posed by Enlightenment humanism, which sought to universalize the definition and achievement of humanity within modernity, but rather enhancing humanity within a specific context: the family, the community, the social agency, the government bureaucracy, the correctional institution, the nursing home, the school, the local council, and so on. This is social work that seeks to define humanity and that seeks to enable others to define and express it, to find ways of respecting that humanity however it is expressed, and to explore the rights and responsibilities that naturally flow from this endeavour.

This can be achieved not just by what social workers do, but by the ways they go about doing it. This includes the way they relate to colleagues, managers, students, and other agencies, as well as the way they relate to the people with whom they are working. Exploring, defining and affirming humanity has in the past been central to social work (Ragg, 1977; Wilkes, 1981). More recently it has been marginalized by managerialism, and its associated positivist world-view, which has emphasized outcomes, evidence and predictability, and sought to stamp out messiness, chaos, contradiction and uncertainty, even though these are inevitably part of the human condition. A social work that emphasizes human rights, from a constructed rights approach of human rights from below, will inevitably challenge this orthodoxy, and will draw more on the questions posed by postmodernism than the answers provided by modernity.

It is common for human rights writers and advocates to talk about a 'common humanity', but this is to impose a single vision of humanity and to require everyone to fit within it. Such utopian vision can readily be oppressive, and the very idea of a common humanity is disempowering and amounts to a potential abuse of human rights, as it gives people no agency in defining that vision of humanity. Rather, the idea of a 'shared humanity' can overcome this. Sharing humanity contains a more active role for the citizen – when we share we contribute as well as take – and it allows for overlapping and differing 'definitions' of what that humanity constitutes. It means we start with what we have, rather than starting with what someone else thinks we should have, and we give as we can, and take as we need. Indeed, sharing one's humanity, and working towards a more general sharing of humanity, is probably as good a 'definition' of social work as one can find.

Conclusion

There are no easy answers, or clear practice prescriptions, for this kind of social work. Rather it is social work that engages in, and indeed relishes, moral struggle, and which requires a social worker to address major questions about the human condition while at the same time helping people to cope with the challenges of daily living, crisis, loss, change, and the structures and discourses of oppression. It is a social work that asks confronting and difficult questions, and that realizes that the answers to those questions are not always – or even usually – clear or 'achievable' in terms of 'outcomes', but that it is in the struggle to answer them that our humanity can be affirmed.

Study Questions

1. Given its complexity and contested status, is the framework of human rights useful for social workers?
2. What are the potential advantages or disadvantages of a human rights framework compared with the more usual 'social justice' perspective?
3. Can the 'constructed rights' approach help to address the conceptual problems raised at the beginning of the chapter?

14

Anti-oppressive Practice

Lena Dominelli

Key Concepts

Citizenship is the status bestowed upon those entitled to live in a particular nation-state and claim the right to its care. Intended to be inclusive, citizenship is disparaged as exclusive for defining those included in a particular territory at the expense of those excluded.

Oppression designates the disadvantage, marginalization and injustice some groups of people experience as part of their everyday life. It involves the devaluation of people's attributes and contributions to society on the grounds of who they are as members of a group socially configured as inferior.

Othering is the process of creating a 'them–us' dichotomy or division between people to include those in the 'us' category and exclude those in the 'them' group because they are deemed inferior.

A **binary dyad** is created when people and their attributes or behaviours are divided into two mutually antagonistic categories that structures one side of that divide as superior and the other as inferior.

Dualist thinking: a binary dyad underpins a dualistic way of thinking that privileges one part at the expense of the other, e.g. man–woman; white people–black people. Dualistic thinking is central to reproducing the dynamics of oppression, othering and social exclusion.

Introduction

Anti-oppressive practice (AOP) has sought to deal with structural inequalities in social work relationships and in broader society since the 1980s. It grew in response to critiques of practice that focused on particular social divisions, e.g. class, 'race' or gender, which featured prominently in radical social work (Bailey & Brake, 1975). It aimed to promote human well-being, eradicate inequality by acknowledging the social construction of social relationships and transform existing power relations that denied people configured as marginal to society the capacity to control their lives while privileging those of others who were part of the dominant group. The values that underpin anti-oppressive practice are rooted in the ideals of equality, egalitarian power relations, social justice, empowerment, human rights and citizenship. Anti-oppressive practitioners address complexity and structural inequalities in a critically reflexive manner that encourages the inclusion of the most marginalized and ignored groups in society.

Anti-oppressive practice encompasses aspects of traditional social work values, such as respect and dignity for the person, self-determination which is turned into empowerment to emphasize service-user agency, contingent confidentiality to replace absolute confidentiality by placing boundaries around what can be treated as confidential, e.g. stating that child sexual abuse or action harming others would be reported to the authorities rather than kept 'confidential' to the worker–service user relationship, and engaged professionalism on the grounds that all positions reflected particular values rather than objectivity and detachment, which simply disguised support for the status quo. Drawing on Paulo Freire's (1972) insight that probing beneath the surface exposed power relations embedded in particular social structures and contexts added another element central to anti-oppressive practice – an understanding of and working with the contexts in which practice takes place.

This chapter examines issues that arise in anti-oppressive practice that promotes the values that are most closely associated with it. To this end, it uses practice examples to identify ethical dilemmas and the limitations of practising anti-oppressively in basically unequal societies. Practising anti-oppressively involves continuous reflection on practice to improve it while critiquing the failure of practitioners and policy makers to support human well-being in complex situations.

Key Ideas

Anti-oppressive practice turns on the inclusive notions of rights, citizenship and social justice, because oppression is considered an exclusionary process that devalues both the presence of certain people and their contributions to society. Understanding the dynamics of oppression is crucial to anti-oppressive practice. From its standpoint, oppression devalues who certain people are and what they do. Oppressive dynamics rely on processes of 'othering' that set up antagonistic social relationships between people by configuring social relations within a 'them–us' binary. 'Them' as 'other' defines those who are different as inferior and devalues their contributions while, at the same time, 'us' privileges those who form the dominant group and whose attributes and achievements are deemed superior and valued. Anti-oppressive practice seeks to undermine the devaluation of the characteristics and contributions of the 'them' in this binary – and questions these depictions as 'natural' aspects of everyday life. It also highlights how the dynamics of oppression are complicated by the use of stereotypes to define 'others' – them – as external to and unwanted by a particular group. Anti-oppressive practice holds that people who are personally unable to accept others as equal cling to personal prejudices and stereotypes that affirm their superiority. It argues that, in so doing, they reproduce the dynamics of oppression in and through their individual behaviour and, collectively, these socially constructed and sanctioned stereotypes endorse the perpetuation of structural inequalities. Anti-oppressive practice challenges this configuration of peoples by exposing inegalitarian power relations and questioning the privileging of the dominant group – us – as a structural feature of modern societies that is then enacted by privileged individuals. To do this, anti-oppressive practitioners have to understand the language and processes of oppression and how they:

- Operate at all levels – personal, institutional and cultural – and in the interstices of everyday life to integrate personal behaviour with society's social structures.
- 'Other' people or create dyads of inclusion and exclusion that marginalize people and disrupt their aspirations for a better life.
- Normalize some people, mainly those in the dominant group, at the expense of others, namely those who have been defined as belonging to a subordinate group.
- Emphasize commonalities within and across social divides while deprecating differences between people whether within or outside a group.
- Deny people agency and control over their lives in the personal, institutional and cultural domains unless they are part of the privileged group.
- Reproduce inegalitarian social relations in the micro-, meso- and macrospheres of society.

By seeking to improve the lives of excluded groups, anti-oppressive practice has modernist aspirations, although it draws upon and contributes to postmodern theories of practice in acknowledging the fluid and multiple dimensions of identity, personal agency and social relations. It grew as a theory and practice in response to service users' critiques of service providers' incapacity to respond to their needs as they saw them. This was particularly important to women who experienced a range of oppressions in their lives, e.g. class, 'race', disability, age and sexual orientation, alongside gender. For example, black feminists demonstrated that their experience of sexism and gender oppression was different from that of white women because racism was an integral part of their oppression, and they had to deal with the complexities of both if they were to achieve real freedom (Lorde, 1984). They could not simply ignore the oppression of black men in racist, white societies. Moreover, they felt that practitioners ignored the constant changes in these relations and divided their everyday experiences into compartments that separated one part of their being from another rather than responding to their needs holistically. For example, black women complained that white practitioners focused on their alleged poor parenting without examining the roles played by racism and limited opportunities for support and resources in producing outcomes they did not want for their children. Particularly significant was social workers' failure to integrate black women's material realities with their emotional and psychological well-being. In focusing on one social division, radical social workers ignore interactions between social divisions and fail to deal with the extensive complexity that configures black women's lives and everyday life practices (ELPs). Anti-oppressive practitioners sought to respond by integrating this multidimensional complexity and fluidity. Dominelli (1993) defined anti-oppressive practice as a new area of study and unfinished project that reflects:

> a form of social work practice which addresses social divisions and structural inequalities in the work that is done with people whether they be users ... or workers and which aims to provide more appropriate and sensitive services which respond to people's needs regardless of ... social status. Anti-oppressive practice embodies a person-centred philosophy, an egalitarian value system concerned with reducing the deleterious effects of structural inequalities upon people's lives; a methodology focusing on both process and outcome; and a way of structuring relationships between individuals that aims to empower users by reducing the negative effects of hierarchy ... AOP is no more and no less than *good practice* operating at the personal, institutional and cultural levels. (p. 11; original emphasis)

By emphasizing *good practice*, this definition indicates that each person is *entitled* to services that meet their needs. It marked a shift away from understanding social work as a charitable activity to one based on human rights and citizenship (see Chapters 13 and 15). Social work educators, through the International Association of Schools of Social Work (IASSW), signalled their commitment to a rights-based approach by arguing for human rights to include social and economic rights alongside the political ones in its mission statement, definition of social work, and ethics and global standards documents. This approach draws upon Articles 22–27 of the Universal Declaration of Human Rights (UDHR), which the IASSW helped formulate in 1947 when it acquired consultative status in the UN. These articles place the right to education, health and social services as one of the responsibilities of signatories to the UDHR, i.e. all member states in the UN.

Overview of the Social Work Literature

Anti-oppressive practice is associated largely with British social work. Its key exponents are Burke and Dalrymple ([1995] 2007), Braye and Preston-Shoot (1995) and Dominelli (1991, 1993, 2002). However, anti-oppressive practice exists in other forms of contemporary social work, e.g. in Britain as empowering practice (Mullender & Ward, 1991); Canada as structural social work (Mullaly, 1997, 2007); the US as 'just' practice (Finn & Jacobson, 2003); various parts of the globe, including New Zealand and Canada, as 'indigenous practice' (Tait-Rolleston & Pehi-Barlow, 2001; Green & Thomas, 2007) and Australia as critical social work (Fook, 2002; Healy, 2000).

Anti-oppressive practice in the UK has been challenged by several writers who objected to practitioners' attempts to address wider social inequalities that are structured into how society is organized and shape people's relationships with each other and opportunities that they can(not) access. These included academics like Martin Davies (1984) and Pinker (1993), who deemed it 'unprofessional', and journalists like Phillips (1993) in the UK, who labelled it 'oppressive'. This has made anti-oppressive practice a contested domain, both in terms of what it means and what it claims as its remit. Despite such opposition, anti-oppressive practice has flourished, at least at the rhetorical level under New Labour's social justice agenda that has chimed with its general tenets. However, it has been transformed into a range of different perspectives that use its general principles to promote participatory, inclusionary and emancipatory social work that includes the voices of previously marginalized groups. Anti-oppressive practice has also spread, albeit unevenly, to cover theory, practice and research, with service users playing a prominent role in these developments, e.g. Aubrey and Dahl (2006).

Application to Social Work Practice

The complex realities that anti-oppressive practitioners seek to address and limited resources in which their work is embedded make practice complicated. Of particular difficulty is the integration of personal and structural issues. Anti-oppressive practitioners need to:

1. Understand the dynamics of oppression – how it is (re)produced in personal thought processes, attitudes and behaviours and embedded in and through institutional and cultural practices that configure professional social work.
2. Appreciate that people are whole human beings who live in specific sociopolitical and historic contexts that require holistic interventions to address the concerns of an individual, group or community.
3. Understand the connections between personal beliefs, institutional policies, cultural practices and service users' concerns and how these interact with and feed off each other.
4. Direct efforts to eradicate oppression in all personal and structural aspects of life and form alliances that include those outside the profession.
5. Support claims that endorse human rights and social justice.

Social work educators can teach students in the classroom and then provide practice placements where they can develop and practise these principles under supervision to become confident and highly proficient anti-oppressive practitioners. Students and practitioners have consistently commented upon the difficulty of practising equality and feeling disempowered by the 'new' managerialism that promotes a techno-bureaucratic professionalism (Dominelli, 2004a, 2004b). The rise of techno-professionalism has diminished relational social work even though worker–user relationships have been central to initiating change in individual behaviour in traditional social work practice (Younghusband, 1978) as in anti-oppressive practice.

In a study by Khan and Dominelli (2000), a social worker expressed her ambiguities about practising anti-oppressively in such an environment, noting that assessments were resource- rather than needs-led: 'I am compelled to adopt this "value" rather than adopt it voluntarily' (p. 12). In critiquing new managerialism, another social worker highlighted the complexities of practice and her powerlessness to overcome them by saying:

> I feel that managerialism and market forces within a supposedly mixed economy of welfare are destroying social work practice. Increasingly, the organisation is driven towards creating an expensive, callous bureaucracy which prides itself on delivering resource-led policies as prime measures of its effectiveness and efficiency. Not content with deskilling a professional workforce, the organisation appears to have effectively distanced itself from accountability and responsibility towards social workers, preferring to devolve such responsibilities to ... individual workers. This has invariably caused untold stress and perpetuates a culture of fear in the workplace. (Dominelli, 2004a, p. 161)

This practitioner highlights the difficulties in achieving social well-being for all and the ethical dilemma that arises when employers' constraints pre-empt the worker's potential to respond to user-defined needs and budget-led priorities dominate the practitioner–user relationship. To succeed, anti-oppressive practice has to address the needs of workers and services users. It is undermined by the adoption of proceduralism over holism that engages service users' realities, processes, inputs and outcomes (Dominelli, 1996). To practice holistically, practitioners need to address the full range of complexities in their interaction with service users and encompass both the personal and structural dimensions of context-specific situations. Figure 14.1 shows

Figure 14.1 Holistic Intervention Chart for Anti-Oppressive Practice

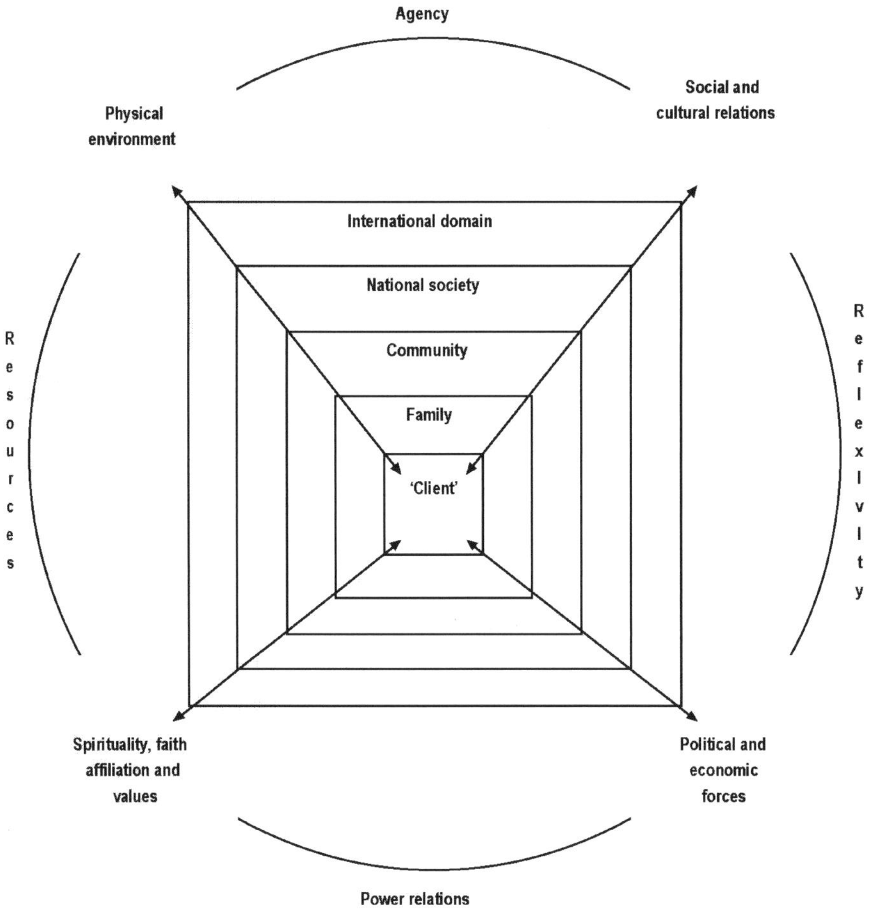

Source: Dominelli (2002, p. 184). Reproduced with permission.

the three levels on which oppression (and anti-oppressive practice) occurs – the personal, institutional and cultural.

The *personal* refers to beliefs and attitudes that individuals hold about themselves and others. Especially important for their practice implications are those that configure others as inferior or lesser humans. The *institutional* dimension includes the legislation, policies and routines of practice that legitimate interventions and define problems in terms of the constraints and contexts within which these occur. The *cultural* element comprises the social norms and values which constitute taken-for-granted assumptions of everyday life. These three dimensions are interactive and feed off and into each other to complicate the reality of oppression and make it difficult to deconstruct if only focusing on the personal element.

Figure 14.1 indicates how holistic practice engages with complexity and the entire range of social, economic, political, cultural and psychosocial factors that impact upon people's needs, experiences of hardship, and capacity to control their lives and exercise initiative. The complexity of levels and dimensions of social life that have to be addressed can sometimes overwhelm practitioners. Social workers reflect this when claiming that they are personally tolerant and do their best to give voice to those who access their services, but feel frustrated by the demands of anti-oppressive practice. This view of anti-oppressive practice focuses on personal practice. Although service users may experience it as preferable to an oppressive individual's work with them, it fails to address the structural elements of oppression embedded in institutional and cultural practices that go beyond individual aspirations as shown in the case study below.

Sally was a 40-year old woman of white British descent living in a cramped bungalow in a suburb of a small English city. A serious car accident left her paralyzed below the waist. Before the accident, Sally had worked as a retail clerk and led an energetic and fulfilling life. She enjoyed her work, had a number of friends and was active in her local church. Now she is a wheelchair user and refuses to go out for fear of something else befalling her, especially as the car accident was not her fault, but that of a drunk driver pushing her off the road and into a deep ditch.

Her changed circumstances led to her losing most of her friends, who found her constant refusal to do things with them 'now that her life had changed forever' difficult, and she became very isolated. The Disability Team in the local social services department had helped her to adapt her house to match her abilities and paid for a personal assistant. Budget restraints limited this to two hours a week. This arrangement meant that Sally could go for several days without seeing anyone. Not having visitors had intensified her feelings of loneliness and she has now been defined as 'clinically depressed', but not 'a danger' to herself or anyone else. Her GP gave her tranquillizers

Case Study (*cont'd*)

to deal with her mood when she told him that she felt left out on a limb by the care she received, although she appreciated what people had done for her. She also described herself as 'useless' and 'lacking purpose'. Madge, a newly qualified social worker, visited Sally following a referral from the GP who felt social workers should assess her needs again.

Madge arrived at the bungalow at the appointed time. No one answered the door. She pounded on it for five minutes and went round the bungalow to see if anyone was at home. However, the curtains were drawn and she could not see inside. She knocked on the doors of several of Sally's neighbours, but they had not seen her. They said this was not unusual; she rarely drew her curtains except when her personal assistant came and did this for her. None of them had maintained their previous relationships with Sally because she did not want their friendships after the accident. Most lamented the loss of a cheerful Sally and her replacement with a morose one who shunned any attempt at chit-chat. Madge returned to the office and phoned Sally intermittently during the rest of the day. Sally did not answer the phone the following day.

Her personal assistant went to see Sally early the next day, but could not get into the house, despite having a key. The police broke in and found Sally slumped over a chair, dead. She had put the chain on the door, pulled a sofa against it and overdosed on drugs. Though not their fault, both Madge and the personal assistant felt distraught. Madge tried to talk about this with her supervisor who responded that 'social work has more than its share of tragic events' and recommended she 'grow a thick skin' if she wanted 'to survive in the profession'. Madge could not think of a riposte and left his office feeling undermined rather than supported.

Sally's situation epitomizes the obstacles encountered by those who want to work in an anti-oppressive manner in a society that is configured to protect the privacy of the individual, curtail public expenditure and emphasize individual self-sufficiency instead of public expressions of concern about others, interdependency and solidarity. This case reflects the patchy and uneven results of practice interventions that deal with people's problems as discrete events rather than responding to them holistically as is called for in anti-oppressive practice. The initial involvement in Sally's circumstances showed respect for the needs of a disabled woman by adapting her home and providing personal care. However, personal assistance could not be given to the full extent of her needs owing to budgetary constraints. As Sally had not requested help to address psychosocial issues linked to adjusting to life as a disabled woman, she was given none. So, the structural oppression of a disabled woman was ignored and Sally was not put in touch with disabled people's organizations so that she could overcome the isolation she felt among able-bodied friends and neighbours now that she had entered what she felt was a 'stigmatized' and dependent status.

This configuration of the matter separated Sally's life into compartments that allowed professionals to draw boundaries around their offers of support. The rationing of resources in this way aims not only to keep within budget but also to spread limited services to a wider group of people. Thus, budget constraints become another way of defining what is and is not possible in practice. As policy, they form a crucial part of the practice context, which can disempower practitioners unable either to challenge them or explore other ways of augmenting meagre resources. For instance, could sending a volunteer to befriend Sally at the beginning of the intervention have supplemented the paid help provided by her personal assistant? Might this have helped Sally explore her changed situation, find new opportunities to fulfil herself in an unhurried manner and enhance her sense of what was now possible for her?

Not looking at Sally's needs holistically meant that her psychosocial well-being was ignored. She was allowed to become isolated and sink into despair while a medical solution was considered the only appropriate form of intervention. Sadly, this provided Sally with the means to take her own life and thereby deal with a situation that she found intolerable. This response reaffirms the professionals' definition of the issue as Sally's failure to come to terms with her altered life situation and blames her for her predicament rather than asking questions about how a system defined her situation so as to disempower her and discredit her feelings about her position. A disabling society that emphasizes bodily fitness, youth and vigour, can precipitate feelings of helplessness and despair in people who are not exposed to alternative possibilities for leading fulfilling and useful lives. The configuration of Sally as less than a whole person, structural inequalities, including the devaluing of the lives of disabled people, and not appreciating their needs for social connection and relationships, formed part of a disablist perspective of her life that contributed to her feeling disempowered by the help she was given. Opportunities for working beyond Sally's material needs were also lost by ignoring her links to her local church, which might have offered love, fellowship and support.

Other structural inequalities were also ignored. For example, white British society values 'independence', and not being able to act as an independent adult placed Sally in a vulnerable, dependent position. This is a disablist view that was intensified by her friends and neighbours believing that 'she should pull herself together'. There was no attempt to deal with her as a valued human being who needed help to adjust to a profound change in her circumstances. That her needs were not seen as significant to the organization was also indicated by those responsible for her care sending a newly qualified social worker instead of a skilled mental health practitioner, given her 'clinical depression'. There was no attempt to see her condition as one requiring the integration of medical and social perspectives on mental health.

Her manager's disdain and lack of care for Madge's response is an oppressive reaction to the emotional impact of witnessing death in awful circumstances. It reflects the belief that the 'detached, objective professional' can deal with upsetting situations in non-emotional ways that have no bearing on their personal or professional identity. It is contrary to anti-oppressive practice that seeks non-oppressive relationships in the workplace to empower workers. Madge's reactions can reflect an engaged professional approach that recognizes both her and Sally's vulnerability. Her concerns should have been taken seriously and considered professionally. A sensitive exploration of these could have strengthened Madge's commitment to the profession and helped address her emotions in facing the unnecessary loss of human life and feelings of disempowerment that accompanied these, especially as it had been the first death that she had encountered. Madge could have been assisted to become a more skilled practitioner if her reaction had been treated with sympathy and empathy by her line manager.

In contrast, an anti-oppressive practitioner working with Sally might have avoided this outcome by: responding to her needs holistically; taking account of her emotional responses to disability; engaging with the structural inequalities that her situation highlighted; and worked with her to resolve issues to her satisfaction. This might have posed problems in terms of finding all the material resources that were needed, but these could have been extended through imaginative use of other available services, e.g. volunteers, and by seeking ways of getting her agency to reconsider its policies. The above scenario suggests that budgetary restraints are a key challenge. But even here, a holistic approach would encourage the practitioner to engage in alliances with others to change policies about supporting people in the community, or alternatively, to look for resources to help Sally gain control of her life, such as supporting a volunteer to respond to Sally's needs, listen to her concerns and work with her and the social worker to solve them. The social worker would also have to be careful not to raise Sally's expectations unfairly and be honest about the extent to which additional resources would be forthcoming. But not all of Sally's needs required material forms of assistance.

Additionally, matters of 'race', ethnicity, gender, class, sexual orientation and disability would have all been considered to answer the question: 'Are these relevant to Sally?' If the reply were 'yes', which ones were they? What was the nature of their impact upon her life? Her replies would have enabled the practitioner to see that Sally had difficulty accepting the loss of 'independence' that had been the lynchpin of her previous life as a white British woman. Together, they would have worked on Sally's views of the situation and drawn upon several different modes of intervention that might have enabled Sally to create another narrative that could have helped her to re-story her life around interdependence, and shown her that she still had a lot to offer people and that there was a lot more she could do with her life.

Dependence is structured into the dominant view of gender relations, and as a woman, she was not helped to see whether she could have continued with some form of paid work that would leave her satisfied with her contribution to society. An anti-oppressive practitioner would have looked for ways to retain Sally's friendships with and links to neighbours and her church congregation and explored whether Sally had any other networks that she could draw upon in readjusting her life. This could include family that she could be put in touch with and those who could have offered her different forms of support. These interventions would have helped Sally maintain her psychosocial health and reduced her emotional vulnerability.

Additionally, a social worker practising in an anti-oppressive manner would seek support for herself as a worker as Madge had done. If rebuffed in the way outlined above, she might have lodged a complaint against her line manager, sought other forms of support or developed a preventative approach earlier to ensure that there were various types of support for practitioners and several mechanisms for accessing these when difficult situations arose. While none of these alternative interventions would have automatically improved Sally's life or Madge's reactions to her death, social workers practising anti-oppressively would have attempted to deal with the complexities in which Sally was embedded and sought to find solutions to them rather than configuring responses in fixed, predetermined ways.

Conclusion

Anti-oppressive practice is an optimistic approach to working with the most marginalized people in society and ambitiously seeks to eradicate oppression at all levels. In conclusion, to promote anti-oppressive practice practitioners should:

1. Reflect upon social inequalities, take action to remove these in practice and, wherever possible, tackle the personal, institutional and cultural dimensions that perpetuate them in society more widely.
2. Be prepared for controversy that jeopardizes livelihoods, including their own, accepting that practising anti-oppressively is not without risk.
3. Be proactive in ending inequalities instead of waiting for others to address the issues.
4. Undertake research that exposes the social construction of all inequalities and capacity for change through both individual and collective actions.

5. Mobilize communities to challenge the belief that oppression is an inevitable part of life by deconstructing it and showing how its dynamics keep people in their places as controlled 'subjects'.
6. Work to articulate alternatives, rooted in egalitarian social relations and controlled by those involved working in partnership with each other.
7. Form alliances with others to eliminate systemic inequalities throughout society.

Study Questions

1. How would you take account of the impact of the values that you hold in your work with service users?
2. How would you explain the link between structural oppression and its impact on your practice as an individual practitioner?
3. What do you think are the contemporary challenges for practising anti-oppressively in your country?

15
Participation and Citizenship

Aila-Leena Matthies

Key Concepts

Civil society is a sphere of social solidarity that is composed of the totality of voluntary civic and social organizations that form the basis of a functioning modern society, as opposed to the regulatory structures of a state and commercial institutions of the market.

User involvement: participating and influencing mainly in the role of service user. The principle is based on professionals and service users being able to get together to work collectively for change and mutual support, sometimes called the 'co-production' of outcomes in recognizing the importance of users making known their own experience, views and ideas.

Citizen participation: participating and influencing mainly in the role of citizen, based on a strong conception of deliberative democracy whereby a trade-off occurs between direct democracy and representative democracy that relies on citizen deliberation to make sound policy.

Introduction

This chapter frames the way in which notions of participation and citizenship play out in social work and how they are understood in different contexts of welfare rationalities. Citizen participation in modern democratic societies seems to be a self-evident value supported by a broad range of agencies and movements. Most developed Western societies have particular programmes for strengthening citizen participation and activating democracy, motivated by the concern for declining traditional political participation and increasing costs of welfare systems. Their motto is 'citizens should just do more themselves' (Active Citizenship Network, 2006; Chanan, 2005; Hvinden &

Johansson, 2007; Matthies, 2006). At the same time, there are debates regarding universal, global citizenship, especially coined in terms of passive citizenship and the protection of human rights. Citizen participation is not merely an idea 'from above', but citizens themselves have become more self-confident, informed and interested in influencing policy decisions on welfare and social work. However, the political elite and citizens seem to have different expectations and understandings of the existing conditions, meaning and purpose of participation. The aim of this chapter is to provide an analysis of contemporary debates on and applications of citizen participation from a social work perspective, i.e. one that directs the focus to values beyond the welfare state debate in welfare politics. To this end, it clarifies why citizen participation is a key value and ethical issue in social work. Taking a sociopolitical frame of analysis, the various roles of citizen participation in contemporary models of new governance and ways of thinking in welfare services are discussed, along with the values beyond these. The chapter also includes an overview of selected relevant literature and critical remarks on user involvement. Thereafter, the challenges and successes of citizen participation and user involvement in social work practice are discussed. Finally, the chapter concludes with a return to the values of social work relating to the distinction between citizen participation and service-user involvement.

Key Ideas

A new timeline of citizen participation

The concept of citizen participation derives from the broader concept of civil society as positively formulated by writers from de Tocqueville to Hegel and Tönnies. Civil society has been a topic of enormous discussion and debate throughout the history of the social sciences. Marx and critical theorists have employed the concept to theorize the very lack of community, the world of egoistic, self-regulating individuals produced by advanced capitalist societies. Social work values reflect some of these critical concerns and have been historically embedded in the ideologies of various national and international citizens' movements which have been a vital part of civil society (Lorenz, 2006). Civil society organizations, like non-government and non-profit organizations (NGOs and NPOs, respectively), still play a central role in social work and welfare services in late modern society. But their function can vary a great deal across market-oriented service companies, assimilated public–private partnerships, advocacy movements and self-help groups. Whether all established civil society organizations still enable strong citizen participation and do indeed incorporate civic society – as assumed by authors like Putnam (2000) – remains a debatable and empirical question.

For the field of social work the participation of citizens is strongly connected to its professional value base and the culture of its institutional systems. It thus permeates the ethics of individual practitioners and their obligations to service users, clients, customers and 'cases'. User involvement and the self-determination of service users have more or less explicitly formed part of the key traditional values and content of social work ethical codes since the profession's inception (Braye & Preston-Shoot, 1995). Since the mid-1990s, with the rise of the Third Way in the UK and anti-welfarist New Right policy in the US, debates on and models of user involvement have become part of broader welfare politics and social policy. They have also become part of debates on social work research methodology, with a strong move towards participatory approaches in research (Branfield & Beresford, 2006; Hanley, 2005; Reason & Bradbury, 2006; Turner & Beresford, 2005).

Although there is widespread agreement that citizen participation is an approach which social work ought to follow, it is not very clear how this should be done in practice. It is foolhardy to expect that generalized 'good participatory practice' or even an empirically tested model of effective user involvement would automatically be a guaranteed recipe for success (Smith, 2004). Far from it; citizen participation is one of the most difficult and important challenges for social work. It requires an advanced reflective ability, professional competence and political acumen. Merely claiming success for user involvement, documenting participatory working processes and listing criteria of self-direction is not sufficient. Such surface accounts of participation cannot effectively challenge authoritarian values and power structures within and beyond the profession. If taken seriously, citizen participation turns crucially on an emancipatory value perspective, a supportive institutional environment, flexible working methods and progressive thinking in social work, all of which are becoming increasingly difficult in the highly managerial environments in which most social workers operate. Yet, to some extent, social work's survival as an autonomous profession hinges on the legitimation received from the citizens and communities which social workers serve.

Enabling or hindering participation of the non-participative?

Citizen participation is primarily associated with traditional political activities, which form the basis of modern Western democracies where the government's role related to nation building and the goal was a cohesive society with a shared national identity. Ongoing surveys on the degree of traditional political participation in processes such as voting and membership of political parties reveal clear evidence of 'non-participation' among certain groups of citizens in most European countries. The shared factor characterizing the most disengaged groups is that they are facing challenges such as low income and educational status, living in deprived areas with high degrees of long-term unemployment, sickness or disability, and discrimination on the grounds of ethnicity and gender (European Citizenship and Participation of Marginalised Network (EUCIPMA), 2007). Importantly for social work, those found to belong to the most non-participative groups are also users of welfare services, i.e. they are often dependent on welfare services and benefits (EUCIPMA, 2007; van Berkel, Coenen, & Vlek, 1998). Hence social work can play a vital role either in strengthening – or hindering – the development of participative citizenship of these marginalized citizens. It follows that the way in which practitioners and welfare systems treat service users can have a direct influence on whether or not they can achieve full citizenship with all its attendant rights and responsibilities and participate fully in democratic processes. However, those usually seen as non-participative, as described above, have often developed their own, independent forms of participation, mutual networking and collective action facilitating their everyday life beyond the expected and organized categories of participation (EUCIPMA, 2007). The question thus arises as to how well positioned social work is to support and encourage more autonomous forms of participation and how far this everyday 'weapon of the weak' (Jordan 1998, 2003) fits the values of social work.

Participation as subjectivization in the work of Adorno

In terms of Theodor Adorno's (1957, 1971) influential critical theory, the ultimate objective of all critical educational engagement – in which I include social work – should be the subjectivization of individuals. By this Adorno means a deeper existential meaning of becoming truly autonomous, self-determining beings, with all the associated rights and responsibilities, i.e. *the realisation of full citizenship*. This means the opposite of being dominated or manipulated by any other persons or external powers in thinking and acting. This part of critical theory describes the highest aim of subjectivization. It explains why participation is so important, especially in social work, which structurally tends to be at risk of the objectivization of service users.

Overview of the Social Work Literature

Typologies of citizenship and participation in welfare governance

Participation and active citizenship are extolled by all political persuasions in contemporary policy discourse. However, more careful analysis reveals a surface of highly value-contaminated metanarratives connected to contemporary political programmes. Håkan Johansson and Bjoern Hvinden (2007) provide a useful typology arising from their analysis of contemporary welfare politics. They identify three mainstream political systems, namely, *socio-liberal, libertarian* and *republican*, tied to different concepts of social citizenship and distinctions between *passive* and *active* citizenship, which reflect the new dynamics of citizenship.

Socio-liberal citizenship, based originally on the work of Marshall (1950), sees citizenship as attached to social rights. Today entitlement to benefits and services is construed as passive citizenship. The active form of socio-liberal citizenship promoted in contemporary Third Way policy attaches benefits to the fulfilment of duties as expressed in the notion of mutual obligation. It makes rights conditional on duties – mainly through participation in paid work.

Libertarian citizenship favours welfare consumerism. Its passive form is visible in the exercise of user choice within quasi-markets, e.g. within provider–consumer relations and managed 'user choice' programmes. Its active dimension involves individual self-responsibility and the exercise of choice in a fully-fledged market, i.e. independent of public provision (Johansson & Hvinden, 2007).

Republican citizenship, in its passive form, involves 'managed' participation through user involvement, informed consent or agency-directed self-help. Its active form comprises self-governed activities, combined with co-responsibility for and commitment to participation in decision making on 'common affairs' (Johansson & Hvinden, 2007, p. 44).

Taking a practice-based approach, Adalbert Evers (2006) outlines five ways of thinking about citizen participation in the daily operations of welfare services:

Welfarism refers to the broader traditional sociopolitical ideology which constructs notions of citizens as equal members of society with social rights and universal access to professionally provided welfare services (as used to be the case in the Nordic countries). Citizen participation is channelled indirectly by corporate groups and representative policy-making structures at the local and national level. A variety of service users and their advocacy organizations are included in commissions and boards only if they are not successful through the traditional political system of voting.

Professionalism is closely connected to welfarism and regards citizens as possessing the same guaranteed rights as professionals. For Evers (2006), old-fashioned paternalism has been replaced by a new 'mild paternalism' (p. 260), i.e. client-centred and anti-oppressive approaches which see the interests of service users as paramount. High levels of professionalism thus require user participation and citizen involvement as equals in the intervention process.

Consumerism is promoted in Third Way policy as the most powerful model for user-centred services since it gives consumers choice. However, it is difficult to transform public goods and personal services into a private market economy based on competition and profit. Most users of welfare services are unable to pay for welfare services but need a tax-financed subvention, which limits their choices. Consumerism thus promotes a deepening of inequality not only in relation to the quality of services but also in terms of access to participation and decision making.

Managerialism holds that welfare should learn from the effectiveness and consumer orientation of the private sector and also take the interests of non-welfare citizens and taxpayers into account. It has led to an overvaluing of managerial and financial outcomes over client involvement and social rights. The users' role is 'managed' by options for individual complaints, e.g. via anonymous call centres, and consumer advice and consultation run increasingly via the Internet.

Finally, Evers (2006) introduces *participationism* as the tendency towards collective self-help and diverse practice models which promote the direct, *in situ* participation of users. Local user- and community-based service providers are strengthened and users are empowered towards self-government in services based on dialogue and service user control. Participationism comes very close to the active dimension of republican citizenship. Its links to the social economy (Nyssens, 2006) and co-operative (Pestoff, 2009) movements are designed to strengthen the local economy. The normative goal of 'citizen-controlled services' is the highest step on Cherry Arnstein's (1969) *ladder of participation* (see also Hart, 1992). In the active dimension of republican citizenship (Johansson & Hvinden, 2007) and participationism (Evers, 2006) the distinction between 'users' and 'citizens' is minimized.

Social work and participation in selected literature

In traditional liberal welfare states and Third Way social policy, where welfare services have already been privatized, like the US and UK, the literature on participation and citizenship in social work and social care continues to grow (e.g. Beresford et al., 1997, 2005; Carr, 2004; Evans, 1996), as does the literature on user-controlled welfare research (Hanley, 2005; Turner & Beresford, 2005). Mirroring the liberal market-oriented model of welfare, the degree of participation in services and in research relates to the level of 'user involvement', but in more radical debates the goal is 'user-controlled' and 'user-led' action. Van Berkel et al.'s (1998) cross-European perspective provides an example of research which makes collective action – or the lack of it – visible in Europe. In Germany, where the traditional corporate welfare state is giving way to active socio-liberal and libertarian models, publications on citizen participation in social work have a broader focus than just user involvement. The citizen's role and influence in local policy and communities, and within voluntary and third-sector agencies, is also discussed along with active forms of republican citizenship (Matthies & Kauer, 2004; Roth & Olk, 2007; Wendt, 1996. *Social Work for the Activating State* (Dahme et al., 2003) reflects critically on the Third Way and provides an overview of various fields where changing concepts of citizenship and participation are reconfiguring social work. Kessl and Otto (2003) make the notion that the new 'activating' governance could enter German politics owing to the declining legitimacy of welfare state-based systems. People felt that the traditional public social security and welfare services failed to take individual life politics into account. But as the authors argue, the new programmes of the 'activating state' are even increasing pressure on individual life politics and encroach into the private areas of citizens' lives. 'Active citizens' communities', 'voluntary engagement' and 'healthy lifestyles' are demanded. Each particular field of welfare practice from aged care to youth work and child protection has faced a turn to a new rationality of 'activating' social work. The aim of social work to support the subjectivization of individuals, groups and communities has changed to mobilization of 'self-entrepreneurship' (Kessl & Otto, 2003, p. 64), i.e. social workers are required to 'reprogramme' themselves and their customers.

In the Nordic countries, where welfarism and professionalism are still strong conceptual models in social work, discussions of citizenship and participation in social work cannot be separated from the broader context of welfare services. The UK debate on user involvement in social work practice is relatively new (Seim & Sletteboe, 2007). Significantly, the literature on collective participation, self-help and mutual aid among marginalized citizens carries a function of making these groups visible in the frame of seemingly equal and universal welfare politics (e.g. Follesø, 2004; Halvorsen, 2002; Nylund, 2000; Seim, 2006). New critical social work literature on citizen participation in casework and family intervention (Uggerhoej, 2009; Valokivi, 2008) or in community work (Matthies, Närhi, & Ward, 2001; Roivainen & al., 2008; Turunen, 2004) attempts to put user involvement on the social work agenda. A comprehensive research overview in the five Nordic countries shows the changing role of Nordic citizens' organizations in the welfare field (Matthies, 2006). Their traditional Nordic function of being the voice of citizens in the services is turning to a function of service provision in public partnership (Wijkström, 2001). Thus forms of welfarism and participationism, i.e. democratic ownership of welfare services, compete with the increasing trend towards privatization in Sweden and Finland, which is bringing multinational care and health companies into welfare provision (Koskiaho, 2008).

Critical perspective on user involvement

As shown above, citizen participation and user involvement are not only solving problems but also creating new ones. New partnerships between the state and civil organizations – NGOs, NPOs and voluntary organizations – often serve the interests of the public sector. For example, Hodgson uses the term 'manufactured' civil society to refer to structures which 'look like civil society, but are in fact a mixture of state/voluntary sector organizations' (Hodgson, 2004, p. 138). Wijkström (2001) refers to 'quasi-NGOs' to denote partnerships involving reduced citizen participation.

Beresford (2001), who has been one of the key figures in advancing user involvement in services and in research in the UK, highlights the tensions and contradictions in contemporary policy. Although welfare service users and their organizations are committed to equal involvement, they are constantly excluded, especially in research settings where service users are asked merely to provide information rather than participate in processes where data is analysed, interpreted and implemented. This raises critical ethical questions about the validity and ownership of knowledge. He regards this as institutionalized discrimination. It is the very thing social work researchers aim to resist in participatory research.

Carey (2009) argues that service user involvement serves the interests of government and welfare organizations within the neoliberal social care market. He provides a long, detailed list of emerging ethical questions. Taking a Foucauldian approach, it could be argued that citizen participation is construed as a sign of self-governance or self-discipline and constitutes a way of governing citizens 'at a distance' (e.g. Dean, 1995; Rose, 1996).

Finally, social work tends to use a more limited definition of participation while more radical notions of participation optimistically regard individual and collective participation as a process which takes place regardless of institutional or professional borders, in the everyday life of citizens, in an endless variety of decisions and actions. This is reminiscent of the feminist idea that the 'personal is political'. Citizen participation is a space, which escapes definition and delimitation, that constantly re-forms subjects and creates its own new places, before researchers discover it, e.g. on the Internet and in the new media (Kansalaislaivurit, 2009).

Application to Social Work Practice

There are inherent ethical dilemmas surrounding participation in social work practice. From a value perspective, social work requires participatory approaches, yet achieving conditions for them is a complex process, keeping in mind the conflicting definitions and critical notion of citizenship participation (discussed above). The service context often does not promote value-based social work notions of participation and self-direction. Those citizens who need social work services are usually not 'active' contributors to or participants in society. The possibilities of enabling user involvement are ethically and practically limited, especially in the case of involuntary or passive service users. If citizens were active and able to participate fully, the need for professional social work would diminish. If a profession is based on the ethical motivation of helping *others*, there might be little room for supporting the self-governing of *others*.

Participatory approaches are indeed not merely methods or techniques to be applied, but demand professional capabilities to identify the unique factors of each context. Jan Fook (2004) uses the term 'contextuality' to refer to the ability to take the whole context or situation into account, including seemingly irresolvable differences. It involves valuing service-user knowledge and viewing the situation from the users' point of view, i.e. from the context of their life-world instead of the narrow windows of the social work agency. In so doing, practitioners might recognize why many well-intentioned efforts for user involvement seem irrelevant from this point of view.

Sarah Banks (2006) includes participation in the core ethical principles of social work, especially through the value of self-determination, emphasized in terms of user participation and empowerment. She distinguishes between negative and positive meanings of self-determination. In its passive form, self-determination can mean an excuse for indifference, expressed as the 'freedom' to reject help when it is clearly needed. In social work self-direction is an active term professionals are encouraged to work towards, creating conditions which enable people to become more self-determining. The difference between these two types of 'self-determination' crystallizes a basic ethical dilemma in social work (see Chapter 5).

The participatory social work perspective approximates the active dimension of republican citizenship as a concept of governance. Rather than agency-led user involvement extolled in Third Way politics, these activities involve broad participation in deliberation, decision making, dialogical processes and service governance. Important for social work is that citizens are not only allowed to participate (the normative dimension) but that they should also receive help, support and encouragement to make full use of opportunities for participation (Johansson & Hvinden, 2007).

Participation is not just a new 'good practice' or an additional action in social work, but if taken seriously, it changes social work as whole. It leads social work to reflect critically on its values concerning its role in clients' lives, not least on who is the expert of the client's life. Following the argumentation of Adorno's critical theory, the subjectivization of individuals, groups and communities is the highest value and aim of all education. Social work is often criticised for its objectivization or manipulation of clients.

Participation as subjectivization also brings new resources and relief for social workers, if responsibility is shared with service users, and they take the primary role in decision making and action. The real difficulty lies in the fact that participatory approaches challenge the explicit and implicit values wherein social work is rooted. It essentially changes the power relations as in user-led services citizens make decisions about the role of professionals. Seen positively, this is a new opportunity for a new type of social work.

Conclusion

Citizenship and participation raise complex issues for social work. In this chapter, I have argued that the core of social work ethics centres on the status of those involved in welfare services. For example, are social workers only allowed to involve service users in a limited frame of service provision wherein they are pushed into activation programmes, like welfare-to-work? Or are service users regarded as human beings of equal worth who enjoy the same status as social workers, who possess full citizenship rights as subjects? What does it mean for marginalized people to have full citizenship when welfare systems are no longer based on social rights? Silvia Staub-Bernasconi (2008) has made a serious suggestion that the purpose – and value base – of the social work profession focus clearly on the realization of the human rights of citizens. This suggestion might be worth serious reflection in the cold era of welfare politics, with its wide range of user-involvement programmes. The service-user and carer-participation agenda is now a global phenomenon, with stakeholder involvement having high priority on many contemporary government policy initiatives. There is also a burgeoning research literature in this area. In recent years, citizens' participation as the co-production of social work interventions has become a veritable showpiece of good intentions on the part of policy makers and welfare agencies (Webb, 2008).

Study Questions

1. The concept of service user and citizen: What are the focal points of distinction?
2. How could a norm of participatory practice apply in a busy social work practice?
3. Imagine yourself as a service user who is the recipient of social services. What kind of access to involvement and what sort of decisions would you expect to participate with in determining the outcomes of your situation?

Part IV
Spiritual Perspectives

Spiritual perspectives have been largely overlooked in the literature of social work ethics and values. For many students, practitioners and clients, a spiritual perspective embodies moral reasons for caring. Indeed, spiritual matters regard the nature and purpose of the human condition, not as a material or biological organism, but as spiritual energy with an eternal relationship beyond the bodily senses, time and the material world. Spirituality may also include the development of the individual's inner life through meaningful practices, such as meditation and prayer. Findings from surveys of social work practitioners and students indicate a need for social work education and practice to focus attention both on the importance of spiritual beliefs in the lives of many service users and on the potential usefulness of religious and spiritual interventions (see Chapter 6).

Part IV examines several spiritual perspectives, namely, Islamic, Christian, and New Age ethics. The contributions in this part reflect this dual focus in social work with Chapters 16 and 17 examining the religions of Islam and Christianity and Chapter 18, New Age spirituality, a dominant form of spirituality in social work (Gray, 2008a). This is the first time religious and spiritual perspectives have been included in the social work ethics and values literature. Here a range of critical but sympathetic treatments are offered that provide for an engagement with spiritual perspectives. These have previously been neglected by most books that students find on their reading lists in social work ethics.

In Chapter 16 on Islam and ethics, Terry Lovat illustrates that the issue of Islam and ethics is far from linear and straightforward, and its complexity is growing with the increasing advance of an Islamist critique of the older tradition, made more complex by the sensitivity of the politics around Islam in current times. For the social worker who engages with Islam in Western societies, be the worker Muslim or non-Muslim, awareness of the realities noted by Lovat is essential, as is an approach to the business of service professionalism that is geared towards agency, dealing with the big picture, engaging with people's wider realities, and looking always to making a difference by reconstructing their worlds, rather than merely repairing their old and possibly fractured ones. Lovat argues that walking the fine line between the boundless respect that Islam deserves and preparedness and skills around transacting with some of its currently fractured reality would be a major challenge for any social worker engaging with a Muslim population in a Western setting.

In Chapter 17 on Christianity and ethics, Russell Whiting re-examines the contribution of Felix Biestek and his fellow secular humanists. He argues that an appreciation of Biestek as a Christian figure, and of some of his core casework principles emerging from a particular positive Christian heritage, is worthwhile and important both for the Christian social worker and for others. Seen in light of the increasing influence of faith-based practice (see Chapter 6), Whiting's discussion of a Christian ethical perspective is as current now as it was in the early beginnings of the Charity Organization Society.

In Chapter 18 on New Age ethics, Dick Houtman and Stef Aupers note the double meaning of the word 'social' in light of changing notions of citizenship (see Chapter 15) and the historical unfolding of three waves of human rights (see Chapter 13), which boils down to a transition from the 'care as favour' of Christian charity to the 'care as right' of modern social policy (Zijderveld, 1999). However, such an account of social policy underestimates its inescapable role as a mode of social control. For Houtman and Aupers, spiritually informed social work does not escape this Janus-faced nature of social policy either. Interpreted as a praiseworthy and progressive liberation from externally imposed controls by some, spiritual social work is regarded as an unprecedented intrusive new mode of social control by others, who understand the infusion of social work with New Age values as a transformation to a new mode of social control that proceeds in two steps. First, it opens up people's inner worlds for public scrutiny by putting human souls on the dissection tables of social workers, therapists and other professionals, and secondly, the soul is refashioned by moulding it in such a way as to produce a self that no longer requires external governance. Thus Houtman and Aupers question whether, from a spiritual – and religious – perspective, social work constitutes the ultimate liberation or the perpetuation of social control.

16
Islam and Ethics

Terry Lovat

Key Concepts

Islam is a monotheistic, Abrahamic religion originating with the teachings of the Islamic prophet Muhammad, a seventh-century Arab religious and political figure.

Islamism refers to the idea that Islam is not only a religion but also a political system; and that modern Muslims must return to their roots of their religion, and unite politically. It is a term that denotes a reactionary, sometimes, violent movement based loosely on Islam. Islamophobia is regarded as a stereotype or series of negative actions that separate communities on the basis of religious cultural differences.

Identity and conflict: Identity denotes the importance of understanding whether a Muslim person identifies with Islam or Islamism and in relation to conflict refers to the juxtaposition between Islam and Islamism.

Introduction

There has been no shortage of recent scholarly and other publications about Islam, especially since the events of 11 September 2001 (Akbarzadeh & Yasmeen, 2005; Ebadi, 2006; El Droubie, 2006; Grieve, 2006; Kamrava, 2006). In one way or another, these works attempt to retrieve, restore and explain the positive story about Islam that is under threat owing to contemporary events. Much of this story seems pertinent to the ethos of modern social work. Before engaging in their application to social work, this chapter begins with an outline of Islam's major social ethics and, in deference to the confused identity of Islam today, juxtaposes these with the dubious ethics of that other face of Islam, known widely by terms such as 'Jihadism', 'Radical Islam' or simply 'Islamism'.

Key Ideas

The confused identities of Islam today

It is increasingly difficult to generalize about Islam with respect to any of its features. An already very disparate tradition, Islam has, in our own times, become fractured by the rapid advance of what might best be described as 'Islamism'. A satisfactory differentiation of Islam and Islamism, or Islamic and Islamist theologies, is both beyond this chapter and beyond pure distinction. In other words, the differentiation is best seen as a construct for the purposes of distinguishing between two different and often opposing streams of thought that are influencing Muslims, the image of Islam and, quite possibly, the ongoing shape and form of Islam itself.

These limits to the differentiation having been established, suffice it to say that 'Islam' pertains to the history, doctrines and values that best stand up to the scrutiny and commentary of scholarship through the ages. 'Islamism', on the other hand, connotes a reaction to certain historical events that most clearly began towards the end of the mediaeval Crusades, has re-emerged from time to time in reaction to further events regarded as threatening to Islam, and has, especially since the Second World War, become an increasingly adhered to set of doctrines with dubious claims on the original tradition. As each 'post-9/11' day passes, for those who understand the true beauty and positive contribution of Islam to civilizing cultures, the sight of its essentially altruistic spirit and ethos of care being colonized by a culture that includes fanaticism and violence constitutes a sad truth.

In a day and age of struggle and confusion between at least two important and often opposing cultures describing themselves as 'Islam', it is vital that a social worker be apprised of both, understanding that the average contemporary Muslim is likely to be influenced by both, and could even be confused by their competing voices. Knowledge and understanding of both cultures constitutes crucial information and insight for a service professional like a social worker who must have an understanding that is more profound and helpful than would be provided by the average media commentary. At the same time, however, social workers cannot afford to be naïve in believing that the more scholarly authenticated perspective on the ethics of Islam would necessarily convey the practical ethics of all who describe themselves as Muslim.

The essential ethics of Islam

Islam's 'Five Pillars of Faith' – its own version of the 'Ten Commandments' – is as characterized by practical guidelines about one's social and moral obligations as about matters of doctrine and religious duty. The responsibility to support the total community through a tithe on a portion of one's steady income is as indispensable to being Muslim as is the duty to prayer. Beyond the duty to one's fellow Muslim, early Islam was characterized by a remarkable tolerance towards members of the community who belonged to other faiths. This tolerance was enjoined on the Muslim because of the fundamental belief that Islam was the fulfilment of the ancient promise to Abraham that God would establish a model community in the midst of the nations. Hence, the *Ummah* was to be inclusive of any devout religious follower, with a very special place reserved for the sibling followers of the 'religions of the Book', Judaism and Christianity (see Armstrong, 2000).

In this context, it is congruous that social welfare systems, together with forms of universal education and health-care schemes, were regular components of the well-constructed *Ummah* of early Islam. The fact of tithing as a religious requirement guaranteed that, from the earliest days, practical social support of a myriad of kinds was available in some measure to all. This 'modern' notion that all members of a community, those of the hegemony and of minority groups, enjoyed such rights was one of the great contributions of Islam to developing consciousness about ways of structuring functional and just societies (Nasr, 2002; Peters, 2003).

A particularly pertinent example for social workers of the ways in which the original inspiration of Islam is impacting on the reconstruction of modern Islam, especially in Western settings, is seen in the women's movement within Islam. The modelling of women's rights in the early Islamic communities is being used increasingly by this movement to reform much of the present-day practice that brings popular disrepute to Islam (Hirsi Ali, 2006, 2007). There is increasing boldness among Muslim women in taking the case to repressive chauvinistic conceptions and harsh political regimes even though, in spite of what has often become popular social and political rhetoric, the hard evidence is that Islam is the last religion that should be used routinely to oppress women. Since the early 1990s, there has been, across the Islamic world, a movement of revival of women's rights among devout Muslim women, rapidly becoming one of its many quieter revolutions designed to withstand the Islamist assault and most likely ultimately to reform Islam from within (Ahmed, 1992, 2006; Ebadi, 2006; Mernissi, 1975, 2006; Wadud, 1999, 2006a, 2006b). Harun Yahya (2002) says of such reform movements: 'Muslims must recapture the true spirit of Islam, and reclaim it from those who have harmed its integrity and honour' (p. 13).

The dubious ethics of Islamism

As implied by Yahya (2002), there is a large contemporary population that describes itself as Muslim yet which would seem to comprise extremely poor emissaries of a religion with its origins and inspirational ethos. Much of the disposition to depict 'the West', and especially Judaic and Christian forces, negatively can be traced to the so-called Christian Crusades of the eleventh to thirteenth centuries (Elisseeff, 1993). Described by Ibn al-Athir, the thirteenth-century Muslim historian, as a 'Christian *Jihad*', the Crusades offered a template by which the essential sacredness of the notion of *Jihad* could be reduced to the vengeful expediency of 'Holy War'. The seeds of Islamism are, therefore, ancient but the growth since around the late 1950s has been prolific.

There are now many faces of Islamism with different geographical and political bases, sometimes quite opposed within themselves but nonetheless united by their virulent and often violent opposition to everything regarded as 'Western'. *HAMAS, Jeemah Islamiyah, Hezbollah, Taliban* and *Al Qa'eda* are just some of the many names with which radical Islamism is associated. Apart from being united in their fundamental opposition to the West, they share in common a tendency towards radical overhaul of the social ethics most traditionally associated with Islam. Gone is the tolerance of difference, even and sometimes especially within Islam. Gone is the commitment to serious social welfare, health care and education, except in the narrowest sense. Gone is the sense of Islam as the *Ummah* that would fulfil the prophetic vision of God's community as one that witnesses to mercy, justice and humility to all at all costs. Most characteristically and of particular pertinence to the women's movement mentioned above, gone are the rights of women as mandated in the constitution of the original *Ummah*. In their place is a tendency towards regressive social ethics, complete with ideologies bent on exclusion and, where necessary, harm to those who stand in the way of it achieving its ends.

For all the fervour and sincerity with which Islamism poses as Islam, its claims to represent the original tradition are all but barren. That having been said, the combination of political circumstances and the relative lack of knowledge of their own tradition by a growing portion of Islam, together with the increasing potency of Islamism as a cogent force with a seemingly effective action plan, has the potential eventually to create fundamental change in Islam. It could become less and less relevant that scholarship is able to puncture the claims of Islamism because it might increasingly be seen to have many of the answers, if not the only answers, that contemporary troubled populations of Islam are seeking.

Overview of the Social Work Literature

Social work as a discipline and profession has been served by a substantial scholarship directed at the challenges presented by the modern polymorphous state and the need to reconceive social work as being about values rather than mere problem solving and about transformation rather than mere repair, a conceptual and practical change towards social work as 'agency' (Banks, 2006; Beckett & Maynard, 2005; DuBois & Miley, 2005; Hugman, 2005; Mama, 2001; Stoesz, 2002). In one way or another, much of this quest is pertinent to the retrieval of Islam's positive story cited above. In the middle, there has been a prolific scholarship that has attempted to draw these two strands together in addressing the issue of a reconceived social work and related human services interfacing with Muslim identity, especially in its Western setting (Ahmad & Sheriff, 2003; Barise, 2005; Becher & Husain, 2003; Faizi, 2001; Fikree, 2005; Haj-Yahia, 2003; Hodge, 2005; Khan, Watson, & Habib, 2005; Koenig et al., 2003; Lyons, Manion, & Carlsen, 2006; Malik, Shaikh, & Suleyman, 2007; Mohammad, 2005; Newland, 2006).

As Ashencaen-Crabtree et al. (2008) imply, much of this latter scholarship is either founded on more generalized issues of racial identity or, where it does deal with issues germane to Islam, does not always do so in ways that betray deep understanding of the distinctive culture that is Islam, nor of the deep affinity between the values of social work and those of Islam. Therefore, even in a book that is ultimately directed at social work practice and practical guidelines for the service professional, Ashencaen Crabtree, Husain, & Spalek (2008) clearly see their priority as ensuring that the reader is offered a solid grounding in Islam's major tenets and beliefs. Only in this way can the important link between the ethos of modern social work and the foundational inspiration of Islam be assured.

Application to Social Work Practice

Social work, Islam and the challenge of agency

The confused identity noted above constitutes part of the dilemma for Westerners trying to understand and address effectively the issue of Islam in its midst and also part of the reason that it is so important that those with significant social responsibilities, like social workers, understand what they are dealing with when they engage with Muslim communities in Western settings. Western social workers can afford to be neither overly arrogant nor *laissez-faire* in the attitude they take into this work. The social worker must be engaged in an informed way that allows both for sensitivity yet also agency to occur. To be sensitive does not mean accepting everything that one might be told. The social worker must understand that there are ethical perspectives to be found in Muslim communities that stand up very well to the origins and historical sources of Islam, but there are ones that do not stand up well at all. In order to have agency, the social worker must know something of the difference. The ramifications are that social workers functioning in a Western context that interfaces with a Muslim population should not merely see themselves being there to receive whatever ethical propositions are put to them but, provided their knowledge is sufficiently well grounded, to play a part in engaging in and transacting the ethical positions they encounter. In a word, the worker's agency should be directed towards *praxis*, practical action for change (Lovat & Gray, 2008). This action is impelled not by mere cross-cultural sensitivity but by deep understanding of Islamic ethics and its differentiation with much of the stereotyped image of Islam, albeit well cultivated and adhered to by many who describe themselves as Muslim.

At all costs, social work agency must avoid patronizing and ethnocentric behaviour. Muslim culture is a proud and elevated one, and its ethics rightly regarded as at least an equal among its peers. Islam is arguably the most corporate of the major religions. That is, consciousness of the good of the community is an ethical imperative. As Hodge (2005) points out, there is, therefore, high compatibility between the ethos of modern social work and the fundamental values of Islam. Indeed, the Muslim in a Western setting might well believe that modern laws around the likes of welfare and non-discrimination, designed to protect and guarantee the rights of all with special emphasis on the poor and disadvantaged, were inspired initially by Islam, a view with considerable substance in scholarship (Amin, 2007; Grieve, 2006; Lewis, 1993; Waardenburg, 2003).

Furthermore, work like that of Ahmad and Sheriff (2003) has shown how much Muslim-based human service can contribute to needs in the non-Muslim community, combining as it does practical care with an explicit religious ethos (see also Barise, 2005; Khan et al., 2005). This work also offers a clue about the potential importance of the social worker being open to engaging with imams and other religious authorities if immersed in an issue that involves Muslim clients. Malik et al. (2007) provide evidence of the importance of such involvement in serving the needs of young Muslims in Britain. Further evidence is available through the work of the UK National Youth Agency (NYA, 2009) that there is a particular need to provide safe and secure space, including spiritual support, for many young Muslims, both immigrant and British-born. It is suggested in the Agency's foundation statement that spiritual support is necessary to ensure that social work agency serves to turn around the negative image, including self-image, that can afflict the young Muslim living in the Western setting. The well-informed and balanced imam is clearly central to this being achieved. By inference, it can be seen that the young Muslim lacking self-esteem and feeling under attack by the surrounding society provides fertile ground for the radical Islamist imam as well.

The NYA raises the spectre of there being an increased need for Muslim workers in the field but that, at this stage, there are few to be found. Granted the demonstrated importance of religious identity and spiritual support, it would seem obvious that this would go a long way to addressing some of the needs identified by the Agency's work. At the same time, the increased presence of Muslim social workers would present other challenges. For a start and as mentioned at the outset, it is increasingly difficult to generalize about Islam and the precise nature of the beliefs, values and practices to be found in Muslim communities. Not only is there the stark opposition noted in this chapter between 'Islam' and 'Islamism' and the many points between the two but, in an older and more ingrained sense, there are vast differences in the nature of the Islam to be found across different ethnicities and cultural backgrounds. This consideration is possibly more crucial when addressing Muslim issues in settings like Britain, Canada and Australia than in Muslim countries because immigration from an array of Muslim provinces has been characteristic of the growth of Muslim populations in these countries. In other words, it is in these countries that the differences within contemporary Islam become so stark. The important rub for a profession like social work is that finding a Muslim practitioner is one thing, while finding one whose Islam is germane to that of the client is quite another thing altogether. It might well be that a Turkish Muslim, for argument's sake, would feel more affinity with a Western social worker than with a Muslim from the Middle East or Asia.

The other challenge associated with having more Muslim workers in the field will be in clearly identifying the scope of their work. Whether they will be employed exclusively to work with Muslim populations or with the general population will be an issue to be addressed. At this stage, the call for more Muslim workers is associated with the need to provide better support for Muslim clients but, once trained and on duty, it would seem inconsistent that they would not then be available for any work with any clientele.

Another issue of contemporary interest to the growth of Islamic culture and populations in Western settings concerns *Sharia*, Islamic Law. The Archbishop of Canterbury created a storm in early 2008 when he described the incorporation of aspects of *Sharia* in Britain as 'unavoidable' (http://news.bbc.co.uk/2/hi/uk_news/7232661.stm). While roundly condemned and urged to resign, the Archbishop defended his view on the basis of the incorporation of Islamic Law into British everyday life being a means of mitigating the demonstrable alienation of British Muslims and so of bolstering social cohesion. In the months since the Archbishop's call, the British government has quietly allowed for this incorporation, with the London *Times* reporting that judges are in fact applying *Sharia* to cases of financial support, divorce and domestic violence (http://www.timesonline.co.uk/tol/news/uk/crime/article4749183.ece).

Such changing practice around the interpretation and application of what is regarded as 'legal' must be incorporated into the practice of a profession like social work. It inevitably will enhance the desirability of having an adequate number of Muslim social workers available to deal with cases liable to be adjudicated by application of *Sharia*.

While many Westerners will bemoan what might appear to be a weakening of their own laws, a well founded appreciation of Islam's social ethics will show that the application of *Sharia* might actually strengthen the social fabric of Western regimes. As Ahmad and Sheriff (2003) demonstrate of social work, a Muslim presence can enhance not only the service of Muslims but of the community in general. Awareness of the mega-ethics in Islam around human rights, social justice and equality, and how these manifest themselves amidst the clash of cultures inherent in Muslims living in Western societies, is the single most important understanding that a social worker striving for agency needs to have. In Islam, the social worker is dealing with the religious ideology that, above all others, established ordinances about social welfare and support that preceded modern welfare systems by a thousand years and more. With the Muslim who knows the faith, the social worker is, in terms of the essential purpose of the profession, dealing with a kindred spirit. At the same time, agency will require sensitivity to the fact that many who call themselves Muslim will have a different understanding of their faith.

Social work, Islam and the practical challenges

Beyond the mega-ethic, the social worker will need to deal with a range of practical issues when engaging with a Muslim community. Although arguably not adequate for dealing with much of the big picture, there is nonetheless a reasonably extensive and updated literature that addresses a number of these practicalities. Burr and Chapman (2004) provide compelling evidence that many of the personal, social and domestic problems that a social worker would deal with are 'somatized' by a larger portion of the Muslim community than is routine in the non-Muslim community. That is, worries and concerns that might be essentially psychological are expressed through bodily pain or ailment more often in the Muslim community. The important practical effect is that many of these problems are more likely to be referred to the health and medical services, rather than social services, at a far greater rate than would apply to the general population. This could result from an unfamiliarity with the nature of a social work service or could amount to the downside of Barise's (2005) insight that many day-to-day problems tend to be 'religionized' by Muslims, so making it arguably more difficult for them to seek help of the secularized type that social work denotes. Indeed, Fikree (2005) has shown that Muslim men and women can both 'religionize' domestic violence, the man in justifying it while the woman in enhancing her own victim status. Douki et al. (2003) and Haj-Yahia (2003) suggest that domestic violence is endemic to Arab settings, whether justified by Islam or not.

Dominelli (1988) is well known for her work on the need for Muslim-sensitive social support provisions to be available, and Faizi (2001) has furthered this work with particular case studies that compare and contrast extant provisions in the US, while advocating for Muslim-sensitive provisions that are, at the same time, not overly exclusivist nor justifying of practices in the 'name of Islam' that are unacceptable in a Western setting and often do not stand up to scrutiny against the principles of Islam anyway. Irfan and Cowburn (2004) meanwhile take the same perspective into their study of certain domestic discipline practices that simply justify forms and levels of abuse that can neither be condoned in Western provinces nor according to an enlightened understanding of Islamic law (see also Ammar, 2000; Koenig et al., 2003). Ashencaen Crabtree and Baba (2001), Halstead and Lewicka (1998) and Mahamud-Hassan (2004) explore the issue of alternative sexual preference in Muslim communities, exposing a scene that is as varied in attitude and practice as would apply to most communities, and this in spite of the rigid norms that are routinely pronounced by Muslim authorities. Homosexuality is a particularly thorny issue for Muslim males, especially with the prominence with which regimes like that in Iran condemn it and hunt down young males who are open in their propensity to be homosexual. Malik et al. (2007) have shown that regular social work service is unlikely to be accessed by the Muslim male facing these or other social difficulties and, as a result, the Muslim Youth Helpline has been established as a religious-based alternative to such service in the UK.

As suggested, the above literature provides a reasonable coverage of some of the practical issues facing a modern Western-based social worker when engaging with the Muslim community. Additionally, the social worker will do well to understand the nature of Muslim prayer and its binding force on the daily timetable, a duty that will need to be accommodated in the context of any social service, be the Muslim a social work employee or client (Al-Krenawi & Graham, 2000). Awareness will also need to be extended to the prohibition on killing of any kind, including abortion except where the mother's life is in danger; on gambling, alcohol and drugs, including tobacco; and on the eating of certain meats.

While the practice is rare, the social worker will need to be alert to the reality of female circumcision within some Muslim communities. While there is no evidence that female circumcision was either enjoined or practised in early Muslim communities, there are significant groups that inherited Islam and went on to continue their traditional practice of female circumcision, eventually incorporating it into their beliefs about Islam. Again, on the theme of social work as agency, it will be important for the social worker to understand that technically there is no connection between such a practice and Islam but that a Muslim from an African tribal group, for instance, might well believe that there is a connection. In the overall interests of women's well-being, this must be a matter for transaction rather than mere reception (Taylor, 2003).

A less serious but nonetheless similarly emotional issue that affects a great number of female Muslims concerns the veil, whether in the form of the lightly veiled *hijab* or fully-veiled *burqa*. Evidence that the veil is enjoined on women by *Qur'anic* testimony is scant but many Muslims – men and women – regard it as a binding injunction and fundamental signal of their submission to God. A growing body of Muslims, both men and especially women, are voicing protest at the practice but it will likely remain an issue of contention and internal tension for some time to come (see Mannson McGinty, 2006).

Conclusion

As illustrated above, the issue of Islam and ethics is far from linear and straightforward, and its complexity is growing with the increasing advance of an Islamist critique of the older tradition, made more complex by the sensitivity of the politics around Islam in current times. For the social worker who engages with Islam in Western societies, be the worker Muslim or non-Muslim, awareness of the realities noted herein is essential, as is an approach to the business of service professionalism that is geared towards agency, dealing with the big picture, engaging with people's wider realities and looking always to making a difference by reconstructing their worlds, rather than merely repairing their old and possibly fractured ones. Walking the fine line between the boundless respect that Islam deserves and preparedness and skills around transacting with some of its currently fractured reality will be a major challenge for any social worker engaging with a Muslim population in a Western setting.

Study Questions

1. Why might a Muslim consider that modern social work is based on an early Islamic tenet of faith?

2. Identify a number of key challenges that face the Western-based social worker who engages with a Muslim community. What might be a reasonable response to each of these challenges?
3. What potential do you see for modern social work and Western-based Muslim communities to enrich each others' understanding of human service?

17

Christianity and Ethics

Russell Whiting

Key Concepts

Christian ethics is not a single entity in that there are competing interpretations of ethics that all claim a basis in Christianity. The following concepts also contribute to an understanding of Christian ethics.

New Testament ethics: The New Testament is not really much concerned with ethics per se and discovery of its ethical import can only result through theological engagement with the text.

Augustinian ethics conceptualizes humanity as sinners. St Augustine devised a scheme for the transmission of original sin through the sexual act. Though this idea is not in the Bible, its continued prominence explains many of Christianity's ethical preoccupations to this day, especially the Church's work with 'fallen women'. Morality for Christianity since Augustine has predominantly been considered in relation to sex and sexuality.

Thomist ethics fuses together Aristotelian ethics and Christian theology grounded in natural law (see Biestek, in this chapter).

Introduction

Social work values and ethics are very closely aligned with the three major Abrahamic faith traditions, namely, Christianity, Judaism and Islam. These are the major faith-based approaches encountered in the developed Western context where social work is predominantly practised. As we saw in Chapter 16, of the three, Islam produces the greatest conflicts because of the politics rather than a proper understanding of the common philosophical roots of these three Abrahamic faiths. As we saw in Part 1 on professional value perspectives, social work has sought hard to divest itself of its religious connections despite its Judeo-Christian value system. But what would happen if social workers were to practise from a faith-based rather than a common professional value or ethical perspective? What would happen if social workers were required to tell clients that they were practising from a Judeo-Christian value perspective, or if they were to openly declare their Christian, Islamic or Buddhist faith, as the case may be? As we saw in Chapter 6, faith-based practice has once again entered the social work lexicon, with interest in religion and spirituality in social work growing as it becomes socially accepted once again to declare one's faith. The rise of the New Right has favoured faith-based social service providers, in the US especially, and brought to the fore the large number of religious providers involved in social and community care provision around the Western world. Buddhist and Hindu ethics have not been developed in social work to the extent that our chosen approaches for inclusion have been, though it is evident in New Age spirituality, which has appropriated Eastern religious perspectives (Gray, 2008a; see Chapter 18).

In this chapter, we re-examine the Judea-Christian values of social work through the work of Jesuit priest Father Felix Biestek, one of the most well-known figures in the development of social work ethics in the West in the twentieth century. His *Casework Relationship* (1961) was used in social work education for many years and a number of sections explicitly affirm his Christian faith. Consequently, he was arguably the most audible Christian voice in the development of professional social work ethics. Eventually, however, that voice became somewhat discredited when Noel Timms (1983) criticized Biestek's list of casework principles and Bill Jordan (1987) directly attacked his faith, commenting that he was bound by 'the constraints and restrictions of traditional Christian moral thinking', adding that clients had more pressing concerns than where their social workers went to church.

This chapter re-examines some material from Biestek's book and argues that Biestek's writing displays a number of theological insights that remain relevant to social work ethics. While a number of these ideas have traditional Catholic – Augustinian and Thomist – underpinnings, Biestek is more usefully thought of as reflecting the Christian humanist tradition, or what might be thought of as a Christianity of an optimistic world-view. This tradition is represented in this chapter by Dutch theologian Erasmus, Anglican poet and clergyman Thomas Traherne and other more recent exponents, particularly Biestek's fellow Jesuits. It is intended that this focus on the positive will have something of a polemic quality, particularly to engage with those who persist in the view that Christianity must necessarily hold an unremittingly negative perception of humanity as miserable sinners and that its influence on the development of social work and social work ethics has been correspondingly negative. This chapter challenges any such presuppositions and makes an effort at realignment.

Key Ideas

Christian humanism and the Christian virtues

In *Civilization and Ethics*, Albert Schweitzer (1923) considered the world religions and their impact on the development of ethics. He divided the religions into those that held optimistic and pessimistic world-views. His critique of the development of Christianity's world-view is complex but stimulating, and worth quoting at length:

> The early Christian conception of the Kingdom of God, which was born of pessimism and, thanks to Augustine, prevailed through the Middle Ages, is rendered impotent, and its place is taken by a conception which is the offspring of modern optimism. This new orientation of the Christian world view, which is accomplished by a slow and often interrupted process between the fifteenth and the end of the eighteenth century, is the decisive spiritual event of the modern age … .
>
> A way is prepared in Erasmus and individual representatives of the Reformation, shyly at first but then more and more clearly, for an interpretation of the teaching of Jesus which corresponds to the spirit of modern times, an interpretation which conceives the teaching as a religion of action in the world. Historically and in actual fact this is a wrong interpretation, for the world view of Jesus is thoroughly pessimistic so far as concerns the future of the natural world. His religion is not a religion of world transforming effort but of awaiting the end of the world … .
>
> But the modern age was right to overlook this paradox, and assuming in Jesus an optimistic world view which corresponded to an ethic of enthusiasm and met with a welcome the spirit of Late Stoicism and that of modern times. For the progress of the spiritual life of Europe this was a necessity. What crisis the latter must have gone through, if it had not without embarrassment to place the new outlook on the universe under the authority of the great personality of Jesus! (Schweitzer, 1923, pp. 63–7)

While one might quibble with Schweitzer's analysis about the pessimism of the earlier traditions, I do not wish to argue with his fundamental position about the development of a positive world-view within Christianity. Erasmus, the definitive and possibly pre-eminent Christian humanist, was known, among other things, for his pacifism. Martin Luther claimed he loved peace more than truth. Also well known were his efforts to preserve the writings of antiquity and to fuse them with the insights of Christianity. Many of Erasmus's writings were concerned about how Christians might best act in the world. Seventeenth-century English Christian humanist Thomas Traherne had similar concerns and accepted that the virtues were not of Christian origin. His *Christian Ethicks* ([1675] 1968) was a product in part of Renaissance thought and recognize the debt Christianity owed in its consideration of the virtues to the writers of antiquity. The book does make a claim however, not an original one anyway, about what Traherne describes as specifically Christian virtues:

> Besides all these, there are some Vertues, which may more properly be called Christian: because they are nowhere else taught but in the Christian Religion, are founded on the love of Christ, and the only Vertues distinguishing a Christian from the rest of the World, of which sort are Love to Enemies, Meekness, and Humility. (Traherne, [1675] 1968, p. 24–5)

In the recovery of the virtues in recent writing in social work ethics, virtues, such as courage and honour, have been highlighted as important for social work identity formation (see, e.g. Clark, 2006; Webb, Chapter 10 in this volume). While not wanting to minimize the importance of such work, this section takes Traherne's three Christian virtues and considers how the Christian humanist tradition has understood and expounded on them. Thereafter, their connection to Biestek's (1961) casework principles and social work ethics more generally is considered. We begin with humility, which surely with an inappropriate expression of pride, the church claimed as its own.

Humility

'For an humble man condescends to look into his Wants, to reflect upon all his Vices, and all his beginnings, with far deeper designs than is ordinarily done' (Traherne, [1675] 1968, p. 212). Christian humility is not to be confused with Aristotelian magnanimity. But, as well as this, there were varieties of Christian humility. In the more pessimistic interpretations of Christianity, humility is based on self-abnegation or self-annihilation. These interpretations are preoccupied with sin and sinfulness. However, such a position is of little use in social work where social workers must know themselves as they do their work through the use, in part, of their own personality. Self-abnegation is simply incompatible with such an approach. Christian humanism's interpretation of humility is not about abnegation or annihilation. Rather, it is a theological interpretation of humility, which is one based, in part, on statements about God, including, among others, God as creator (see also Bowpitt, 2000). This idea has been a central one for Christian humanists. Dutch Christian humanist and contemporary of Biestek, Edward Schillebeeckx (1971), extends it in his writing about what he calls humble humanism:

> Humility is not a diminution or a denial of human values, pusillanimity or smallness of soul, or a compulsive denigration as evil of something which man regards, in his heart, as nonetheless inwardly valuable and precious to him. True humility predisposes a loyal acceptance of human greatness but it regards this precisely as a creaturely value ... Humility includes experience and awareness of self, but awareness of ourselves as God's gift ... Awareness of being a creature is thus the basis of humble humanism. (p. 23)

In a very similar vein, South African John de Gruchy (2006) writes: 'Acknowledging the whole cosmos as God's creation, Christian humanists recognise that all of life is bound together in an amazingly complex evolutionary web that evokes humility and awe' (p. 30). The importance of the concept of creatureliness also cannot be overestimated in Biestek's formulation of social work, as shall be seen below, and it is a clear indicator of his connection to this tradition.

Meekness

'Meekness respecteth other faults; humility and penitence our own' (Traherne, [1675] 1968, p. 206). If humility were concerned with the individual's perception of himself in relation to the world and to God, meekness would be concerned with an individual's relations with others. Christians have not always been meek in their approach to 'good works'. Even those organizations with a reputation for meekness today cannot claim that. For example, Elizabeth Isichei (1970), in her account of Victorian Quakers, claims that:

> The very structure of a Victorian philanthropy, with its phalanx of honorary Vice-Presidents, its host of offices, and its printed subscription lists, encouraged the charitable to seek the bubble reputation. Critics ... attributed Quaker philanthropy to 'a love of distinction, which they can in no other way indulge. (p. 215)

Social work today is more egalitarian than Victorian philanthropy but the bubble reputation still finds ways to emerge. We must, however, avoid falling into the common trap of writing about the vice of pride rather than the virtue of meekness. Meekness is directly related to humility and ideas about commonality. It is underlined by the belief that all people are Children of God. Jesus told the story of the Pharisee who prayed: 'God, I thank thee, I am not as other men are, extortioners, unjust, adulterers or even as this publican' (Luke 18:11).

'I am not as other men' is not something a social worker might say. One reason social workers find to do social work is that they recognize a bond or a sense of sameness with the person with whom they are working. Jordan (1987), in amongst his already cited criticisms of Biestek, writes of service users or clients: 'The only difference between us and them is that they look to social workers to help sort it out, whereas we, usually, look elsewhere' (p. 27).

What would a social work based on humility and meekness look like? It is interesting that Traherne ([1675] 1968) uses the phrase 'Meekness *respecteth* others' faults', because there is a also a connection with the concept of respect here. Boros (1968), another twentieth-century Christian humanist in the Society of Jesus, elucidates the connection between respect and meekness:

> Respect for a person is really reverence. The German word for this is *Ehrfurcht* – a strange word combined of 'fear' *(Furcht)* and 'honour' *(Ehre)*. Fear which shows honour. It is a holy respect for what is great in the other person. In it a man renounces the possession of the other person, the using of him for his own purposes. He takes his hand away instead of grabbing. A true humanity is created only where a man steps back, where he does not force himself forward, does not snatch at things; in this way a free space is created in the world in which the other person can flourish in his own nature, dignity and beauty. (p. 20)

This is a description of a kind of social work in practice, a social work of meekness.

Love of enemies

Although he cited love of enemies as one of the three Christian Virtues, Traherne ([1675] 1968) does not give the topic its own chapter in *Christian Ethicks* as he had done with humility and meekness. A certain complacency in Traherne's writing on this topic is evident. He certainly does not challenge the social order and is, perhaps, a typical Restoration figure seeking stability and order instead of the quest for a 'New England'. Of humility, Traherne ([1675] 1968) writes:

> It need not be observed that sweetness of conversation, that civility, and courtesie, that springs from humility. The meek and the Lowly are the same men: the Kind, and the Charitable, and the Affable and the good are all of them Humble, and so are all they that prefer others above themselves, and render themselves amiable by honouring their inferiours, and giving place to their Equals. (p. 215)

Traherne had no wish to destabilize the social order as he had seen the bloodshed such an attempt had caused and he saw love of enemies very much in that light. For the modern-day social worker, however, there are considerable problems in this thinking. The implication is that the humble render themselves amiable by their ability to overlook social inequality. This line of criticism is picked up by contemporary Christian ethicist, Stanley Haeurwas (1983), specifically in relation to Christian humanism:

> In fact behind the emphasis on the 'human' character of Christian ethics is a deep fear that there might be a radical discontinuity between a Christian culture and their culture. The result, I fear, is that natural law assumptions function as an ideology for sustaining some Christians' presuppositions that their societies – particularly societies of Western democracies –are intrinsic to God's purposes. (p. 59)

Haeurwas (1983) is a thoroughgoing pacifist who reserved special ire for recent US wars fought, in part, in the name of Christianity. If the reader thinks we are moving away from social work here, we need only reflect on the presence of conflict and violence encountered in everyday social work practice.

Traherne ([1675] 1968) has a short section, however, where he links meekness and love of enemies: 'When we understand the perfection of the love of God, the excellency of immortal Souls, the price and valour of our Saviour's Blood ... *and the Joyes of which our sorest enemies are capable* ... compassion itself will melt us into meekness' (p. 204; emphasis added). This is all of a piece with the earlier writing. Love of enemies is based on a conception on commonness, of common humanity. Whether these lines are anything more than poetic and contain matter of substance is another question.

If Christian humanists have little to say on love for enemies, there are other Christians whose formulations of this idea are relevant for social work ethics. The modern writer who speaks most plainly on the topic is Dietrich Bonhoeffer (1948). His own position develops and changes but, specifically in regard to loving one's enemies, he writes:

> To the natural man, the very notion of loving his enemies is an intolerable offence, and quite beyond his capacity: It cuts right across his idea of good and evil. More important still, to man under the law, the idea of loving his enemies is clean contrary to the law of God, which requires men to sever all connection with their enemies and to pass judgement on them. Jesus however takes the law of God in his own hands and expounds its true meaning. The will of God, to which the law gives expression, is that men should defeat their enemies by loving them. (p. 127)

The reference to judgement brings us back to Biestek. Bonhoeffer here is implying that judgement can be made once connections are severed. Non-judgementalism, one of Biestek's principles, therefore, necessitates the maintenance of contact with those who are deemed enemies or, perhaps more appropriately, those with whom one is in conflict.

Overview of the Social Work Literature

Christian humanist theology and The Casework Relationship

Biestek's highly influential *Casework Relationship* was published in the UK in 1961. When I trained in the early 1990s, his list of seven casework principles was still being used in 'Introduction to social work ethics' sessions. Banks (2006) refers to the book as 'surprisingly influential' (p. 31), but it is not, in fact, so surprising as the book is ideally suited to a single introductory lecture on social work ethics. It provides a frequently repeated list of principles, or what have since become thought of as social work values: individualization, purposeful expression of feelings, controlled emotional involvement, acceptance, a non-judgemental attitude, client self-determination and confidentiality, and proceeds with emboldened definitions of these principles. Almost every social work text that has referred to *The Casework Relationship* has confined itself to citing these principles. I do not intend to cite them here but refer the reader to the original. Lying behind these principles is an ethical framework based, in large part, on Christian theology. It is a richly hued theology and certainly not one that can be characterized simply as 'traditional moral thinking', although it does have something of that. For example, in describing the right to confidentiality, Biestek (1961) draws on the Thomist conception of natural law:

> The natural law is the will of the Creator as manifested in nature. Because of the infinite intelligence of the Creator each thing is assigned a function and a purpose. As long as the thing performs its function, order reigns and there is a serenity and a growth in its life ... Concretely, the natural law spells out man's duties to himself, to his fellow men, to his family, to society and to God. (p. 122)

In other sections, an Augustinian emphasis on the sins of humanity is evident, even, for example, in saying that 'Today social work accepts the Christian concept that it is possible to love the sinner without loving his sin' (Biestek, 1961, p. 91). There are other general religious comments that cannot be categorized as either traditionally moral or as Christian humanist. Examples of these are, where in commencing his chapter on individualization, Biestek (1961) notes that Christ expected his followers to 'individualize their love' (p. 23). He also cites St Francis of Assisi, St Vincent de Paul and Frederic Ozanan as individualizers and precursors of modern caseworkers. Above and beyond these general and traditional comments are a series of statements that Biestek makes, which closely accord with Christian humanist writing on the Christian virtues. It is in the chapter on acceptance that the theological references reach their peak. The whole basis of Biestek's (1961) conception of acceptance is theological:

> Man has a unique value in the universe. This intrinsic value is derived from God, his creator, and is not affected by personal success or failure in things physical, economic, social or anything else ... The social failures, just as the socially successful, are made in the image of God, are children of the infinitely loving heavenly Father and heirs of heaven. Even unacceptable acts, such as violations of the civil law or the moral law, do not deprive the person of his fundamental God-given dignity ... It is necessary to stress the source of human dignity. It does not come from personal success; it does not originate in a Bill of Rights or in a democratic constitution –these merely proclaim the worth of the individual rather than bestow it. The origin of the dignity of humanity is divinity. (pp. 73–4)

Biestek's reason why caseworkers must accept their clients was very simple. It is because she and they are creatures, that is, created beings. For students of social work, the important point is that Biestek has a reason for acceptance of others. Students might not have the same reason as Biestek or as a Christian theologian for accepting a person but they must have a reason. Otherwise the principle of acceptance is no more than a simple and unfounded assertion. This is perhaps a challenge of Christian humanism to secular humanism, to establish an alternative rationale for acceptance:

> our natural recognition of the value and dignity of both our God and His divine images around us in men, must prompt us once more to approach our God, and almost also our fellow man – upon our knees. (Cronin, cited in Biestek, 1961, p. 75)

This is a clear justification for a social work of the meek. In the final sentences of his book, Biestek (1961) reiterates the emphasis on the worker's fraternity with those he (*sic*) is working with and produces a formulation for egalitarianism:

> As an idealist he sees each client as a precious child of the heavenly Father. As a realist he sees the client as he really is, with attitudes and behaviour which perhaps are quite unlike to God's. With the motive of love, he strives for skill in the use of the wisdom of sciences to help his brother in need. The caseworker hopes that he is, in some small way, an instrument of Divine Providence. (p. 137)

This quotation encapsulates Biestek's articulation of the conception of fraternity and he does so using Christian humanist theology. Another challenge to secular humanists might be to query the secular basis of fraternity.

In summary, it is important to note that Felix Biestek was not just a Christian. He was also a Jesuit. Almost all the Christian humanists of note in the twentieth century were also Jesuits, including Teilhard de Chardin, Alfred Delp, Karl Rahner, Edward Schillebeecx and Ladislaus Boros, to name but a few, and all were from different European countries (see also Modras, 2004 for more on the Jesuit Christian humanist heritage). So when Biestek makes theological references in *The Casework Relationship* he was working from this base and background. Biestek's own theological comments are numerous but limited. If this chapter does nothing else, it has hopefully shown how Biestek's thoughts about social work ethics chime with some of the deeper thinking of his contemporary fellow Christian humanists and that their thinking is relevant to a consideration of social work ethics even today.

One of the reasons why Biestek was chosen as the focus of this chapter is that he stands more or less alone as a Christian figure focusing on ethics in social work. There is not a large literature on social work and Christianity generally, and even less specifically on social work ethics. For the most part, theologians and social workers have managed to avoid one another. What literature there is mostly has a North American focus, such as was found in the journal *Social Work and Christianity,* or was produced some time ago (Hnik, 1938; Niebuhr, 1932). In recent years, there has been a range of material in the *British Journal of Social Work* on spirituality but not necessarily on Christianity, with the exception of Bowpitt (1998, 2000).

Application to Social Work Practice

In considering the application of the Christian virtues of love for enemies, humility and meekness to contemporary social work practice, child protection is an obvious example. This is because in work of this kind the conflicts and tensions inherent in the social worker's task are closest to the surface. It is indeed a role in which social workers may face considerable aggression. Yet social workers' response to such situations of need might rather be seen as practical love in action, as motivated by compassionate concern. As such, child protection might also be seen as a field in which meekness and humility on the part of the worker are positive assets. Eileen Munro (1999), in her seminal article on common mistakes in child protection work, highlighted how social workers become wedded to their first impressions of people and situations and fail to conduct proper reviews, in part because doubting their judgements would mean doubting their professional selves. A genuinely humble worker would never hold on to her own views simply because they were her own. She would be doubly suspicious of her own views and judgements until they had been thoroughly tested and checked. In summary, the humble and meek social worker would be someone able to form working relationships with individuals, no matter how difficult the circumstances. In addition, she would maintain close relationships with colleagues whom she would expect to closely scrutinize her performance.

Conclusion

This chapter does not attempt to revive Biestek but to chart its continuing relevance. Many of the criticisms made of his views and his list of principles, from wherever they emerged, hit their target. Yet still I would argue that an appreciation of Biestek as a Christian figure, and of some of his core casework principles emerging from a particular positive Christian heritage, is worthwhile and important both for the Christian social worker and for others. At a recent conference of social work academics, practice assessors and others involved in developing the social work profession in Britain, a visiting panel of civil servants assessing the state of the profession, asked a series of questions about the competence and 'fitness for practice' of newly qualified social workers. Finally, the proceedings were pulled up sharply, at least temporarily, by one participant at the event who asked, 'What about humility?' The clear implication of the question is that what is expected of newly qualified social workers is some awareness, not just of their inadequacies but also, framed positively, of what they yet need to know, how they have yet to develop and the importance of being cautious, in line with Boros's (1968) comments above of not forcing themselves forward and not snatching at things in others.

Study Questions

1. To what extent are meekness and humility currently desired attributes in a social worker?
2. Is a pacifist social work (Christian or otherwise) possible?
3. What are the differences between Christian humanism, as described in this chapter, and secular humanism? Are those differences significant for social work?

18

New Age Ethics

Dick Houtman and Stef Aupers

Key Concepts

Esotericism: A 'spiritual' Western tradition, rooted in the fifteenth-century Renaissance, that is critical of dogmatic religion and rational science and presents 'gnosis', or personal experience, as a 'third way' to determine what is true, just and beautiful.

New Age: A secularized offshoot of esotericism that emerged in the 1960s, which assumes the existence of a 'spiritual' or 'divine' self that is part of a universal spirit or life force that permeates and connects all that exists and that makes itself known through one's emotions and intuitions.

Spiritual turn: The increased interest in New Age spiritual perspectives in Western, particularly north-western European, countries from the 1960s onwards.

Introduction

Sociologists of religion increasingly doubt that the decline of the Christian churches in the West produces a turn to a non-religious world-view. Even more so, they doubt the validity of hard-boiled, rationalist notions of secularization, according to which reason and rationality, or faith in science and technology, increasingly replaces belief in a transcendent personal God. The late Bryan Wilson (1982), for example, assumed that 'In contemporary society, the young come to regard morality – any system of ethical norms – as somewhat old-fashioned. For many young people, problems of any kind have technical and rational solutions' (p. 136), while Karel Dobbelaere (1993) maintains that 'People increasingly think that they can control and manipulate "their" world. They act more in terms of insight, knowledge, controllability, planning and technique and less in terms of faith' (p. 15). Voices such as these meet with increased scepticism these days.

There is, of course, no doubt that, especially in north-western European countries with a largely Protestant heritage, such as Britain, Germany, the Netherlands, Denmark, Norway and Sweden, the Christian churches have declined strongly, while adherence to traditional Christian doctrines, values and practices has also eroded substantially since the 1960s (e.g. Bruce, 2002). It is, however, much more doubtful that, during this same period, a rationalist world-view has become more widespread and has somehow pushed aside and effectively replaced Christian world-views. Indeed, theories of reflexive modernization and postmodernization maintain that, since the 1960s, we have been witnessing a simultaneous decline of religious traditionalism and rationalist faith in science and technology (e.g. Beck, 1992; Giddens, 1991; Inglehart, 1997; Seidman, 1994).

This twofold cultural erosion constitutes a mainstreaming of the values of the 1960s counter-culture, which entailed a double protest against moral traditionalism and intellectual rationalism in the name of individual liberty, personal authenticity and respect for cultural diversity (Campbell, 2007; Marwick, 1998; Zijderveld, 1970). Indeed, the subtitle of Theodore Roszak's (1968) classic, *The Making of a Counter Culture*, itself a counter-cultural pamphlet as much as a social-scientific study, underscores the counter-culture's protest against not only moral traditionalism, but rationalism, as well: *Reflections on the Technocratic Society and Its Youthful Opposition*. Sociologist Daniel Bell (1976) has gone so far as to maintain that 'though [the counter-culture] appeared in the guise of an attack on the "technocratic society" [its ideology] was an attack on reason itself' (p. 143).

Although New Age is very much the spiritual heir of this counter-culture (Campbell, 2007; Zijderveld, 1970), it has deeper historical roots than this. It is basically a secularized offshoot of the tradition of Western esotericism, which is a markedly 'Eastern' spiritual undercurrent in the West that has its historical roots in the fifteenth-century Renaissance (Campbell, 2007; Hanegraaff, 2002). Esotericism, like New Age, features a simultaneous rejection of religious faith and intellectual rationalism, presenting itself as a superior synthesis of, and hence alternative to, each of these (Heelas, 1996; Hanegraaff, 1996).

In this chapter, we begin by discussing how the emergence of New Age in the counter-culture of the 1960s and 1970s, and especially its mainstreaming since the 1980s, needs to be understood from a cultural-sociological point of view. We then argue that the portrayal of New Age in the social-scientific literature as featuring an incoherent 'spiritual marketplace' dominated by individualized seekers is flawed and one-sided, because the indisputable diversity on the ground is itself an unavoidable outcome of a doctrine that is uncontested and provides the spiritual milieu with much more unity than typically acknowledged. Finally, we demonstrate that it is precisely this shared doctrine that accounts for New Age's public significance in the contemporary Western world, and in the field of social work.

The Spiritual Turn in Late Modernity

Problems of meaning and identity

The shift towards New Age spirituality since the 1960s flies in the face of the notion of a transition from traditional theistic Christianity characterized by belief in a transcendent personal God to a rationalism that is characterized by faith in reason, science and technology. Paul Heelas and Linda Woodhead (2005) even suggest that a 'spiritual revolution' may be under way – a major transition from dogmatic 'religion' to 'spirituality' that motivates 'people to live in accordance with the deepest, sacred dimensions of their own unique lives' (p. 7). Colin Campbell (2007) goes so far as to observe 'a fundamental revolution in Western civilization, one that can be compared in significance to the Renaissance, the Reformation, or the Enlightenment' (p. 41).

Much of this shift from theistic Christian religiosity to New Age spirituality is driven by secularization and detraditionalization. These are not unambiguous blessings, because they rob people of the protective cloaks of tradition-grounded 'pre-given' and 'self-evident' answers to questions of meaning and identity. As a result, many late-modern individuals in the West feel thrown back upon themselves and are endlessly haunted by existential questions of the type: 'What is it that I really want?', 'Is this really the sort of life I want to live?', 'What sort of person am I, really?' (Beck, 1992; Beck & Beck-Gernsheim, 2002; Giddens, 1991). It is this cultural condition that makes not only late-modern individuals, but also social work and a wide range of other institutional domains, highly receptive to New Age spirituality (Gray, 2008a; Henery, 2003).

To explain precisely why this is the case, the emergence of this new cultural condition can be usefully put in classical Weberian terms. According to sociologist Max Weber, who wrote almost a century ago about processes of cultural change in the Occident, a 'disenchantment of the world' erodes belief in a transcendent 'other world' that gives meaning to 'this world'. A disenchanted world is hence a world without foundations, a world in which 'there are no mysterious incalculable forces that come into play' (Weber, [1919] 1948, p. 139), and in which 'the world's processes ... simply "are" and "happen" but no longer signify anything' (Weber, 1978; 1921, p. 506). With traditional religious systems of meaning becoming less plausible, these lose much of their former capacity to provide late-modern selves with convincing explanations of what the world's processes 'really' mean. The problems of meaning and identity discussed in the above-mentioned sociological studies are, in other words, inevitable side effects of Max Weber's disenchantment of the world.

Cultural rationalization

Weber was well aware that the world's disenchantment sparked new quests for meaning, witnessing, as he did, many of his fellow intellectuals taking refuge in utopian experiments, alternative religions and esoteric movements. Nevertheless, he adopted a rationalist stance (Weber, [1919] 1948), and firmly dismissed spiritual tendencies such as these as 'weakness not to be able to countenance the stern seriousness of our fateful times' (p. 149). It is unfortunate that Weber did not study these attempts to re-enchant the modern world systematically, especially since his sociology of culture constitutes a promising point of departure for such an analysis. Indeed, Campbell (2007) applies some of Weber's most fundamental theoretical insights and methodological principles to arrive at an empirically informed and truly Weberian theory of the shift towards New Age spirituality since the 1960s. Especially vital to this theory is Weber's assumption of a universal human need to give meaning to an essentially meaningless world and his conception of culture as 'the endowment of a finite segment of the meaningless infinity of events in the world with meaning and significance from the standpoint of human beings' (Schroeder, cited in Campbell, 2007, p. 11).

As to the explanation of cultural change, Weber's notion of 'cultural rationalization' is vital. This notion refers to the reconstruction of belief systems so as to make them less vulnerable to loss of plausibility through the occurrence of events they cannot account for, or even blatantly contradicting them. Precisely such a process of cultural rationalization accounts for the emergence and subsequent mainstreaming of New Age since the 1960s. With traditional meanings understood by many as no longer 'natural' or 'self-evident', and hence implausible, unconvincing and unsatisfactory, New Age constitutes a system of meaning that is less vulnerable to disenchantment than doctrinal Christianity. It accomplishes this by emphasizing personal experience rather than conformity to doctrines and propositional truths, hence going beyond the need to 'believe' or 'have faith'. As long as experiences are seen from the 'emic' perspective of the experiencing person, they are, after all, 'true' and 'real' by definition. This is what distinguishes them from, for instance, 'errors' or 'sinful deeds', i.e. notions which rely on external standards of legitimacy. While traditional theistic types of religion give meaning to personal experiences through religious doctrines, in short, New Age constructs such experiences as spiritual lessons about oneself and the sacred.

More specifically, New Age understands emotions, such as love, pain, pleasure, anger or happiness, as personal reactions to events in the outer world that convey vital spiritual knowledge about one's inner world – about the sort of person one 'really' is 'at the deepest level'. Thus New Age does not rely on a radically transcendent personal God, who has revealed what the world's events and processes 'really' mean, but rather on a notion that the sacred lies 'within' each person (Heelas & Houtman, 2009).

Key Concepts

Self-spirituality

The foregoing implies that New Age, despite its emphasis on the primacy of personal experience, is not free of doctrine. Indeed, as seen from the 'etic' perspective of the detached intellectual observer, New Age is based on the assumption that people have basically not one, but two selves: a 'mundane,' 'conventional' or 'socialized' self is demonized as the 'false' or 'unreal' product of society and, as such, contrasted with a 'higher,' 'deeper,' 'true' or 'authentic' self that is understood as sacred. The latter is seen as one's 'natural' or 'real' self – a self that is basically unpolluted by society and its roles and institutions. Paul Heelas (1996) argued that 'the most pervasive and significant aspect of the *lingua franca* of the New Age is that the person is, in essence, spiritual' (p. 18). Getting in touch with this 'spiritual self' is a moral imperative in the New Age milieu since it is the only avenue towards spiritual growth, the good life and, basically, salvation from modern alienation.

This, then, is the principal doctrine of New Age spirituality: the belief that in the deepest layers of the self the 'divine spark' – to borrow a term from ancient Gnosticism – is still smouldering, waiting to be stirred up and supersede the socialized self. Notwithstanding the centrality of this doctrine, New Age is often characterized as a 'pick-and-mix religion' (Hamilton, 2000), 'religious consumption à la carte' (Possamai, 2003) or a 'spiritual supermarket' (Lyon, 2000), because of its marked tendencies towards syncretism and *bricolage* (Luckmann, 1996). The principal source of such claims is Thomas Luckmann's *The Invisible Religion* (1967), in which he argues that a 'market of ultimate significance' emerges where religious consumers shop for strictly personal packages of meaning, based on individual tastes and preferences. Since Luckmann published his path-breaking work, accounts of modern religion as radically privatized and fragmented have almost attained the status of sociological truisms. Kelly Besecke (2005) correctly points out that 'Luckmann's characterization of contemporary religion as privatized is pivotal in the sociology of religion; it has been picked up by just about everyone and challenged by almost no one' (p. 186). What is wrongly neglected in this literature, however, is that the indisputable fragmentation of the contemporary spiritual milieu stems from the doctrine of self-spirituality. Ironically, then, this fragmentation does not prove the absence of a shared doctrine, but rather its presence. Given that established religious traditions need to be rejected, while one needs to 'choose one's personal path' by taking personal experiences, feelings and intuition seriously, New Age cannot present itself otherwise than as a 'consumerist market religion' in which the individual spiritual seeker-consumer rules sovereign (Aupers & Houtman, 2006).

Holism

Re-establishing contact with the 'true' or 'divine' self is held to enable one to reconnect to a sacred realm that holistically connects 'everything' and to overcome one's state of alienation. This brings us to holism as the second major tenet of New Age. The 'deeper' self is essentially spiritual, because it is part of an impersonal spirit or life force that permeates 'everything' – nature, the cosmos and human beings alike. To put it more simply, human beings are seen as nodes in a field of spiritual energy that connects 'everything' as a universal and impersonal spirit or life force. In this way, contacting the spiritual self through meditation, yoga or other spiritual exercises enables one to 'get connected' with all that exists – nature, the cosmos and people. In other words, self-spirituality assumes holism – the belief that an invisible unity exists beyond the world's dualisms and fragmentation. One can, of course, also argue the other way around to the effect that holism assumes self-spirituality, so that 'getting connected' enables one to experience the sacred in the deeper layers of one's own consciousness. In short, the doctrines of self-spirituality and holism assume one another, so that neither is more 'fundamental' than the other: without a belief in a deeper spiritual self one cannot connect to the cosmos and without a belief in holism one cannot believe that one has a self that is essentially sacred.

Belief in self-spirituality and holism motivate New Agers to reject 'pre-given' authoritative sources that provide meaning and identity. Instead of relying on answers offered by the Christian churches and scientific specialists, they trust on the 'internal' compass of the spiritual self. This means, as we have seen above, that, epistemologically speaking, New Age entails a third way of 'gnosis' that rejects religious faith as well as scientific reason as vehicles of truth (Hanegraaff, 1996). Instead, it opts for taking personal experience seriously, i.e. listening to one's 'inner voice' and trusting one's 'intuition'. Hence the major difference with theistic Christianity is not so much that a shared religious doctrine is absent, but rather that New Age is less susceptible to disenchantment because only personal experiences are taken seriously. To put this somewhat bluntly: as long as one personally experiences the self as spiritual, and 'everything' as essentially connected, no further 'proof' is needed.

The spiritual turn

There is unfortunately not much hard evidence for the contemporary presence of New Age as a more 'modernity proof' conception of the sacred than theistic Christianity, mostly because questionnaires used by sociologists – even sociologists of religion – still have a clear Christian bias. As a consequence, the large comparative international surveys are much more useful for documenting the breakdown of the Christian past than for mapping the gradual expansion of its New Age successor. Despite this, surveys increasingly produce findings that make researchers raise their eyebrows. In 2006, to give just one example, no less than 36 per cent of the Dutch population believed that 'there must be a higher force that controls life', while a mere 24 per cent still believed in 'a God who personally occupies himself with every single human being' (Bernts, Dekker, & de Hart, 2007, p. 133).

Although the virtual absence of good questionnaires in the large comparative international surveys unfortunately leaves too much room for speculation, it is pretty clear that a marked shift from theistic Christian religiosity to New Age spirituality is taking place, and this is documented in the social work literature on spirituality (Gray, 2008a) and other empirical studies (Heelas & Woodhead, 2005; Houtman & Aupers, 2007; Houtman & Mascini, 2002). Particularly in heavily secularized and formerly Protestant northwestern European countries, such as Britain, the Netherlands and Scandinavia, enormous numbers of people nowadays say that they believe in 'an impersonal spirit or life force' rather than in 'a personal God' (Heelas, 2007; Houtman & Aupers, 2007; Houtman & Mascini, 2002). There is, moreover, suggestive evidence that in some of the massively Catholic countries of southern Europe, particularly Portugal, a major 'spiritualization' of Christian religiosity may be taking place that calls for more detailed empirical study in the future (Heelas & Houtman, 2009; Houtman, Aupers, & Heelas, 2009).

Overview of the social work literature

New Age's role in the public domain

As a corollary to the portrayal of New Age as an incoherent collection of strictly personal meaning systems, it is commonly maintained that it remains confined to 'the life-space that is not directly touched by institutional control' (Luckmann, 1996, p. 73) and hence fails to 'generate powerful social innovations and experimental social institutions' (Bruce, 2002, p. 97). Again following Luckmann's (1967) lead, almost a generation of sociologists of religion have argued repeatedly that, under conditions of modernity, religion can only appear as 'privatized' – as a matter of personal choice – and hence as lacking wider social and public significance. Modern religion has thus long been seen as 'almost an exclusively psychological phenomenon, with very limited and indirect social consequence' (Besecke, 2005, p. 187). Things seem to be changing rapidly in recent years, however, with ever more publications coming up on the emergence of New Age in the public sphere.

Given its conception of the sacred as immanent rather than transcendent and its ensuing rejection of the notion of a 'religious' domain that can somehow be separated from a 'secular' sphere, it is, in fact, not even surprising that New Age deeply affects the public domain. Because it understands the sacred as permeating 'everything', basically everything – literally from sexuality to work – attains spiritual meaning and significance (Campbell, 2007, p. 37). Precisely because of this, New Age cannot even be banned from public life as easily as Christian religiosity, and spiritual discourses about the self have indeed increasingly come to permeate the public sphere. We have been witnessing a major interest in New Age spirituality in 'hard' fields like management and business leadership and 'soft' ones like health and social work alike. While many of today's largest and most successful corporations and organizations, such as Guinness, General Dynamics, Boeing Aerospace and even the US army (Heelas, 1996) have put spirituality to work by offering their employees spiritual courses and training (e.g. Aupers & Houtman, 2006; Grant, O'Neilen, & Stephens, 2004; Heelas, 2006, 2008), we also see a clear resurgence of interest in spirituality (and in its wake religion as well) in social work (see Chapters 6, 16 and 17). Given New Age's rejection of narrowly conceived Christian doctrines and secular rationalism alike, it comes as no surprise that pleas for the introduction of this type of spirituality in social work meet with widespread scepticism. This is because social work is firmly rooted in nineteenth-century Christian charity and philanthropy (see Chapter 6), which has itself largely been displaced during the twentieth century by a secular rationalist-professional model.

New Age and social work

In nineteenth-century Britain, 'the Methodist sick-visitor was qualified by her faith, not her professional training, and the effectiveness of her work depended upon spiritual power rather than technical skill' (Bowpitt, 1998, p. 681). From the end of the nineteenth century onwards, however, the secularization of social work set in, especially with the British Charity Organization Society working towards its professionalization by reorienting it towards secular goals, to be attained by the systematic application of social science methods (Bowpitt, 1998). The radically secularized practices of social work that emerged in the second half of the twentieth century are lamented in an article in the *Catholic Social Science Review*, where the author bitterly observes that 'a secular mindset unconcerned with and increasingly hostile to God's centrality ... has replaced ... [the Catholic and Christian heart of social service programs]' (Brandyberry, 2002, p. 5). He adds that 'social work has rejected many of the fundamentals of Christian sexual morality and norms related to the sanctity of life', which has, 'sadly, contributed more to the widespread brokenness of [North] American families than to healing' (ibid., pp. 7–8). According to his own experiences, 'schools of social work are presently operating almost as centers of indoctrination into secularist, Enlightenment values and ideas' (ibid., p. 11).

This struggle between the Christian heritage and its rational-secular competitor informs much of the contemporary controversies about the introduction of New Age spirituality in social work. Those who identify with the rationalist model tend to associate spirituality with religion and the latter with 'narrow, rigid religious traditions, personal pathology, or an underlying coercive religio-political agenda', which is understood as 'antithetical to social work goals and values, such as respect for personal autonomy and self-determination, non-judgmental attitudes, and equality' and hence feeds understandable fears of 'pathological consequences of religious expression, such as passivity, excessive guilt, or gender inequality' (Praglin, 2004, p. 72). Those who are sympathetic to New Age spirituality, on the other hand, understand it as precisely antithetical to traditional Christian religiosity. Hence they invoke essentially identical social work goals and values in pleading against 'sectarianism and exclusivity' (Canda, cited in Praglin, 2004, p. 75) and for more attention to what essentially boils down to self-spirituality and holism. Indeed, pointing out the marked presence of the 'spirituality-religion binary' in the social work literature, Neil Henery (2003) observes that 'For the spirituality project, religion is a resource to be handled with care. In particular, the customs and dogma must be avoided. Spirituality is about the opposite. It is about self expression and individual experience' (p. 1109). It is quite clear, in short, that the introduction of New Age spirituality in social work – as elsewhere – meets with considerable scepticism or even downright hostility from those who would prefer a reinstallation of Christian models and those who wish to defend a rationalist and secular professional profile.

Application to social work

Unleashing the God within

The doctrine of self-spirituality that requires living in a 'natural' and 'authentic' way, i.e. being true to who one 'really' or 'at the deepest level' is, constitutes the great refrain of therapeutic applications of New Age spirituality. This doctrine is not just understood as important for 'people with problems', as in applications in health care or social work, but basically for everyone, because it holds that 'one doesn't need to be sick to get better'. This 'getting better' requires taking one's personal feelings and intuitions, understood as emanations of the 'God within', seriously in guiding one in life's choices so as to be able to live life to the full.

The understanding of the spiritual self as essentially good, pure and tied up with a life force that permeates everything informs New Age's understanding of personal problems. Frustrations, bitterness, unhappiness, mental disorders, depressions, illness, family violence, child abuse and whatever other problems people may encounter in their lives are all understood as stemming from disconnections from the God within, i.e. as failures to live 'in tune' with the person one really is. Given the essential goodness of the spiritual self, these disconnections are understood as caused by external impositions – mostly obsessive conformity to external orders, demands and standards (e.g. one's spouse or family, the company one works for, and the rich and famous taken as role models) or externally imposed emotional damage, as in all sorts of victimization (an unhappy childhood, sexual abuse, bullying at work, or whatever). External causes such as these are hence understood as preventing one from being whom one 'really' or 'at the deepest level' is.

These disconnections can only be undone by re-establishing the lost contact with the spiritual self. Applications of New Age in social work hence boil down to encouraging and helping people to listen to their 'inner voices' – to take their own feelings, emotions and desires more seriously and learn to dissociate from institutional demands and bad experiences that prevent them from doing so. In this way, the aim is replacing concerns about 'what others expect me to do' or 'what others have done to me' by personal answers to fundamental questions of the type, 'What is it that I really want?', 'Is this really the sort of life I want to live?', 'What sort of person am I, really?'

Answers to questions such as these are understood as a vital starting point for re-establishing contact with the spiritual self and bringing one's life back 'in tune'. Knowledge about oneself is hence understood as enabling liberation from externally imposed forces and unleashing the God within by tapping into powers and resources that have hitherto remained hidden and unexploited in the deeper layers of consciousness. To help people re-encounter who they really are and attain the self-knowledge needed to follow their personal paths and realize their hidden potential, social work can apply a wide range of psychodynamic and psychotherapeutic techniques, ranging from the spiritual to the psychological.

Conclusion

As the double meaning of the word 'social' already indicates, social work and social policy have a Janus face. After all, the notion of 'social' implies caring for the individual in society *and* connotes the interest of society as a whole (Jones, 1985). Because of this ambiguity of the word 'social', social scientific accounts of the roles, functions and consequences of social work, social policy and the welfare state have always tended to come in strongly different flavours. On the one hand, there have always been those who have portrayed social policy as directed at the promotion of individual well-being by caring for the sick, the poor, the elderly and, more generally, those seen as incapable of caring for themselves. The best known example of this tendency is probably T.H. Marshall's (1965) account of modern citizenship as the historical unfolding of three waves of human rights (see Chapter 13). Such an unfolding of citizenship thus boils down to a transition from the 'care as favor' of Christian charity to the 'care as right' of modern social policy (Zijderveld, 1999).

The problem with such an account of social policy, which constructs it as being of a 'caring-sharing' nature, is that it fails to take into account its role in providing (post-) industrial societies with skilled, healthy and motivated workforces by means of state-supported systems of education, health care, social security, social work, and so on (Higgins, 1981). In other words, it underestimates its inescapable role as a mode of social control. The latter not only applies to the poor laws from the sixteenth century onwards (e.g. Slack, 1988), but also to later systems of social policy. Many of the latter have relied on clear moral boundaries between the 'impotent' and 'able-bodied' poor, while notions of 'deservingness' have typically loomed large (e.g. Houtman, 2000; Macarov, 1980). Spiritually informed social work does not escape this Janus-faced nature of social policy either. Interpreted as a praiseworthy and progressive liberation from externally imposed controls by some, spiritual social work is regarded as an unprecedented intrusive new mode of social control by others. Echoing Michel Foucault (1977, 1988), authors such as Nikolas Rose (1986) and Frank Furedi (2003) exemplify the latter position. They understand the infusion of social work with New Age values as a transformation to a new mode of social control that proceeds in two steps. First, it opens up people's inner worlds for public scrutiny by putting human souls on the dissection tables of social workers, therapists and other professionals: 'Through a relation permissiveness – what today would be called being nonjudgemental – therapists are able to gain a privileged access to people's subjectivity' (Furedi, 2003, p. 95). Secondly, the soul is refashioned by moulding it in such a way as to produce a self that no longer requires external governance – a self that conceives of itself as obliged to be free and self-governing, a self that no longer needs to be forced or bribed into conformity. In Furedi's (2003) words:

> the management of people's internal life ... transforms the private feelings of people into a subject matter for public policy-making and cultural concern. ... The cultivation of certain emotional attitudes and the repression of others is systematically pursued by institutions and professionals devoted to the management of how people ought to feel. (p. 197)

Does spiritual social work constitute the ultimate liberation or the ultimate social control, then? It seems inevitable to conclude that it is in fact both, just like all systems of social policy that preceded it.

Study Questions

1. How widespread are New Age ethics, self-spirituality and holism in contemporary social work?
2. How can this 'spiritual' turn and the rejection of the (social) scientific approach in social work be understood from a psychological, sociological and historical perspective?
3. How is the implementation of New Age ethics in social work evaluated by the various groups involved (e.g. policy makers, social workers and clients)?

19
Conclusion: Practising Values in Social Work

Mel Gray and Stephen A. Webb

Social workers face especially hard moral choices. They are often caught between a rock and a hard place. There are situations in which, whatever they do, moral blame and guilt will result. Thus it seems that moral goodness is not always within the grasp of social workers. The problem of what is called moral 'dirty hands' always looms as a possibility with the realities of front-line practice. 'Dirty hands' are said to result when a social worker encounters a conflict of duties or values and must choose between alternatives, none of which is entirely satisfactory. In such cases social workers find themselves in situations where they can be morally sullied by doing what is morally permissible or even obligatory. There are some situations where social workers experience moral guilt or regret for doing the right thing. A social worker who is complicit in having an older person admitted to a residential nursing home because she is at risk of falling but knows that institutional life will inevitably hasten her dementia is one possible case of moral dirty hands. Under such difficult circumstances you often hear people gingerly remark that 'it was for the best'. In social work moral dilemmas are genuine even when the right solution is clear. The question of how a social worker is to act in the public good when circumstances are not ideal for its realization is a very common problem. Student social workers will argue about whether providing a favourable low-threshold assessment for an older person so they can receive a generous home support allowance, in the face of the possibility that such a lax assessment will necessarily reduce the overall amount for people to receive such support, gets to the heart of the dirty hands problem. The central claim here is that an act may be the wrong thing to do in utilitarian terms but may still leave the social worker doing the right thing in relation to a particular client's needs. Here we are confronted with the moral question of to what extent a social worker's obligation to a client depends crucially on what other social workers are doing in similar situations. It is unlikely that moral principles in social work are executed from a single consistent system. Here we may also ask the difficult question of whether social workers are progressively hardened to become insensitive to principled moral stances because of their exposure to the political realities of a system that does not consistently work to the benefit of clients. According to Aristotle in *Nicomachean Ethics*, 'habits build character' (1976), therefore a social worker who sacrifices his or her own principles one time becomes more likely to do so again in the future. It may be the case that social workers who set aside what once were their moral views become progressively desensitized to the sorts of violations that previously caused moral indignation. In such cases social workers may become habituated to accept what once seemed morally unacceptable. These hard-edged examples may have induced a sense of gloom for some readers and, indeed, for others may harden a realist recognition of this is 'how things really are in social work'. Well, yes and no. While the kinds of dirty hands situations discussed above may well reflect the harsh realities of certain situations in social work we wish to contend these are the political exception rather than the moral rule. Indeed, the good achieved by using dirty hands will far outweigh the bad consequences of using dirty means. In identifying this distinction we wish to offer a dose of moral comfort and optimism to social workers involved in the practice of values. In fact what the 'dirty hands' examples illustrate is the point at which morality and politics collide within social work agencies. That is, the way that moral intentions on behalf of the practitioner get caught up and often mauled by political expediencies, such as limited resources and conflicting agency priorities. The evaluative aspect of moral decision is compromised. In the section that follows we argue that, as a class of evaluative agents, social workers *and* social work are distinctive in the significant moral good they contribute to society.

One of the central themes of this book is how an adherence to an ethical stance is a defining strength of social work and something that makes it most distinctive. Across the range of chapters, we have shown how social work refuses to drop the notion that society can be a vehicle for the translation of private troubles into public concerns and how the democratically generated search for community, solidarity and justice is worth pursuing. In a society in which the narrow pursuit of material self-interest is the norm, adherence to an ethical stance is more radical than people realize. In the face of a dominant culture of materialism and instrumental rationality, social work as a profession is almost unique in that it remains committed to the values of compassion, social justice and care in an economic climate of self-interest.

Practising values and believing in them is an active process that depends on ethical commitment. Commitment to an ethical stance is a virtue because it indicates the seriousness, necessity and deliberative nature of moral decisions and actions. Why are social workers committed to an ethical stance? The short answer to this is that they are what Charles Taylor calls 'strong evaluators'. He introduces the notion of 'strong evaluation' in his 'Responsibility for Self' (1976), where he is not just interested in what it is right to do, but what it is good to be. For Taylor the character of the self is constituted by ethical concerns, that is, the self is partly constituted in and through the taking of moral stances. His concern is *how* we orient ourselves in relation to the good, and the way in which we negotiate and move in an ethical location as human agents. It strikes us that this orientation to the good is what enables social workers to establish durable and trusting relations with clients, that is, as embodied agents who encounter people with concern and care.

Taylor distinguishes between what he calls 'weak evaluation' and 'strong evaluation'. The former is about how we weigh up the way we want to satisfy our desires, deciding which we want to satisfy best. This might involve thinking about whether we want to buy a new car, instead of taking a holiday. As Smith (2002) points out, 'the decisive issue in my evaluation is just what I happen to feel like' (p. 89). Taylor (1976) refers to this as 'weak evaluation'. In weak evaluation the statement that 'A is better than B' remains inarticulable, because there is nothing else to say about it. The statement, 'I just like A better because it just feels better' is just a matter of *de facto* desires or preferences. The person weighs desired actions 'simply to determine convenience, or how to make different desires compossible or how to get the overall satisfaction' (Taylor, 1976, p. 282). Such simple weighing of alternatives is possible without any qualitative distinction in the intrinsic desirability of the desires in question. Taylor recognizes, however, that another kind of evaluation is at play in the way we think about ourselves. Sometimes we find ourselves evaluating desires in terms of what they are worth. He calls this 'strong evaluation'. As Smith (2002) goes on to explain, 'What counts now is the way I locate or interpret the feelings, that is, how I characterize them as something base and petty, or as something higher and more admirable' (p. 89). Roughly speaking, to characterize this type of evaluation refers to the times we beat ourselves up over things we do to ourselves or others. It involves a standard or judgement of worth or what some call conscience. Strong evaluators exercise an ethical sensibility and judgement that is based on their ability to contrast the value or worth of things. This provides them with standards and characteristics by which they judge the quality of human life.

It seems to us that it is promising to position social workers, in general, as strong evaluators. Positioning social workers in such a way means that they are different from say politicians, bankers, businessmen, lawyers and the police. We accept that this kind of claim requires some empirical justification, but it would not be too difficult to devise instruments that test the differences across professions and between strong and weak when evaluating social workers. The evaluative understanding of social workers is a matter of practical judgement and habituation, emotional sensitivity and personal experience, rather than a kind of cognitive knowledge acquired by detached reasoning or through learning theories. Most crucially, as is shown throughout this book, social workers exhibit commitment to an ethical life. As strong evaluators, they can articulate the reasons for their preferences on the basis of qualitative distinctions of worth. They are likely to be involved in supererogation that goes beyond the call of duty. Strong evaluation makes a difference to one's motivation. The difference to one's motivation is not simply on a judgement-by-judgement basis, but rather one has strong attachments to certain strongly valued ends. Taylor (1989) suggests this is because:

> I see certain of my other properties as admitting of only one kind of strong evaluation by myself, because these properties so centrally touch what I am as an agent, that is, as a strong evaluator, that I cannot really repudiate them in the full sense. For I would be thereby repudiating myself, inwardly riven and hence incapable of fully authentic evaluation. (p. 34)

One can read this passage as Taylor advocating the following kind of reasoning: 'Because I am filthy rich, I would be repudiating myself if I were an egalitarian, so the value of equality cannot be applied to me.' Or, 'I am not a nice guy, so demands of considerateness do not apply to me.'

Our claim about social workers as strong evaluators is a generic claim. We are, however, aware that there are strong and weak evaluators working within social work. The weak evaluative practitioner is a simple 'weigher of alternatives', an opportunist making discrete judgement-by-judgement decisions that takes no stand at all concerning the qualitative worth of different value options. He or she is unconcerned with the evaluative aspects of the objects of evaluation. If it were true that social workers were, on the whole, strong evaluators, it is likely that we could locate the identity of social work as a profession as one that *in-potentia* is a source for the articulation of strong evaluative goods. Thus the constitutive good of social work provides the constituting ground of its worth or goodness for social workers. Indeed, for social workers, contact with the constitutive good of social work is a source of ethical motivation for their moral agency. Social work is a *constitutive socio-ethical good* that has a generative power for the social worker in that it permits an ethical life to be articulated and channelled towards that which has intrinsic worth. Some institutional settings permit this more than others. Here we can see how the social worker as a strong evaluator and social work as a constitutive ethical good are mutually reinforcing aspects that embed a moral life. By acting within an ethical framework, social workers have a moral sensibility of qualitative distinctions in which some basic evaluative commitments orient them in positive terms and give horizons to the constitutive ground of their moral identity. Indeed, in part, the justification for such a book as this is to acknowledge the ethical good of social work and celebrate its moral sources. Implicit throughout the various chapters is the suggestion that social workers have an inchoate form of ethical sensibility which constitutes a part of their moral identity and which is expressed in the way that particular situations are evaluated for the ethical challenges that might be inherent in them. Social work is one of the very few professions in modern times that openly acknowledges, reflects on and struggles with these ethical challenges. It is for this very reason that social work itself has distinct value as a constitutive ethical good. The 'practice of value' sits at the very core of social work (Webb, 2006, p. 200–10).

Finally, we would like to conclude with some comments about the value of moral pluralism for social work. A key organizing theme of this book has been to affirm and endorse the plurality of values in social work. Thus we have not tried to show that there is one fundamental value, such as human rights, from which all other values are derived. As the influential moral philosopher Thomas Nagel (1979) remarked:

> I do not believe the source of value is unitary ... I believe that value has fundamentally different kinds of sources, and that they are reflected in the classification of values into types. Not all values represent the pursuit of some single good in a variety of settings. (p. 131–2)

On this view, a professional code of ethics that denies the plurality of values is mistaken. A stronger argument for the plurality of values in social work would be to claim that the reduction of values involves the degeneration and impoverishment of human life. In fact, this argument is central to Martha Nussbaum's (1983) *The Fragility of Goodness*, where she claims that openness to different and incommensurable values is a condition for a rich and full life. Furthermore, for Nussbaum, valuing autonomy – as social work does – leads to moral pluralism. Social work needs an approach which takes account of the plurality of values people hold, one that recognizes that values are chosen and cannot be imposed on people and that acknowledges the changing nature of values. Values change in response to contexts. They change in relation to external social, political, cultural and economic forces. Personal values alter as individuals develop, affected by, among other things, life experience, social and political awareness, a greater understanding of other people and their life struggles, and a desire for increased tolerance of differences. Professional values change as a result of theoretical, empirical, ideological and practical developments. And they reflect diverse professional, moral, social and spiritual perspectives.

References

AASW *see* Australian Association of Social Work.

Abbott, A. (2002). Measuring social work values: A cross-cultural challenge for global practice. *International Social Work*, 42(4), 455–70.

Adams, P. (2008). The code of ethics and the clash of orthodoxies: A response to Spano and Koenig. *Journal of Social Work Values and Ethics*, 5(2), 6–26. Retrieved on 08–11–08 from: http://www.socialworker.com/jswve/index2.php?option=com_content&do_pdf=1&id=94.

Addams, J. ([1902] 1964). *Democracy and social ethics*. New York: Macmillan. Republished with an introductory life of Jane Addams by A.F. Scott, Cambridge, MA: Harvard University Press.

Adorno, T.W. (1971). Erziehung nach Auschwitz [Education after Auschwitz]. In Adorno, T.W. *Erziehung zur Mündigkeit* [Education for the majority]. Frankfurt/M. Suhrkamp, pp. 00–00.

Africans Unite against Child Abuse (AFRUCA) (2006). *AFRUCA proposal for a UK law against diagnosing children as witches*. Retrieved on 27–02–08 from: http://www.bnlf.org.uk/Documents/Afruca_Econsultation_feb07.pdf

AFRUCA *see* Africans Unite against Child Abuse.

Ahmad, F., & Sheriff, S. (2003). Muslim women of Europe: Welfare needs and responses. *Social Work in Europe*, 8, 30–55.

Ahmed, L. (1992). *Women and gender in Islam: Historical roots of a modern debate*. New Haven, CT: Yale University Press.

Ahmed, L. (2006). Women and the rise of Islam. In M. Kamrava (ed.), *The new voices of Islam: Reforming politics and modernity*. New York: I.B. Tauris, 177–20.

Akbarzadeh, S., & Yasmeen, S. (2005). *Islam and the West: Reflections from Australia*. Sydney: University of NSW Press.

Al-Krenawi, A., & Graham, J. (2000). Islamic theology and prayer: Relevance for social work practice. *International Social Work*, 43, 289–304.

Amin, O. (2007). *Influence of Muslim philosophy on the West*. Retrieved 10.11.08 from: http://www.renaissance.com.pk/JunRefl2y3.html

Ammar, N. (2000). Simplistic stereotyping and complex reality of Arab-American immigrant identity: Consequences and future strategies in policing wife battery. *Islam and Christian-Muslim Relations*, 11, 51–69.

Aristotle (1976). *Nicomachean ethics*. Harmondsworth: Penguin.

Armstrong, H. (1991). *Taking care: A church response to children, adults and abuse*. London: National Children's Bureau. (Revised edn 1997.)

Armstrong, K. (2000). *A history of God*. London: Vintage.

Arnstein, S.R. (1969). A ladder of citizen participation. *Journal of the American Institute of Planners*, 35(4), 216–24.

Ashencaen Crabtree, S., & Baba, I. (2001). Islamic perspectives in social work education. *Social Work Education*, 20, 469–81.

Ashencaen Crabtree, S., Husain, F., & Spalek, B. (2008). *Islam and social work: Debating values, transforming practice*. Bristol: Policy Press.

Asquith, M., & Cheers, B. (2001). Morals, ethics and practice: In search of social justice. *Australian Social Work*, 54(2), 15–26.

Atherton, C.R., & Bolland, K.A. (2003). Postmodernism: A dangerous illusion. *International Social Work*, 45(4), 421–33.

Aubrey, C., & Dahl, S (2006). Children's voices: The views of vulnerable children on their service providers and the relevance of services they receive. *British Journal of Social Work*, 36(1), 21–40.

Aupers, S., & Houtman, D. (2006). Beyond the spiritual supermarket: The social and public significance of New Age spirituality. *Journal of Contemporary Religion*, 21, 201–22.

Australian Association of Social Work (1999). *Code of Ethics*. Canberra: AASW.

Australian Association of Social Work (n.d.). *Australian Association of Social Workers Acknowledgement Statement to Aboriginal and Torres Strait Islander People*. Retrieved 10.03.08 from: http://www.aasw.asn.au/adobe/advocacy/recog_ack_statement_AUG04.pdf

Ayer, A.J. (1969). *Philosophical essays*. New York: St. Martin's Press, 271–84.

Bailey, R., & Brake, M. (1975). *Radical social work*. London: Edward Arnold.

Banks, S. (1998). Professional ethics in social work: What future? *British Journal of Social Work*, 28(2), 213–31.

Banks, S. (ed.) (2001). *Ethics and values in social work*. Basingstoke: Palgrave Macmillan.

Banks, S. (2002). Professional values and accountabilities. In R. Adams, L. Dominelli, & M. Payne (eds) *Critical practice in social work*. Basingstoke: Palgrave Macmillan.

Banks, S. (2003a). *Ethics, accountability and the social professions*. Basingstoke: Palgrave Macmillan.

Banks, S. (2003b). From oaths to rule books: A critical examination of codes of ethics for the social professions. *European Journal of Social Work*, 6(2), 133–44.

Banks, S. (2006). *Ethics and values in social work*. 3rd edn. Basingstoke: Palgrave Macmillan.

Banks, S. (2008a). Critical commentary: Social work ethics. *British Journal of Social Work*, 38(6), 1238–49.

Banks, S. (2008b). Ethics and social welfare: The state of play. *Ethics and Social Welfare*, 2(1), 1–9.

Banks, S., & Gallagher, A. (2009). *Ethics in professional life*. Basingstoke: Palgrave Macmillan.

Barise, A. (2005). Social work with Muslims: Insights from the teachings of Islam. *Critical Social Work Online*, 6(2).

Baron, M. (1997). Kantian ethics. In M. Baron, Pettit, P., & Slote, M. (eds), *Three methods of ethics: A debate*. Oxford: Blackwell, pp. 3–91.

BASW *see* British Association of Social Workers.

Battin, M.P. (1992). *Ethics in the sanctuary: Examining the practices of organized religion*. New Haven, CT: Yale University Press

Bauman, Z. (1989) *Modernity and the holocaust*. Cambridge: Polity Press.

Bauman, Z. (1993) *Postmodern ethics.* Oxford: Blackwell.

Bauman, Z. (1995). The making and unmaking of strangers. *Thesis Eleven*, 43, 1–16.

Bauman, Z. (1998). What prospects of morality in times of uncertainty? *Theory, Culture & Society*, 15(1), 11–22.

Bauman, Z. (1999). The world inhospitable to Levinas. *Philosophy Today*, 43(2), 151–67.

Beauchamp, T.L. & Childress, J.F. (2001). *Principles of Biomedical Ethics.* 5th edn. Oxford: Oxford University Press.

Becher, H., & Husain, F. (2003). *South Asian Muslims and Hindus in Britain: Developments in family support.* London: National Family and Parenting Institute.

Beck, U. (1992). *Risk society: Towards a new modernity.* London: Sage.

Beck, U., & Beck-Gernsheim, E. (2002). *Individualization: Institutionalized individualism and its social and political consequences.* London: Sage.

Beckett, C., & Maynard, A. (2005). Values and ethics in social work. London: Sage.

Bell, D. (1976). *The cultural contradictions of capitalism.* New York: Basic Books.

Bennett, B., & Zubrzycki, J. (2003) Hearing the stories of Australian Aboriginal and Torres Strait Islander social workers: Challenging and educating the system. *Australian Social Work*, 56(1), 61–70.

Beresford, P. (2001). Service users, social policy and the future of welfare. *Critical Social Policy,* 21(4), 494–512.

Beresford, P., Croft, S., Evans, C., & Harding, T. (1997). Quality in personal social services: The developing role of user involvement in the UK. In A. Ever, R. Haverinen, K. Leichsenring, & G. Wistow (eds), *Developing quality in personal social services: Concepts, cases and comments.* Aldershot: Ashgate, 63–80.

Beresford, P., Shamash, M., Forrest, V., Turnerand, V., & Branfield, F. (2005). *Developing social care: Service users' vision for adult support,* London: Social Care Institute for Excellence. Retrieved 27.08.09 from: http://www.scie.org.uk/publications/reports/report07.pdf

Bergland, N. (2008). Opponents marched against gay marriage law. *Aftenposten,* 14 April. Retrieved 18.06.09 from: http://www.aftenposten.no/english/local/article2367161.ece (18 June 2009)

Berman, M. (2000). *Wandering God: A study in nomadic spirituality.* New York: State University of New York Press.

Bernts, T., Dekker, G., & de Hart, J. (2007). *God in Nederland, 1966–2006* [God in the Netherlands, 1966–2006]. Kampen: Ten Have.

Besecke, K. (2005). Seeing invisible religion: Religion as a societal conversation about transcendent meaning. *Sociological Theory,* 23(2), 179–96.

BHA *see* British Humanist Association.

Biestek, F.P. (1961). *The casework relationship.* London: Allen & Unwin.

Biestek, F.P., & Gehrig, C.C. (1978). *Client self-determination in social work: A fifty year history.* Chicago: Loyola Press.

Bilson, A. (2007). Promoting compassionate concern in social work: Reflections on ethics, biology, and love. *British Journal of Social Work,* 37(8), 1371–86.

Bisman, C. (2004). Social work values: The moral core of the profession. *British Journal of Social Work,* 34, 109–23.

Blaug, R. (1995). Distortion of the 'face-to-face': Communicative reason and social work practice. *British Journal of Social Work,* 25, 423–39.

Bonhoeffer, D. (1948). *The cost of discipleship*. London: Camelot Press.

Boros, L. (1968). *Meeting God in man*. London: Search Press.

Borrmann, S. (2005). Ethical dilemmas in social work with right-wing youth groups: Solutions based on the document *Ethics in Social Work, Statement of Principles*, by the IFSW. *Journal of Social Work Values and Ethics*, 2(1). Retrieved on 13.03.01 from: http://www.socialworker.com/jswve/content/view/15/34/

Borrmann, S. (2007). Ethische Dilemmata in der Sozialen Arbeit: Erscheinungsformen und Umgangsweisen im Internationalen Vergleich [Ethical dilemmas in social work: An international comparison of social work practice]. In E. Engelke, K. Maier, E. Steinert, S. Borrmann, & C. Spatscheck (eds), *Forschung für die Praxis: Zum gegenwärtigen Stand der Sozialarbeitsforschung* [Research for social work practice: New developments in social work research]. Freiburg im Breisgau: Lambertus Verlag, 224–6.

Botvin, G.J., Schinke, S.P., Epstein, J.A., Diaz, T., & Botvin, E.M. (1995). Effectiveness of culturally focused and generic skills training approaches to alcohol and drug abuse prevention among minority adolescents: Two-year follow up study. *Psychology of Addictive Behaviors*, 9(3), 183–94.

Bowles, W., Collingridge, M., Curry, S., & Valentine, B. (2006). *Ethical practice in social work: An applied approach*. Sydney: Allen & Unwin.

Bowpitt, G. (2000). Working with creative creatures: Towards a Christian paradigm for social work theory, with some practical implications. *British Journal of Social Work*, 30, 349–64.

Boyle, D.P., & Springer, A. (2001). Toward a cultural competence measure for social work with specific populations. *Journal of Ethnic and Cultural Diversity in Social Work*, 9(3/4), 53–72.

Brandyberry, T. (2002). Catholic social work models for the future: From social worker to Catholic social servant? *Catholic Social Science Review*, 7. Retrieved 01.07.08 from: http://www.catholicsocialscientists.org/cssr2002/Article—Brandyberry.pdf

Branfield, F., & Beresford, P. with contributions from others (2006). Making user involvement work: Supporting service user networking and knowledge. York: Joseph Rowntree Foundation. Retrieved 28.02.09 from: http://www.jrf.org.uk/knowledge/findings/socialcare/1966.asp

Braye, S., & Preston-Shoot, M. (1995). *Empowering practice in social care*. Buckingham: Open University Press.

Brill, C.K. (2001). Looking at the social work profession through the eye of the NASW code of ethics. *Research on Social Work Practice*, 11(2), 223–34.

Briskman, L., & Noble, C. (1999). Social work ethics: Embracing diversity. In B. Pease & J. Fook (eds), *Transforming social work practice*. St. Leonards, NSW: Allen & Unwin, 57–69.

British Association of Social Workers (1979). *A Code of Ethics for Social Workers*. Birmingham: BASW.

British Association of Social Workers (2002). *Code of Ethics*. Birmingham: BASW.

British Humanist Association (2007). *Quality and Equality: Human Rights, Public Services and Religious Organisations*. London: British Humanist Association.

Bruce, S. (2002). *God is dead: Secularisation in the West*. Oxford: Blackwell.

Bryant, C.C. (2004). Collaboration between the Catholic Church, the mental health, and the criminal justice systems regarding clergy sex offenders. In T.G. Plante (ed.), *Sin against the innocents: Sexual abuse by priests and the role of the Catholic church.* Westport, CT: Praeger, 115–22.

Bunge, M. (1967). *Scientific research II: The search for truth.* New York: Springer.

Bunge, M. (1989). *Ethics: The good and the right.* Dordrecht: Kluwer.

Bunge, M. (1996). *Finding philosophy in social science.* New Haven, CT: Richard Henderson.

Bunge, M. (1998). *Philosophy of science, Vol. 2: From explanation to justification.* London: Transaction.

Burke, A. (2001). *In fear of security: Australia's invasion anxiety.* Annandale, NSW: Pluto Press.

Burke, A. (2002). The perverse perseverance of sovereignty. *Borderlands* (e-journal), 11(1). http://www.borderlandsejournal.adelaide.edu.au/issues/vol1no1.html

Burke, A., & Dalrymple, B. ([1995] 2007). *Anti-oppressive practice : Social care and the law.* Buckingham: Open University Press.

Burr, J., & Chapman, T. (2004). Contextualizing experiences of depression in women from South Asian communities: A discursive approach. *Sociology of Health and Illness*, 26, 433–52.

Busuttil, J., & ter Haar, G. (2002). (eds) *The freedom to do God's will: Religious fundamentalism and social change.* London: Routledge.

Butler, J. (2000). Ethical ambivalence. In M. Garber, B. Hanssen, & R.L.Walkowitz (eds), *The turn to ethics.* London: Routledge, pp. 15–28.

Campbell, C. (2007). *The Easternization of the West: A thematic account of cultural change in the modern era.* Boulder, CO: Paradigm.

Campbell, T., Ewing, K., & Tomkins, A. (eds) (2001). *Sceptical essays on human rights.* Oxford: Oxford University Press.

Canadian Association of Social Workers (1994). *Code of Ethics.* Ottawa: CASW.

Canda, E.R. (1998). *Spirituality in social work.* Binghampton NY: Haworth Press.

Canda, E.R., & Furman, L.D. (1999). *Spiritual diversity in social work practice: The heart of helping.* New York: Free Press.

Cardemil, E.V., Reivich, K.J., & Seligman, M.E. (2002). The prevention of depressive symptoms in low-income minority middle school students. *Prevention & Treatment*, 5(1). Retrieved 06.10.08 from: http://www.ajph.org/cgi/content/abstract/91/5/761

Carey, M. (2009). Happy shopper? The problem with service user and carer participation. *British Journal of Social Work*, 39, 179–88.

Carlson Brown, J., & Parker, R. (1989). For God so loved the world. In R. Carlson, J. Brown, & C.R. Bohn (eds), *Christianity, patriarchy, and abuse: A feminist critique.* Cleveland, OH: Pilgrim Press.

Carr, S. (2004). *Has service user participation made a difference to social care services?* Bristol: Polity Press.

Carroll, J. (2004). *The wreck of Western culture: Humanism revisited.* Revised edn. Carlton North: Scribe.

CASW *see* Canadian Association of Social Workers.

Catholic Office for the Protection of Children and Vulnerable Adults (2002–7). *Annual Reports.* Birmingham: COPCA. Retrieved 25.07.08 from: http://www.copca.org.uk/

Catholic Office for the Protection of Children and Vulnerable Adults (2006). *Healing the wound: National policy for the Catholic Church in England & Wales for the support of those who have suffered abuse and those accused of abuse*. Birmingham: COPCA. Retrieved 04.10.07 from: http://www.copca.org.uk/publicdocuments/SupportPolicyFinalReleasedAug06.pdf

CCETSW *see* Central Council for Training and Education in Social Work.

Cemlyn, S. & Briskman, L. (2003). Asylum, children's rights and social work. *Child and Family Social Work,* 8(3), 163–78.

Central Council for Training and Education in Social Work (1976). *Values in social work*. London: CCETSW.

Chaiklin, H. (1982). Social work education in Israel: An analysis and some suggestions. *Journal of Jewish Communal Service,* 59, 35–42.

Chambré, S.M. (2001). The changing nature of 'faith' in faith-based organisations: Secularization and ecumenicism in four AIDS organisations in New York City. *Social Service Review,* 75, 435–55.

Chanan, G. (2005). *Active citizenship and community involvement: Getting to the roots*. Retrieved 28.02.09 from: http://www.eurofound.europa.eu/pubdocs/1997/57/fi/1/ef9757fi.pdf

Chang-Muy, F., & Congress, E. (eds) (2008). *Social work with immigrants and refugees: Legal issues, clinical skills, and advocacy issues*. New York: Springer.

Cheetham, J. (ed.) (1982). *Social work and ethnicity*. London: Allen & Unwin.

Chenoweth, L., & McAuliffe, D. (2008). *The road to social work and human service practice*. Melbourne: Cengage.

Children's Society (2008). *Our mission and values*. Retrieved 18.04.08 from: http://www.childrenssociety.org.uk/all_about_us/who_we_are/our_vision/Our_vision_mission_and_values_1081.html

Chodorow, N. (1978). *The reproduction of mothering*. Berkeley: University of California Press.

Christian Institute (2002a). *Adoption law: Sidelining stability and security*. Newcastle-upon-Tyne: Christian Institute. Retrieved 18.12.07 from: http://www.christian.org.uk/html-publications/adoption_briefing2.htm

Christian Institute (2002b). *Same-sex parenting is bad for kids*. Newcastle-upon-Tyne: Christian Institute. Retrieved 18.12.07 from: http://www.christian.org.uk/pressreleases/2002/february_06_2002.htm ()

Clark, C.L. (1999). Observing the lighthouse: From theory to institutions in social work ethics. *European Journal of Social Work,* 2(3), 259–70.

Clark, C.L. (2006). Moral character in social work. *British Journal of Social Work,* 36, 75–89.

Clark, C.L. (2007). Professional responsibility, misconduct and practical reasoning. *Ethics and Social Welfare,* 1(1), 56–75.

Clark, C.L., with Asquith, S. (1985). *Social work and social philosophy: A guide to practice*. London: Routledge & Kegan Paul.

Clifford, D., & Burke, B. (2009). *Anti-oppressive ethics and values in social work*. Basingstoke: Palgrave Macmillan.

Cnaan, R. (1999). *The newer deal: Social work and religion in partnership*. New York: Columbia University Press.

Collingridge, M., Miller, S., & Bowles, W. (2001). Privacy and confidentiality in social work. *Australian Social Work,* 54(2), 3–13.

Community Care News (2003a). Social workers warned not to plead conscience clause in same-sex cases. *Community Care,* 15 May. Retrieved 18.12.07 from:

http://www.communitycare.co.uk/Articles/2003/05/15/40761/social-workers-warned-not-to-plead-conscience-clause-in-same-sex.html?key=YOUTH%20OR%20SERVICES

Community Care News (2003b). Debate on a conscience opt out clause for social workers. *Community Care,* 19 June. Retrieved 18.12.07 from: http://www.communitycare.co.uk/Articles/2003/06/19/41155/debate-on-a-conscience-opt-out-clause-for-social-workers.html?key=CHILDREN%20OR%20SERVICES

Community Care Special Edition (2008). *Seeing red on conduct: How the GSCC's conduct system has worked for social worker.* Community Care, 3 September.

Congress, E. (1992). Ethical decision-making of social work supervisors. *Clinical Supervisor* 10(1), 157–69.

Congress, E. (1993). Teaching ethical decision-making to a diverse community of students: Bringing practice into the classroom. *Journal of Teaching in Social Work,* 7(2), 23–36.

Congress, E. (1999). *Social work values and ethics: Identifying and resolving professional dilemmas.* Belmont, CA: Wadsworth.

Congress, E., & Gummer, B. (1996). Is the *code of ethics* as applicable to agency administrators as direct service providers? In E. Gambrill & R. Pruger, *Controversial issues in social work ethics, values and obligations.* Boston: Allyn & Bacon, pp. 137–50.

Congress, E., & Healy, L. (2006). International ethical document adopted. *Social Work Education Reporter,* 54(1), 18–19.

Congress, E., & Lynn, M. (1994). Group work programs in public schools: Ethical dilemmas and cultural diversity. *Social Work in Education,* 16(2), 107–14.

Congress, E., & McAuliffe, D. (2006). Professional ethics: Social work codes in Australia and the United States. *International Social Work,* 49(2), 165–76.

COPCA *see* Catholic Office for the Protection of Children and Vulnerable Adults.

Cowburn, M., & Nelson, P. (2008). Safe recruitment and social justice and ethical practice: Should people who have criminal convictions be allowed to train as social workers? *Social Work Education,* 27(3), 293–306.

Crabtree, S.A., Husain, F., & Spalek, B. (2008). *Islam and social work: Debating values, transforming practice.* Bristol: Policy Press.

Crisp, B.R. (2008). Social work and spirituality in a secular society. *Journal of Social Work,* 8(4), 363–75.

Crompton, M. (1996). *Children, spirituality and religion: A training pack.* London: CCETSW.

Crompton, M. (1998). *Children, spirituality, religion and social work.* Aldershot: Ashgate.

Cross, T., Brazron, B., Dennis, K., & Isaacs, M. (1989). *Towards a culturally competent system of care: A monograph on effective services for minority children who are severely emotionally disturbed.* Washington, DC: CASSP Technical Assistance Center, Georgetown University Child Development Center.

Cumberlege Commission Report (2007). *Safeguarding with confidence: Keeping children and vulnerable adults safe in the Catholic church.* London: Incorporated Catholic Truth Society. Retrieved 06.10.08 from: http://www.cathcom.org/mysharedaccounts/cumberlege/report/Chapter2.asp?Section=2&FontSize=13

Dahme, H-J., Otto, H-U., Trube, A., & Wohlfahrt, N. (Hrsg.) (2003). *Soziale Arbeit für den aktivierenden Staat* [Social work for the activating state]. Opladen: Leske+Budrich.

Daly, M., & Lewis, J. (2000). The concept of social care and the analysis of contemporary welfare states. *British Journal of Sociology*, 52(2), 281–98.

Davies, M. (1984). *The essential social worker*. Aldershot: Gower.

de Anda, D. (ed.) (1997). *Controversial issues in multiculturalism*. Boston: Allyn & Bacon.

De'Ath, E. (2004). The historical role of charities in addressing social exclusion. Paper presented at the National Evaluation of the Children's Fund Conference, *Understanding prevention: Children, families and social inclusion*. Online conference, 17–24 June. Retrieved 25.12.08 from: http://www.ne-cf.org/conferences/show_paper.asp?section=000100010001&conferenceCode=000200080011&id=116&full_paper=1)

de Gruchy, J.W. (2006). *Being human: Confessions of a Christian humanist*. London: SCM.

Derezotes, D.M., Poertner, J., & Testa, M.F. (2005). *The overrepresentation of African American children in the system: Race matters in child welfare*. Washington, DC: Child Welfare League of America.

Devore, W., & Schlesinger, E.G. ([1981] 2006). *Ethnic-sensitive social work practice*. 5th edn. St. Louis, MO: C.V. Mosby.

Diamond, J. (1999). *Guns, germs and steel*. New York: W.W. Norton.

Dobbelaere, K. (1993). Individuele godsdienstigheid in een geseculariseerde samenleving [Individual religiosity in a secularized society]. *Tijdschrift voor Sociologie*, 14, 5–29.

Dolgoff, R., Loewenberg, F., & Harrington, D. (2009). *Ethical decisions for social work practice*. 8th edn. Belmont, CA: Thomson, Brooks Cole.

Dominelli, L. (1988). Deprofessionalizing social work: Anti-oppressive practice, competencies and postmodernism. *British Journal of Social Work*, 26: 153–76.

Dominelli, L. (1991). Anti-oppressive practice. In L. Dominelli, N. Patel, & W. Thomas Bernard (eds), *Anti-oppressive paradigms for practice*. Sheffield: Sociological Studies, Sheffield University.

Dominelli, L. (1993). *Social work: Mirror of society or its conscience?* Inaugural Lecture, Sociological Studies, Sheffield University, 26 May.

Dominelli, L. (1996). Deprofessionalizing social work: Anti-oppressive practice, competencies and postmodernism. *British Journal of Social Work*, 26, 153–75.

Dominelli, L. (2002). *Anti-oppressive social work theory and practice*. London: Palgrave Macmillan.

Dominelli, L. (2004a). Practising social work in a globalising world. In N.T. Tan & A. Rowlands (eds), *Social work around the world III*. Berne: International Federation of Social Workers, 151–73.

Dominelli, L. (2004b). *Social work: Theory and practice for a changing profession*. Cambridge: Polity Press.

Dominelli, L. (2008). *Anti-racist social work*. 3rd edn. Basingstoke: Palgrave Macmillan.

Dominelli, L., Lorenz, W., & Soydan, H. (eds) (2001). *Beyond racial divides: Ethnicities in social work practice*. Aldershot: Ashgate.

Douki, S., Nacef, F., Belhadj, A., Bousaker, A., & Ghachem, R. (2003). Violence against women in Arab and Islamic countries. *Archives of Women's Mental Health*, 6, 165–71.

Douzinas, C. (2000). *The end of human rights: Critical legal thought at the turn of the century*. Oxford: Hart.

Douzinas, C. (2007). *Human rights and Empire: The political philosophy of cosmopolitanism*. Abingdon: Routledge.

DuBois, B., & Miley, K. (2005). *Social work: An empowering profession*. Boston: Pearson.

Dumka, L.E., Lopez, V.A., & Carter, S.J. (2002). Parenting interventions adapted for Latino families: Progress and prospects. In J. Contreras, K.A. Kerns, and A.M. Neal-Barnett (eds), *Latino children and families in the United States: Current research and future directions*. Westport, CT: Praeger, 203–33.

Dunne, T., & Wheeler, N. (eds) (1999). *Human rights in global politics*. Cambridge: Cambridge University Press.

Ebadi, S. (2006). *Iran awakening: A memoir of revolution and hope*. New York: Random House.

Ejaz, F.K. (1991). Self-determination: Lessons to be learned from social work practice in India. *British Journal of Social Work*, 21(2), 127–42.

El Droubie, R. (2006). *My Muslim life*. London: Hodder Wayland.

Elisseeff, N. (1993). The reactions of the Syrian Muslims after the foundation of the first Latin Kingdom of Jerusalem. In M. Shatzmiller (ed.), *Crusaders and Muslims in twelfth-century Syria*. Leiden: E.J. Brill, 162–72.

Ellis, K. (2007). Direct payments and social work practice: The significance of 'street-level bureaucracy' in determining eligibility. *British Journal of Social Work*, 37(3), 405–22.

Eskridge, W.N., & Spedale, D.R. (2006). *Gay marriage: For better or for worse? What we've learned from the evidence*. Oxford: Oxford University Press.

EUCIPMA *see* European Citizenship and Participation of Marginalised Research Network.

European Citizenship and Participation of Marginalised Research Network (2007). New practices and concepts in enabling participatory European citizenship of groups usually classified as 'the most non-participative'. Unpublished research proposal.

Evans, C. (1996). Service users acting as agents of change. In P. Bywaters & E. McLeod (eds), *Working for equality in health*. London: Routledge, 81–93.

Everitt, A., & Hardiker, P. (1996). *Evaluating for good practice*. London: Macmillan.

Evers, A. (2006). Complementary and conflicting: The different meanings of 'user involvement' in social services. In A-L. Matthies (ed.), *Nordic civic society organisations and the future of welfare services*. Copenhagen: Nordic Council of Ministers, 255–76. Retrieved 28.02.09 from: http://www.norden.org/pub/velfaerd/social_helse/sk/TN2006517.pdf

Faizi, N. (2001). Domestic violence in the Muslim community. *Journal of Women and the Law*, 10, 15–22.

Farrell, D. (2004). An historical viewpoint of sexual abuse perpetrated by clergy and religious. *Journal of Religion and Abuse*, 6(2), 41–80.

Farrell, D. (2009). Sexual abuse perpetrated by Roman Catholic priests and religious. *Mental Health, Religion and Culture*, 12(1), 39–53.

Featherstone, B. (2004). *Family life and family support: A feminist analysis*. Basingstoke: Palgrave Macmillan.

Featherstone, B. (forthcoming). *Contemporary fathering: Theory, policy and practice*. Bristol: Policy Press.

Featherstone, B., & Evans, H. (2004). *Children experiencing maltreatment: Who do they turn to?* London: NSPCC.

Ferreira, M.J. (2001). 'Total altruism' in Levinas's 'Ethics of the Welcome'. *Journal of Religious Ethics*, 29(3), 443–70.

Fikree, F. (2005). Attitudes of Pakistani men to domestic violence: A study from Karachi, Pakistan. *Journal of Men's Health and Gender*, 2, 49–58.

Follesø, R. (2004). *Bruker eller brukt? Landsforeningen for barnevernsbarn: Analyse av en interesseorganisasjon i møte med dagens barnevern*[User or used? The organization for youth in care: An analysis of an interest organization's encounter with the present child welfare]. Trondheim: Norges teknisk-naturvitenskapelige universitet.

Fook, J. (2002). *Social work: Critical theory and practice*. London: Sage.

Fook, J. (2004). What professionals need from research: Beyond evidence-based practice. In D. Smith (ed.), *Social work and evidence-based practice*. London: Jessica Kingsley, 29–46.

Foucault, M. (1970). *The order of things: An archaeology of the human sciences*. London: Routledge.

Foucault, M. (1977). *Discipline and punish*. New York: Pantheon.

Foucault, M. (1988). Technologies of the self. In L.H. Martin, H. Gutman, and P.H. Hutton (eds), *Technologies of the self: A seminar with Michel Foucault*. London: Tavistock, 16–49.

Franklin, D.L. (1986). Mary Richmond and Jane Addams: From moral certainty to rational inquiry in social work practice. *Social Service Review*, 60(4), 504–525.

Fraser, H., & Briskman, L. (2005). Through the eye of a needle: The challenge of getting justice in Australia if you're Indigenous or seeking asylum. In I. Ferguson, M. Lavalette, & E. Whitmore (eds), *Globalisation, global justice and social work*. London: Routledge.

Freeguard, H. (ed.) (2007). *Ethical practice for health professionals*. Melbourne: Thomson.

Freire, P. (1972). *Pedagogy of the oppressed*. Harmondsworth: Penguin.

Frister, R. (2000) *The cap: The price of a life*. New York: Grove Press.

Frogget, L. (2002). *Love, hate and welfare: Psychosocial approaches to policy and practice*. Bristol: Policy Press.

Furedi, F. (2003). *Therapy culture: Cultivating vulnerability in an uncertain age*. London: Routledge.

Furman, L.D., Benson, P.W., Grimwood, C., & Canda, E.R. (2004). Religion and spirituality in social work education and direct practice at the millennium: A survey of UK social workers. *British Journal of Social Work*, 34(6), 767–92.

Furness, S. (2003). Religion, belief and culturally competent practice. *Journal of Practice Teaching in Health and Social Care*, 15(1), 61–74.

Furness, S., & Gilligan, P. (2009). *Religion, belief and social work: Making a difference*. Bristol: Policy Press.

Galtung, J. (1994). *Human rights in another key*. Cambridge: Polity Press.

Gamble, D. (2002). *Time for action: Sexual abuse, the churches and a new dawn for survivors*. London: Churches Together in Britain and Ireland.

Garber, M., Hanssen, B., & Walkowitz, R.L. (2000). Introduction: The turn to ethics. In M. Garber, B. Hanssen, & R.L. Walkowitz (eds), *The turn to ethics*. New York: Routledge.

Garcia, J.G., Cartwright, B., Winston, S.M., & Borzuchowska, B. (2003). A transcultural integrative model for ethical decision-making in counselling. *Journal of Counseling and Development*, 81, 268–77.

General Social Care Council (2002). *Codes of practice*. London: GSCC.

General Social Care Council (2008). *Raising standards in social work conduct in England.* Retrieved 03.09.08 from: http://www.gscc.org.uk/Conduct/Publications+and+useful+documents/

Giddens, A. (1991). *Modernity and self-identity: Self and society in the late modern age.* Cambridge: Polity Press.

Giddens, A. (1998). *The Third Way.* Cambridge: Polity.

Gidron, B. (1983). Comment on 'Social work education in Israel: An analysis and some suggestions. *Journal of Jewish Communal Service,* 59, 259–62.

Gilligan, C. (1982). *In a different voice: Psychological theory and women's development.* Cambridge, MA: Harvard University Press.

Gilligan, P. (2003). 'It isn't discussed'. Religion, belief and practice teaching: Missing components of cultural competence in social work education. *Journal of Practice Teaching in Health and Social Care,* 5(1), 75–95.

Gilligan, P. (2008). Child abuse and spirit possession: Not just an issue for African migrants. *childRIGHT,* 245, 28–31.

Gilligan, P. (forthcoming). Considering religion and beliefs in child protection and safeguarding work: Is any consensus emerging? *Child Abuse Review.*

Gilligan, P., & Furness, S. (2006). The role of religion and spirituality in social work practice: Views and experiences of social workers and students. *British Journal of Social Work,* 36(4), 617–37.

Goffman, E. (1975). *Frame analysis: An essay on the organization of experience.* Harmondsworth: Penguin.

Goldstein, H. (1987). The neglected moral link in social work practice. *Social Work,* 32(3), 181–7.

Goodale, M., & Merry, S. (eds) (2007). *The practice of human rights: Tracking law between the global and the local.* Cambridge: Cambridge University Press.

Goode, H., McGee, H., & O'Boyle, C. (2003). *Time to listen: Confronting child sexual abuse by Catholic clergy in Ireland.* Dublin: Liffey Press.

Gordon, R. (2000). Critical race theory and international law: Convergence and divergence racing American foreign policy. In *Proceedings of the American Society of International Law 2000.* Washington, DC: American Society of International Law, 260–6.

Graham, M. (2007). *Black issues in social work and social care.* Bristol: Policy Press.

Grant, D., O'Neilen, K., & Stephens, L. (2004). Spirituality in the workplace: New empirical directions in the study of the sacred. *Sociology of Religion,* 65, 265–83.

Graves, J. (2004). *The race myth.* New York: Dutton.

Gray, M. (1993). *The relationship between social work, ethics and politics.* PhD thesis, University of (Kwa-Zulu) Natal, Durban, South Africa.

Gray, M. (1995). The ethical implications of current theoretical developments in social work. *British Journal of Social Work,* 25(1), 55–70.

Gray, M. (1996). Moral theory for social work. *Social Work/Maatskaplike Werk,* 32(4), 289–95.

Gray, M. (2008a). Viewing spirituality in social work through the lens of contemporary social theory. *British Journal of Social Work,* 38(1), 175–96.

Gray, M. (2008b). Unpublished correspondence.

Gray, M. (2009). Moral sources: Emerging ethical theories in social work. *British Journal of Social Work.* Advance Access, 22 Sept. doi:10.1093/bjsw/bcp104. 1–18.

Gray, M., Coates, J., & Yellow Bird, M. (2008). *Indigenous social work around the world: Towards culturally relevant social work practice*. Aldershot: Ashgate.

Gray, M., & Gibbons, J. (2007). There are no answers, only choices: Teaching ethical decision making in social work. *Australian Social Work*, 60(2), 222–38.

Gray, M., & Lovat, T. (2006). The shaky high moral ground of postmodernist 'ethics'. *Social Work/Maatskaplike Werk*, 42(3/4), 201–12.

Gray, M., & Lovat, T. (2007). Horse and carriage: Why Habermas's discourse ethics gives virtue a praxis in social work. *Ethics and Social Welfare*, 1(3), 310–28.

Gray, M., & Lovat, T. (2008). Practical mysticism, Habermas and social work praxis. *Journal of Social Work*, 8(2), 149–63.

Gray, M., & Stofberg, J.A. (2000). Social work and respect for persons. *Australian Journal of Social Work*, 53(3), 55–61.

Gray, M., & Webb, S.A. (2008). Social work as art revisited. *International Journal of Social Welfare*, 17(1), 182–93.

Gray, M., & Webb, S.A. (2009). The return of the political in social work. *International Journal of Social Welfare*, 18(1), 111–15.

Green, J. W. (1982, 1995). *Cultural awareness in the human services: A multi-ethnic approach*. Boston: Allyn & Bacon.

Green, R.G., Kiernan-Stern, M., & Baskind, F.R. (2005). White social workers' attitudes about people of color. *Journal of Ethnic and Cultural Diversity in Social Work*, 14(1/2), 47–68.

Green, J., & Thomas, R. (2007). Learning through our children, healing through our children: Best practice in First Nations communities. In L. Dominelli (ed.), *Revitalising communities in a globalising world*. Aldershot: Ashgate, pp. 175–92.

Grieve, P. (2006). *Islam history, faith and politics: The complete introduction*. London: Robinson.

GSCC *see* General Social Care Council.

Guttmann, D., & Cohen, B-Z. (1995). Israel. In T.D. Watts, D. Elliott, & N.S. Mayadas, *International Handbook on Social Work Education*. Westport, CT: Greenwood Press, 305–20.

Haakonssen, K. (1996). *Natural law and moral philosophy: From Grotius to the Scottish Enlightenment*. Cambridge: Cambridge University Press.

Habermas, J. (1971). *Knowledge and human interests*. Boston: Beacon.

Habermas, J. (1990). *Moral consciousness and communicative action*. Cambridge: Polity.

Habermas, J. (1991). *Justification and application*. Cambridge: Polity.

Haj-Yahia, M. (2003). Beliefs about wife beating among Arab men from Israel; The influence of their patriarchal ideology. *Journal of Family Violence*, 18, 193–206.

Halstead, M., & Lewicka, K. (1998). Should homosexuality be taught as an acceptable alternative lifestyle? A Muslim perspective. *Cambridge Journal of Education*, 28, 18–22.

Halvorsen, R. (2002). *The paradox of self-organisation among disadvantaged people: A study of marginalised citizenship*. Trondheim: Norges Teknisk-naturvitenskapelige Universitet.

Hamilton, M. (2000). An analysis of the festival for mind-body-spirit, London. In S. Sutcliffe and M. Bowman (eds), *Beyond New Age: Exploring alternative spirituality*. Edinburgh: Edinburgh University Press, 188–200.

Handy, C. (1994). *The age of paradox*. Watertown, MA: Harvard Business School Press.

Hanegraaff, W.J. (1996). *New Age religion and Western culture: Esotericism in the mirror of secular thought.* Leiden: Brill.

Hanegraaff, W.J. (2002). New Age religion. In L. Woodhead, P. Fletcher, K. Kawanami, and D. Smith (eds), *Religion in the modern world.* London: Routledge, 249–63.

Hanley, B. (2005). *Research as empowerment? Report of a series of seminars organised by the Toronto Group.* York: Joseph Rowntree Foundation. Retrieved 09.03.09 from: http://www.jrf.org.uk/bookshop/eBooks/1859353185.pdf

Harrington, D., & Dolgoff, R. (2008). Hierarchies of ethical principles for ethical decision making in social work. *Ethics and Social Welfare,* 2(2), 183–96.

Harris, J. (2008). State social work: Constructing the present from moments in the past. *British Journal of Social Work,* 38(4), 662–79.

Harris, J., & Kirk, B. (2000). Jugendgerichtssystem und Managerialismus in England [Youth justice and managerialism in England]. In H-U. Otto & S. Schnurr (eds), *Privatisierung und Wettbewerb in der Jugendhilfe: Marktorientierte Modernisierungsstrategien in Internationaler Perspektive* [Privatization and competition in work with young people: an international perspective on market-focused modernization strategies]. Neuwied: Luchterhand.

Hart, R. (1992). *Children's participation from tokenism to citizenship.* Florence: UNICEF Innocenti Research Centre.

Hauerwas, S. (1983). *The peaceable kingdom: A primer in Christian Ethics.* London: SCM.

Hayden, P. (ed.) (2001). *The philosophy of human rights.* St Paul, MN: Paragon House.

Hayes, D., & Houston, S. (2007). Lifeworld, system and family group conferences: Habermas' contribution to discourse in child protection. *British Journal of Social Work,* 37, 987–1006.

Hayes, D., & Humphries, B. (eds) (2004). *Social work, immigration and asylum: Debates, dilemmas and ethical issues for social work and social care practice.* London: Jessica Kingsley.

Healy, K. (2000). *Social work practices: Contemporary perspectives on change.* London: Sage.

Healy, K., & Meagher, G. (2004). The reprofessionalization of social work: Collaborative approaches for achieving professional recognition. *British Journal of Social Work,* 34(2), 240–60.

Healy, L. (2001). *International social work: Professional action in an interdependent world.* New York: Oxford University Press.

Heelas, P. (1996). *The New Age movement: The celebration of the self and the sacralisation of modernity.* Oxford: Blackwell.

Heelas, P. (2006). The infirmity debate: On the viability of New Age spiritualities of life. *Journal of Contemporary Religion,* 21, 223–40.

Heelas, P. (2007). The spiritual revolution of Northern Europe: Personal beliefs. *Nordic Journal of Religion and Society,* 20, 1–28.

Heelas, P. (2008). *Spiritualities of life: New Age romanticism and consumptive capitalism.* Oxford: Blackwell.

Heelas, P., & Houtman, D. (2009, forthcoming). RAMP findings and making sense of the 'God within each person, rather than out there'. *Journal of Contemporary Religion,* 23.

Heelas, P., & Woodhead, L. (with B. Seel, B. Szerszynski, & K. Tusting) (2005). *The spiritual revolution: Why religion is giving way to spirituality.* Oxford: Blackwell.

Hekman, S. (1995). *Moral voices, moral selves.* Cambridge: Polity Press.

Helms, J.E., Jernigan, M., & Mascher, J. (2005). The meaning of race in psychology and how to change it. *American Psychologist*, 60, 27–45.

Henery, N. (2003). The reality of visions: Contemporary theories of spirituality in social work. *British Journal of Social Work*, 33, 1105–13.

Herbert, G. (2003). *A philosophical history of rights*. New Brunswick, NJ: Transaction.

Hicks, S. (2003). The Christian Right and homophobic discourse: A response to evidence that lesbian and gay parenting damages children. *Sociological Research Online*, 8(4). Retrieved 18.12.07 from: www.socresonline.org.uk/8/4/hicks.html

Higgins, J. (1981). *States of welfare: Comparative analysis in social policy.* Oxford: Basil Blackwell.

Hill, M., Glaser, K., & Harden, J. (1995). A feminist model for ethical decision-making. In E. Rave & C. Larsen (eds), *Ethical decision-making in therapy: Feminist perspectives.* New York: Guildford Press, 18–37.

Hirsi Ali, A. (2006). *The caged virgin: A Muslim woman's cry for reason.* London: Free Press.

Hirsi Ali, A. (2007). *Infidel: My life*. London: Free Press.

Hnik, F.M. (1938). *The philanthropic motive in Christianity: An analysis of the relations between theology and social service*. Oxford: Blackwell.

Hobbes, T. ([1651] 1968). *Leviathan*. Harmondsworth: Penguin.

Hodge, D. (2005). Social work and the house of Islam: Orientating practitioners to the beliefs and values of Muslims in the United States. *Social Work*, 50, 162–73.

Hodge, D.R. (2001). Spiritual assessment: A review of major qualitative methods and a new framework for assessing spirituality. *Social Work*, 46(3), 203–14.

Hodge, D.R. (2005). Developing a spiritual assessment toolbox: A discussion of the strengths and limitations of five different assessment methods. *Health and Social Work*, 30(4), 314–23.

Hodgson, L. (2004). Manufactured civil society: Counting the cost. *Critical Social Policy*, 24, 139–64.

Holland, T., & Kilpatrick, A. (1991). Ethical issues in social work: Toward a grounded theory of professional ethics. *Social Work*. 36(2), 138–44.

Hollis, F. (1966). *Casework: A psychosocial therapy*. New York: Random House.

Hollway, W. (2006). *The capacity to care*. London: Routledge.

Hölscher, D. (2005). A postmodern critique of the SACSSP's Draft Code of Ethics, *Social work/Maatskaplike Werk*, 41(3), 237–50.

Honderich, T. (n.d.). *Free will, determinism, and moral responsibility*. Retrieved 16.09.08 from: http://www.ucl.ac.uk/~uctytho/ted12.htm

Honneth, A. (1995). *The struggle for recognition: The moral grammar of social conflicts*. Cambridge: Polity Press.

Houston, S. (2003). Establishing virtue in social work: A response to McBeath and Webb. *British Journal of Social Work*, 33, 819–24.

Houston, S. (2008). Communication, recognition and social work: Aligning the ethical theories of Habermas and Honneth. *British Journal of Social Work*, Advance Access, 1–17.

Houtman, D. (2000). The working class and the welfare state: Support for economic redistribution, tolerance for nonconformity, and the conditionality of solidarity with the unemployed. *Netherlands' Journal of Social Sciences*, 36, 37–55.

Houtman, D., & Aupers, S. (2007). The spiritual turn and the decline of tradition: The spread of post-Christian spirituality in fourteen Western Countries (1981–2000). *Journal for the Scientific Study of Religion*, 46, 305–20.

Houtman, D., Aupers, S., & Heelas, P. (2009). Christian religiosity and New Age spirituality: A cross-cultural comparison. *Journal for the Scientific Study of Religion*, 48(1), 170–80.

Houtman, D., & Mascini, P. (2002). Why do churches become empty, while New Age grows? Secularization and religious change in the Netherlands. *Journal for the Scientific Study of Religion*, 41, 455–73.

Hugman, R. (2003). Professional values and ethics in social work: Reconsidering postmodernism. *British Journal of Social Work*, 33(8), 1025–42.

Hugman, R. (2005). *New approaches in ethics for caring professions*. Basingstoke: Palgrave Macmillan.

Hugman, R., & Smith, D. (1995). Ethical issues in social work: An overview. In R. Hugman & D. Smith (eds), *Ethical issues in social work*. London: Routledge, pp. 1–15.

Hunt, L. (2007). *Inventing human rights*. New York: Norton.

Hursthouse, E. (1999). *On virtue ethics*. Oxford: Oxford University Press.

Hvinden, B., & Johansson, H. (eds) (2007). *Citizenship in Nordic welfare states: Dynamics of choice, duties and participation in a changing Europe*. London: Routledge.

Ife, J. (2005). A culture of human rights and responsibilities. Alice Tay Memorial Lecture, Parliament House, Canberra, Australia.

Ife, J. (2006). Human rights beyond the three generations. In E. Porter & B. Offord, *Activating human rights*. Oxford: Peter Lang.

Ife, J. (2008). *Human rights and social work: Towards rights-based practice*. Revised edn. Cambridge: Cambridge University Press.

IFSW *see* International Federation of Social Workers.

Inglehart, R. (1997). *Modernization and postmodernization: Cultural, economic, and political change in 43 countries*. Princeton, NJ: Princeton University Press.

International Federation of Social Workers (IFSW) (2004). *Ethics in social work: Statement of principles*. Retrieved 20.11.08 from: http://www.ifsw.org/en/f38000032.html

Irfan, S., & Cowburn, M. (2004). Disciplining, chastisement and physical child abuse: Perceptions and attitudes of the British Pakistani community. *Journal of Muslim Affairs*, 24, 89–98.

Iser, M. (2003). *Habermas and virtue*. Retrieved 11.08.08 from: http://www.bu.edu/wcp/Papers/Cont/ContIser.htm

Isichei, I. (1970) *Victorian Quakers*. Oxford. Oxford University Press.

Jayaratne, S., Croxton, T., & Mattison, D. (1997). Social work professional standards: An exploratory study. *Social Work*, 42(2), 187–19.

Jepson, P. (2000). Racist incident monitoring: Progress by the police. *New Law Journal*, 562–3.

Johansson, H., & Hvinden, B. (2007). What do we mean by active citizenship? In B. Hvinden & H. Johansson (eds), *Citizenship in Nordic welfare states: Dynamics of choice, duties and participation in a changing Europe*. London: Routledge, 32–49.

Jones, C. (1985). *Patterns of social policy: An introduction to comparative analysis*. London: Tavistock.

Jordan, B., with Jordan, C. (2000). *Social work and the Third Way: Tough love as social policy*. London: Sage.

Jordan, W. (1987). Fallen idol. In T. Philpot (ed.), *On second thoughts: Reassessments of the literature of social work*. Wallington: Community Care, pp. 00–00.

Kamrava, M. (ed.) (2006). *The new voices of Islam: Reforming politics and modernity.* New York: I.B. Tauris.

Kansalaislaivurit (2009). *Onko Suomessa aitoa kansalaisyhteiskuntaa? Blogi keskustelua kansalaisyhteiskunnasta* [Citizen navigators: Does an authentic civic society exist in Finland? A blog contribution at the platform discussion on civic society]. Retrieved 28.02.09 from: http://kansalaisyhteiskunnasta.vuodatus.net/

Kant, I. ([1785] 1948). *Groundwork to a metaphysics of morals.* London: Hutchinson.

Kellner, D. (1998). Zygmunt Bauman's postmodern turn. *Theory, Culture & Society,* 15(1), 73–86.

Kelly, D.R., & Popkin, R.H. (eds) (1991). *The shapes of knowledges from the Renaissance to the Enlightenment.* New York: Springer.

Kennedy, M. (2000). Christianity and child sexual abuse: The survivors' voice leading to change. *Child Abuse Review,* 9(1), 124–41.

Kennedy, M. (2003). *Christianity and child sexual abuse: Survivors informing the care of children following abuse.* Paper presented to the Royal College of Psychiatrists. Retrieved 20.12.07 from: http://www.rcpsych.ac.uk/pdf/Margaret%20Kennedy%201.11.03%20Christianity%20and%20Child%20Sexual%20Abuse%20–%20Survivors%20informing%20the%20care%20of%20children%20following%20abuse.pdf

Kennison, P. (2008). Child abuse in a religious context: The abuse of trust. In P. Kennison and A. Goodman (eds), *Children as victims.* Exeter: Learning Matters, 61–77.

Kessl, F., & Otto, H-U. (2003). Aktivierende Soziale Srbeit: Anmerkungen zur neosozialen Programmierung Sozialer Arbeit [Activating social work: Remarks to the neo-social programme of social work]. In H-J. Dahme, H.U. Otto, A. Trube, & N. Wohlfahrt (eds), *Soziale Arbeit für den aktivierenden Staat* [Social work for the activating state]. Opladen: Leske+Budrich, 57–74.

Khan, P., & Dominelli, L. (2000). *Social work and globalisation: A report.* Southampton: Centre for International Social and Community Development, Southampton University.

Khan, Z., Watson, P., & Habib, F. (2005). Muslim attitudes towards religion, religious orientation and empathy among Pakistanis. *Mental Health, Religion and Culture, 8:* 49–61.

Kjørstad, M. (2005). Between professional ethics and bureaucratic rationality: The challenging ethical position of social workers who are faced with implementing a workfare. *European Journal of Social Work,* 8(4), 381–98.

Klein, M. (1995) Responsibility. In T. Honderich (ed.), *The Oxford companion to philosophy.* Oxford: Oxford University Press.

Koenig, M., Ahmed, S., Hossein, M., & Mozumder, K. (2003). Women's status and domestic violence in rural Bangladesh. *Demography,* 40, 269–88.

Koh, K. (2006). Analysis of religious organizations' contribution to social welfare facilities in Korea: 2001–2003. *Health Welfare Policy,* 115, 65–73.

Koskiaho, B. (2008). *Hyvinvointipalvelujen tavaratalossa* [In the supermarket of welfare services]. Tampere: Vastapaino.

Kristjánsson, K. (2007). *Aristotle, emotions, and education.* Aldershot: Ashgate.

Kugelman, W. (1992). Social work ethics in the practice arena: A qualitative study. *Social Work in Health Care,* 17(4), 59–77.

Kulis, S., Marsiglia, F.F., Elek, E., Dustman, P., Wagstaff, D.A., & Hecht, M.L. (2005). Mexican/Mexican American adolescents and keepin' it REAL: An evidence-based substance use prevention program. *Children & Schools*, 27(3), 133–45.

Kutchins, H. (1991). The fiduciary relationship: The legal basis for social work responsibilities to clients. *Social Work*, 36(2), 106–13.

Lago, C., & Thompson, J. (1996). *Race, culture and counseling*. Buckingham: Open University Press.

Larkin, H. (2007). The ethics of social work practise in a nursing home setting: A consultants' dilemma. *Journal of Social Work Values and Ethics*, 4(3). Retrieved 18.12.08 from: http://www.socialworker.com/jswve/content/view/67/54/

Levinas, E. ([1974] 1991). *Otherwise than Being; or, Beyond Essence*, trans. Alphonso Lingis. Dordrecht: Kluwer Academic.

Levinas, E. (1998). *Entre nous: On thinking of the Other*, trans. Michael B. Smith and Barbara Harshav. New York: Columbia University Press.

Levinas, E. (1999). *Alterity and transcendence*. New York: Columbia University Press.

Levy, C.S. (1983). Client self-determination. In A. Rosenblatt & D. Waldvogel (eds), *Handbook of clinical social work*. San Francisco: Jossey Bass, pp. 000.

Lewis, B. (1993). *Islam and the West*. New York: Oxford University Press.

Lewis, J. (ed.) (2003). *The new rights of man*. London: Constable & Robinson.

Ling, H.K. (2008). The development of culturally appropriate social work practice in Sarawak, Malaysia. In M. Gray, J. Coates, & M. Yellow Bird (eds), *Indigenous social work around the world: Towards culturally relevant education and practice*. Aldershot: Ashgate, pp. 97–106.

Linzer, N., Conboy, A., & Ain, E. (2003). Ethical dilemmas of Israeli social workers. *International Social Work*, 46(1), 7–21.

Lipsky, M. (1980). *Street-level bureaucracy dilemmas of the individual in public services*. New York: Russell Sage.

Locke, J. ([1690] 1946). *The second treatise on civil government*. Oxford: Blackwell

Lorenz, W. (2006). *Perspectives on European social work: From the birth of the nation state to the impact of globalisation*. Opladen: Barbara Budrich.

Lorde, A. (1984). *Sister outsider: Essays and speeches*. Berkeley, CA: Crossing Press.

Louden, R.B. (1997). On some vices of virtue ethics. In D. Statman (ed.), *Virtue ethics: A critical reader*. Edinburgh: Edinburgh University Press, pp.000.

Lovat, T., & Gray, M. (2008). Towards a proportionist social work ethics: A Habermasian perspective. *British Journal of Social Work*, 38, 1100–14.

Luckmann, T. (1967). *The invisible religion: The problem of religion in modern society*. New York: Macmillan.

Luckmann, T. (1996). The privatisation of religion and morality. In P. Heelas, S. Lash, & P. Morris (eds), *Detraditionalisation: Critical reflections on authority and identity*. Oxford: Blackwell, 1996, pp. 72–86.

Lum, D. (1996). *Social work practice and people of color: A process stage model*. Monterey, CA: Brooks/Cole.

Lynch, E.W., & Hanson, M. J. (1992). *Developing cross-cultural competence: A guide for working young children and their families*. Baltimore. MD: Paul H. Brookes.

Lyon, D. (2000). *Jesus in Disneyland: Religion in postmodern times*. Oxford: Polity.

Lyons, K., Manion, K., & Carlsen, M. (2006). *International perspectives on social work*. Basingstoke: Palgrave Macmillan.

Macarov, D. (1980). *Work and welfare: The unholy alliance.* Beverly Hills, CA: Sage.

MacIntyre, A. (1985). *After virtue: A study in moral theory.* 2nd edn. Notre Dame, IN: University of Notre Dame Press.

MacKenzie, N., & MacKenzie, J. (eds) (1982). *The diary of Beatrice Webb, Vol. 1.* Cambridge, MA: Cambridge University Press.

Mahamud-Hassan, N. (2004). It doesn't happen in our society. *Index on Censorship,* 33, 38–41.

Malik, R. Shaikh, A. & Suleyman, M. (2007). *Providing faith and culturally sensitive support services to young British Muslims.* Leicester: National Youth Agency.

Mama, R. (2001). Preparing social work students to work in culturally diverse settings. *Social Work Education,* 20, 373–82.

Mannson McGinty, A. (2006). *Becoming Muslim.* New York: Palgrave Macmillan.

Mapp, S. (2008). *Human rights and social justice in a global perspective: An introduction to international social work.* New York: Oxford.

Marshall, T.H. (1950). *Citizenship and social class and other essays.* Cambridge; Cambridge University Press.

Marshall, T.H. (1965). Citizenship and social class. In T.H. Marshall (ed.), *Class, citizenship and social development.* New York: Anchor, 71–134.

Marwick, A. (1998). *The sixties: Cultural revolution in Britain, France, Italy, and the United States,* c.*1958*–c.*1974.* New York: Oxford University Press.

Maslow, A. H. (1943). A theory of human motivation. *Psychological Review,* 50, 370–96.

Matthies, A., & Kauer, K. (eds) (2004). *Wiege des sozialen Kapitals* [A cradle for social capital]. Bielefeld: Kleine Verlag.

Matthies, A-L. (ed.) (2006) *Nordic civic society organisations and the future of welfare services.* Copenhagen: Nordic Council of Ministers. Retrieved 28.02.09 from: http://www.norden.org/pub/velfaerd/social_helse/sk/TN2006517.pdf

Matthies, A-L., Närhi, K., & Ward, D. (eds) (2001). *The eco-social approach in social work.* Jyväskylä: University of Jyväskylä.

Mattison, M. (2000). Ethical decision-making: The person in the process, *Social Work,* 45, 201–12.

McAuliffe, D. (1999). Clutching at codes: Resources that influence social work decisions in cases of ethical conflict. *Professional Ethics: A Multidisciplinary Journal,* 7(3–4), 9–24.

McAuliffe, D., & Chenoweth, L. (2008). Leave no stone unturned: The inclusive model of ethical decision making. *Ethics and Social Welfare,* 2(1), 38–49.

McAuliffe, D., & Sudbery, J. (2005). Who do I tell? Support and consultation in cases of ethical conflict. *Journal of Social Work,* 5(1), 21–43.

McBeath, G., & Webb, S. (1991). Social work, modernity, and postmodernity. *Sociological Review,* 39(4), 745–62.

McBeath, G., & Webb, S.A. (2002). Virtue ethics and social work: Being lucky, realistic, and not doing one's duty. *British Journal of Social Work,* 32(8), 1015–36.

McGoldrick, M., Giordano, J., & Pearce, J.K. (eds) (1996). *Ethnicity and family therapy.* 2nd edn. New York: Guilford Press.

McLaughlin, K. (2007). Regulation and risk in social work: The General Social Care Council and the social care register in context. *British Journal of Social Work,* 37(7), 1263–77.

Meacham, M.G. (2007). Ethics and decision making for social workers. *Journal of Social Work Values and Ethics*, 4(3). Retrieved 18.12.08 from: http://www.socialworker.com/jswve/content/view/70/54/

Meijer, M. (ed.) (2001). *Dealing with human rights: Asian and Western views on the value of human rights*. Utrecht: Netherlands Humanist Committee on Human Rights (HOM).

Meleyal, L. (2009). *Reframing conduct in the context of social work registration conduct case outcomes*. Doctoral thesis, University of Sussex.

Mernissi, F. (1975). *Beyond the veil*. Cambridge, MA: Schenkman.

Mernissi, F. (2006). Muslim women and fundamentalism. In M. Kamrava (ed.), *The new voices of Islam: Reforming politics and modernity*. New York: I.B. Tauris, 205–12.

Miley, K.K., O'Melia, M., & Dubois, B. (2004) *Generalist social work practice: An empowering approach*. Boston: Allyn & Bacon.

Miner, M.H. (2006). A proposed comprehensive model for ethical decision-making. In S. Morrissey & P. Reddy (eds), *Ethics and professional practice for psychologists*. Melbourne: Thomson. 25–37.

Miranda, J., Bernal, G., Lau, A., Kohn, L., Hwang, W-C., & LaFramboise, T. (2005). State of the science on psychosocial interventions for ethnic minorities. *Annual Review of Clinical Psychology*, 1(1), 113–42.

Mission Australia (2007). *Our Vision 2007–2017*. Sydney: Mission Australia. Retrieved 24.07.08 from: http://www.missionaustralia.com.au/document-downloads/doc_details/62–mission-australia-strategic-plan-20072017

Mittwoch, F. (1983). An exchange on Israeli social work education (letter). *Journal of Jewish Communal Service*, 59, 361–2.

Modras, R. (2004). *Ignatian humanism: A dynamic spirituality for the 21st century*. Chicago: Loyola Press.

Mohammad, R. (2005). Negotiating spaces of the home, the education system and the labor market. In G. Falah & C. Nagel (eds), *Geographies of Muslim women*. New York: Guildford, 178–202.

Monshipouri, M., Englehart, N., Nathan, A., & Philip, K. (eds) (2003). *Constructing human rights in the age of globalization*. Armonk, NY: M.E. Sharpe

Moore, A. (2007). Ethical theory, completeness and consistency. *Ethical Theory and Moral Practice*, 10(3), 297–308.

Mulholland, H. (2005). Unmarried and same-sex couples free to adopt. *Guardian*, 30 December. Retrieved 25.07.08 from: http://www.guardian.co.uk/society/2005/dec/30/adoptionandfostering.childrensservices

Mullaly, B. (2007). *The new structural social work*. 3rd edn. Don Mills, Ontario: Oxford University Press.

Mullaly, R. (1997). *Structural social work*. Toronto: McClelland & Stewart.

Mullender, A., & Ward, D. (1991). *Self-directed groups: User action for empowerment*. London: Whiting & Birch.

Muñoz, R.F., Penilla, C., & Urizar, G. (2002). Expanding depression prevention research with children of diverse cultures. *Prevention & Treatment*, 5(1). Retrieved 06.10.08 from: http://psych.unn.ac.uk/pdf/prev/pre0050013c.html

Munro, E. (1999). Common errors of reasoning in child protection work. *Child Abuse and Neglect*, 23, 745–758.

Murdoch, I. (1970). *The sovereignty of good*. London: Routledge & Kegan Paul.

Nagel, A. (2006). Charitable choice: The religious component of the US-welfare-reform – theoretical and methodological reflections on 'faith-based organizations' as social service agencies. *Numen*, 53(1), 78–111.

Nagel, T. (1979) *Mortal questions*. Cambridge: Cambridge University Press.

Narey, M. (2007). *Our basis and values*. Ilford: Barnardos. Retrieved 18.04.08 from: www.barnardos.org.uk

Nasr, S. (2002). *The heart of Islam*. San Francisco: Harper/National Association of Social Workers.

NASW see National Association of Social Workers.

National Association of Social Workers (1999). *Code of Ethics*. Washington, DC: NASW. Available online at: http://www.naswdc.org/pubs/code/code.asp

National Youth Agency (2009). *The national youth agency*. Retrieved 18.06.09 from: www.nya.org.uk

Nealon, J. (1998). *Alterity politics: Ethics and performative subjectivity*. Durham, NC and London: Duke University Press.

Niebuhr, R. (1932). *The contribution of religion to social work*. New York: Columbia University Press.

Newland, L. (2006). Female circumcision: Muslim identities and zero tolerance policies in rural West Java. *Women's Studies International Forum*, 29, 394–404.

Nolan, Lord (2001). *A programme for action: Final report of the independent review on child protection in the Catholic Church in England and Wales*. London, Catholic Bishops' Conference of England and Wales. Retrieved 15.09.08 from: http://www.bishop-accountability.org/resources/resource-files/reports/NolanReport.pdf

Nozick, R. (1974). *Anarchy, state, and utopia*. Oxford: Blackwell.

Nussbaum, M. ([1983] 1986) *The Fragility of Goodness*. Cambridge: Cambridge University Press.

NYA *see* National Youth Agency.

Nylund, M. (2000). *Varieties of mutual support and voluntary action*. Helsinki: Finnish Federation for Social Welfare and Health.

Nyssens, M. (ed.) (2006). *Social enterprise at the crossroads of market, public policies and civil society*. London: Routledge.

Obrecht, W. (2001). *Das Systemtheoretische Paradigma der Disziplin und der Profession der Sozialen Arbeit: Eine transdisziplinäre Antwort auf das Problem der Fragmentierung des professionellen Wissens und die unvollständige Professionalisierung der Sozialen Arbeit* [The systemic paradigm of social work: An answer to the problem of fragmentation of knowledge in social work]. Zurich: Hochschule für Soziale Arbeit Zürich.

Obrecht, W. (2005). *Umrisse einer biopsychologischen Theorie menschlicher Bedürfnisse: Geschichte, Probleme, Struktur, Funktion* [A biopsychosocial Theory of human needs: History, Problems, structure and function]. Vienna: Skript zur gleichnamigen Lehrveranstaltung im ISMOS der Wirtschaftsuniversität Wien.

O'Donoghue, P. Bishop (2007). *To all at Catholic caring services and the parishes of the Diocese*. Letter, 9 July. Retrieved 18.12.07 from: http://www.lancasterrcdiocese.org.uk/bishop/caring-services.pdf

Orend, B. (2002). *Human rights: Concept and context*. Peterborough ONT: Broadview.

Orme, J., & Rennie, G. (2006). The role of registration in ensuring ethical practice. *International Social Work*, 49(3), 333–44.

Outhwaite, W. (1996). *The Habermas reader*. Oxford: Polity.

Park, G. (1990). Making sense of religion by direct observation: An application of frame analysis. In S.H. Riggins (ed.), *Beyond Goffman: Studies on communication, institution, and social interaction*. New York: Mouton de Gruyter, pp. 235–76.

Park, Y. (2005). Culture as deficit: A critical discourse analysis of the concept of culture in contemporary social work discourse. *Journal of Sociology and Social Welfare*, 32(3), 11–33.

Parton, N. (1994). 'Problematics of government', (post)modernity and social work. *British Journal of Social Work*, 24(1), 9–32.

Parton, N. (2003). Rethinking professional practice: The contributions of social constructionism and the feminist 'ethics of care'. *British Journal of Social Work*, 33, 1–16.

Patel, N., Nalk, N., & Humphries, B. (1998). *Visions of reality: Religion and ethnicity* in social work. London: Central Council for Education and Training in Social Work.

Payne, M. (2005). *The origins of social work: Continuity and change*. Basingstoke: Palgrave Macmillan.

Pearson, D. (2007). *Child abuse linked to belief in spirit possession: New DfES guidelines will fail children without concerted action now*. Churches Child Protection Advisory Service Press Release, 2 February. Retrieved 01.03.08 from: http://www.ccpas.co.uk/Press%20releases/2%20Feb%202007.htm

Pereira, W. (1997). *Inhuman rights: The Western system and global human rights abuse*. Penang: The Other India Press/Apex Press/Third World Network.

Perez-Koenig, R., & Rock, B. (eds) (2001). *Social work in the era of devolution: Toward a just practice*. New York: Fordham University Press.

Perlman, H.H. (1965). Self-determination: Reality or illusion? *Social Service Review*, 39(4), 410–21.

Perlman, H.H. (1976). Believing and doing: Values in social work education. *Social Casework*, 57(6), 381–98.

Pestoff, V.A. (2009). *A democratic architecture for the welfare state*. London: Routledge.

Peters, F. (2003). *Islam*. Princeton, NJ: Princeton University Press.

Phillips, M. (1993). An oppressive urge to end oppression, *Observer*, 1 August.

Phoca, S., and Wright, R. (1999) *Introducing postfeminism*. Cambridge, Icon.

Pinker, R. (1993). A lethal kind of looniness, *Times Higher Educational Supplement*, 10 September.

Plante, T. (2002). *A perspective on clergy sexual abuse*. Retrieved 18.06.09 from: http://www.psychwww.com/psyrelig/plante.html

Plante, T.G. (ed.) (2004). *Sin against the innocents: Sexual abuse by priests and the role of the Catholic Church*. Westport, CT: Praeger.

Possamai, A. (2003). Alternative spiritualities and the cultural logic of late capitalism. *Culture and Religion*, 4, 31–45.

Prager, E. (1988). American social work imperialism: Consequences for professional education in Israel. In I. Benshahak, R. Berger, & Y. Kadman (eds), *Social work in Israel*. Tel-Aviv: Israel Association of Social Workers.

Praglin, L.J. (2004). Spirituality, religion, and social work: An effort towards interdisciplinary conversation. *Journal of Religion and Spirituality in Social Work*, 23, 67–84.

Price, S. (2008). Agency bows to pressure over same-sex adoptions: Working with law 'only way to save service'. *The Universe*, 27 July.

Putnam, R. (2000). *Bowling alone: The collapse and revival of American community*. London: Simon & Schuster.

Ragg, N. (1977). *People not cases: A philosophical approach to social work*. London: Routledge & Kegan Paul.

Rajagopal, B. (2003). *International law from below: Development, social movements and third world resistance*. Cambridge: Cambridge University Press.

Rankin, P. (2006). Exploring and describing the strength/empowerment perspective in social work. *Journal of Social Work Theory and Practice,* 14. Retrieved 06.10.08 from: http://www.bemidjistate.edu/academics/publications/social_work_journal/issue14/articles/rankin.htm

Rawls, J. (1971). *A theory of justice*. Oxford: Oxford University Press.

Reamer, F.G. (1983). The concept of paternalism in social work. *Social Service Review,* 57(3), 254–71.

Reamer, F.G. (ed.) (1991). *AIDS and Ethics*. New York: Columbia University Press.

Reamer, F.G. (1998a). *Current controversies in social work ethics: Case examples*. Washington, DC: NASW.

Reamer, F.G. (1998b). The evolution of social work values and ethics. *Social Work,* 43(6), 488–500.

Reamer, F.G. (2001a). *Ethics education in social work*. Alexandria, Victoria: CSWE.

Reamer, F.G. (2001b). *The social work ethics audit: A risk management tool*. Washington, DC: NASW Press.

Reason, P., & Bradbury, H. (eds) (2006). *Handbook of action research*. London: Sage.

Reichert, E. (2003). *Social work and human rights: A foundation for policy and practice*. New York: Columbia University Press.

Reichert, E. (2006). *Understanding human rights: An exercise book*. London: Sage.

Reichert, E. (ed.) (2007). *Challenges in human rights: A social work perspective*. New York: Columbia University Press.

Reid, J. (2007). To register or not: The relevance of the social work codes of practice for the social work lecturer. *Ethics and Social Welfare,* 1(3), 336–41.

Rhodes, M.L. (1986). *Ethical dilemmas in social service*. Boston: Routledge & Kegan Paul.

Rhodes, M.L. (1991). *Ethical dilemmas in social work practice*. Milwaukee: Families Service America.

Rice, D. (1975). The Code: A voice for approval. *Social Work Today,* 18 October, 381–2.

Richmond, M.E. (1922). *What is social case work? An introductory description*. New York: Russell Sage Foundation.

Robertson, C., & Fadil, P. (1999). Ethical decision-making in multinational organisations: A culture-based model. *Journal of Business Ethics,* 19(4), 385–92.

Robinson, W., & Reeser, L. (2000). *Ethical decision-making in social work*. Boston: Allyn & Bacon.

Rodriguez, G. (2007). *Mongrels, bastards, orphans and vagabonds. Mexican immigration and the future of race in America*. New York: Pantheon.

Roivainen, I., Nylund, M., Korkiamäki, R., & Raitakari.S. (eds) (2008). *Yhteisöt ja sosiaalityö* [Communities and social work]. Jyväskylä: PS-Kustannus.

Rose, N. (1986). *Governing the soul: The shaping of the private self*. London: Routledge.

Rose, N. (1996). *Inventing ourselves*. Cambridge: Cambridge University Press.

Rossiter, A., Prilleltensky, I., & Walsh-Bowers, R. (2000). A postmodern perspective on professional ethics. In B. Fawcett, B. Featherstone, J. Fook, & A. Rossiter (eds),

Postmodern feminist perspectives: Practice and research in social work. London: Routledge, 83–103.

Roszak, T. (1968). *The making of a counter culture: Reflections on the technocratic society and its youthful opposition.* New York: Doubleday.

Roth, R., & Olk, T. (2007). *Mehr Partizipation wagen: Argumente für eine verstärkte Beteiligung von Kindern und Jugendlichen* [Daring to participate more: arguments for increased involvement amongst children and young people]. Gütersloh: Bertelsmann Stiftung.

Rothman, J. (2005). *From the front-lines: Student cases in social work ethics.* Boston: Pearson.

Rousseau, J. ([1762] 1913). *The social contract.* London: Dent.

Sandel, M. (1982). *Liberalism and the limits of justice.* Cambridge: Cambridge University Press.

Sanderson, T. (2007). Government minister says social work done by Christians is superior. *Newsline.* National Secular Society. Retrieved 12.10.08 from: http://www.secularism.org.uk/governmentministersayssocialwork1.html

Schillebeecckx, E. (1971). *World and church.* London: Sheed & Ward.

Schlesinger, E.G., & Devore, W. (1979). Social workers view ethnic minority teaching. *Journal of Education for Social Work,* 15(3), 20–7.

Schlesinger, E.G., & Devore, W. (2007). Ethnic sensitive social work practice: Back to the future. *Journal of Ethnic and Cultural Diversity in Social Work,* 16(3/4), 3–29.

Schweitzer, A. (1923). *Civilization and ethics.* London: Unwin.

Seedhouse, D. & Lovett, L. (1992). *Practical medical ethics.* Chichester: John Wiley.

Segal, L. (1987). *Is the future female?* London: Virago.

Seidman, S. (1994). *Contested knowledge: Social theory in the postmodern era.* Cambridge, MA: Blackwell.

Seim, S. (2006). *Egenorganisering blant fattige: En studie av initiativ, mobilisering og betydning av Fattighuset* [Self-organization among poor people: A study of the poor house initiative, mobilization and outcome]. Gothenburg: Department of Social Work, Gothenburg University.

Seim, S., & Sletteboe, T. (eds) (2007). *Brukermedvirkning i barnvernet* [User involvement in child care]. Oslo: Universitetsforlaget.

Sevenhuijsen, S. (1998). *Citizenship and the ethics of care.* London: Routledge.

Sevenhuijsen, S. (2000). Caring in the Third Way: The relation between obligation, responsibility and care in Third Way discourse. *Critical Social Policy,* 20(1), 5–37.

Sheridan, M.J., & Amato-von Hemert, K. (1999). The role of religion and spirituality in social work education and practice: A survey of student views and experiences. *Journal of Social Work Education,* 35(1), 125–41.

Sherman, N. (1997). *Making a necessity of virtue.* Cambridge: Cambridge University Press.

Sibeon, R. (2004). *Rethinking social theory.* London: Sage.

Silverman, M., & Rice, S. (1995). Ethical dilemmas of working with individuals who have HIV disease. *Journal of Gay and Lesbian Social Services,* 3(4), 53–68.

Siporin, M. (1983). Morality and immorality in working with clients. *Social Thought,* 9(4), 10–28.

Skehill, C. (1999). Reflexive modernity and social work in Ireland: A response to Powell. *British Journal of Social Work, 29,* 797–809.

Slack, P. (1988). *Poverty and policy in Tudor and Stuart England.* London: Longman.

Slote, M. (1997). From morality to virtue. In D. Statman (ed.), *Virtue ethics: A critical reader.* Edinburgh: Edinburgh University Press, pp. 00–00.

Smedley, A., & Smedley, B.D. (2005). Race as biology is fiction, racism as a social problem is real. *American Psychologist,* 60, pp. 16–26.

Smith, B.H. (1988). *Contingencies of value: Alternative perspectives for critical theory.* Cambridge, MA: Harvard University Press.

Smith, D. (ed.) (2004). *Social work and evidence-based practice.* London: Jessica Kingsley.

Smith, N.H. (2002). *Charles Taylor: Meanings, morality and modernity.* Cambridge: Polity.

Solas, J. (2008). Social work and social justice: What are we fighting for? *Australian Social Work,* 61(2), 124–36.

Sonnenberg, K. (2003). *The social work profession as qualified by the aspects of efficiency and ethics: A comparison between Germany and England.* Birmingham: BASW/Venture Press.

South African Council of Social Services Professions (SACSSP) (n.d.). *The Council's Ethics.* Retrieved 28.11.08 from: http://www.sacssp.co.za/index.php?pageID=34&pagename=/PROFESSIONAL-CONDUCT/)

Spano, R., & Koenig, T. (2008). A response to Paul Adams: The codes of ethics and the clash of orthodoxies. *Journal of Social Work Values and Ethics,* 5(2), 5–9. Retrieved 01.10.08 from: http.//www.socialworker.com/jswve/content/view/93/65/

Spicker, P. (1990). Social work and self-determination. *British Journal of Social Work,* 20(3), 221–36.

Squires, J. (ed.) (1993). *Principled positions: Postmodernism and the rediscovery of value.* London: Lawrence & Wishart.

Stafford, W. (1996). International human rights instrument and racial discrimination in the United States. *International Policy Review,* 6 (1), 68–89.

Staub-Bernasconi, S. (2008). *Menschenrechte in ihrer relevanz für die Soziale Arbeit als theorie und praxis* [Human rights and their relevance for social work theory and practice]. In M. Vyslouzil, T. Schmidt, & P. Pantucek (eds), *Recht. So. Menschenrechte und Probleme der Sozialarbeit* [Justice. Thus. Human rights and problems associated with social work]. Vienna: Mandelbaum-Verlag, pp. 10–34.

Steinman, S.O., Richardson, N., Franks, N., & McEnroe, T. (1998). *The ethical decision-making manual for helping professionals.* Pacific Grove, CA: Brooks/Cole.

Sternberg, R.J., Grigorenko, E.L., & Kidd, K.K. (2005). Intelligence, race, and genetics. *American Psychologist,* 60, 46–59.

Stobart, E. (2006). Child abuse linked to accusations of possession and witchcraft'. London: Department for Educational Skills. Retrieved 25.07.08 from: http://www.dfes.gove.ul/research/data/uploadfiles/RR750.pdf

Stocker, M. (1997). Emotional identification, closeness and size. In D. Statman (ed.), *Virtue ethics: A critical reader.* Edinburgh: Edinburgh University Press, pp. 00–00.

Stoesz, D. (2002). From social work to human services. *Journal of Sociology and Social Welfare,* 29, 19–37.

Strom-Gottfried, K. (1999). Professional boundaries: An analysis of violations by social workers. *Families in Society,* 80, 439–49.

Swanton, C. (1997). Virtue ethics and satisficing rationality. In D. Statman (ed.), *Virtue ethics: A critical reader*. Edinburgh: Edinburgh University Press pp. 00–00.

Tait-Rolleston, W., & Pehi-Barlow, S. (2001). A Maori social work construct. In L. Dominelli, W. Lorenz, & H. Soydan (eds), *Beyond racial divides: Ethnicity in social work*. Aldershot: Ashgate, pp. 00–00.

Tascón, S. (2002). Australia's new Other: Shaping compassion for onshore refugees. *Journal of Australian Studies*, 77, 5–14.

Tascón, S. (2006). *Refugees and volunteers: Deconstructing borders, reshaping compassion*. Thesis, University of Western Australia

Tascón, S. (2009). I'm falling in your love: Cross-cultural romance and the refugee film. In R. Murawska, Simpson, C., & Lambert, A. (eds), *Diasporas of Australian cinema*. Sydney: Intellect.

Taylor, C. (1976). Responsibility for self. In A. Rorty (ed.), *The identities of persons*. Berkeley: University of California Press, 81–99. Reprinted in Gary Watson (ed.), (1982), *Free will*. Oxford: Oxford University Press, 111–26.

Taylor, C. (1979). Determinism and the theory of agency. In S. Hook (ed.), *Determinism and freedom*. New York: Macmillan, 224–30.

Taylor, C. (1989). *Sources of the self: The making of the modern identity*. Cambridge: Cambridge University Press.

Taylor, V. (2003). Female genital mutilation: Cultural practice or child abuse? *Paediatric Nursing*, 15, 31–3.

Thompson, N. (2006). *Anti-discriminatory practice*. London: Palgrave Macmillan.

Thorpe, R. (1996). Indigenous challenges to the social work and welfare work codes of ethics in Australia. Paper presented at the *Third National Conference for Australian Association for Professional and Applied Ethics*, Charles Stuart University, Wagga Wagga, 3–6 October.

Timms, N. (1983). *Social work values: An enquiry*. London: Routledge & Kegan Paul.

Traherne, T. ([1675] 1968). *Christian ethicks*. New York: Cornell University Press.

Tronto, J. (1993). *Moral boundaries*. London: Routledge.

Trotter, J., Kershaw, S., & Knott, C. (eds) (2008). Sexualities. *Social Work Education*, Special Issue, 27(2), 117–225.

Turner, M., & Beresford, P. (2005). *User controlled research: Its meanings and potential*. Shaping Our Lives and the Centre for Citizen Participation, Brunel University. Retrieved 28.02.09 from: http://www.shapingourlives.org.uk/Downloads/Usercontrolledresearch%20report.pdf

Turunen, P. (2004). *Samhällsarbete I Norden* [Community work in the Nordic countries]. Acta Wexionesia 47. Växjö: Växjö University Press.

Uggerhoej, L. (2009, forthcoming). Creativity, fantasy, role-play and theatre in social work: A voice from the past or steps for the future? *Social Work & Social Sciences Review*.

United Nations Centre for Human Rights (1994). *Human rights and social work: A manual for schools of social work and the social work profession*. New York: UN.

University of Southern California School of Social Work (n.d.). Mission statement. Los Angeles: USC School of Social Work.

Valokivi, H. (2008). *Kansalainen asiakkaana: Tutkimus vanhusten ja lainrikkojien osallisuudesta, oikeuksista ja velvollisuuksista* [Citizen as client: A study on participation, rights and responsibilities of elderly people and offenders]. Acta Universitatis Tamperensis. Tampere University.

van Berkel, R., Coenen, H., & Vlek, R. (eds) (1998). *Beyond marginality: Social movements of social security claimants in the European Union.* Retrieved 28.02.09 from: http://www.shapingourlives.org.uk/Downloads/Usercontrolledresearch%20report.pdf

van den Bersselaar, O.D. (2005). Virtue-ethics as a device for narratives in social work: The possibility of empowerment by moralising. *Lectoraat Reflectie op het handelen.* Retrieved 20.11.08 from: http://www.reflectietools.nl/documentatie/Virtue_Ethics_VvdB.pdf

Waardenburg, J. (2003). *Muslims and others: Relations in context.* Berlin: Walter de Gruyter.

Wadud, A. (1999). *Qur'an and woman: Re-reading the sacred text from a woman's perspective.* New York: Oxford University Press.

Wadud, A. (2006a). Aishah's legacy: The struggle for women's rights within Islam. In M. Kamrava (ed.), *The new voices of Islam: Reforming politics and modernity.* New York: I.B. Tauris, 201–4.

Wadud, A. (2006b). *Inside the gender Jihad: Women's reform in Islam.* Oxford: Oneworld.

Walden, T., Wolock, I., & Demone, H. (1990). Ethical decision making in human services. *Families in Society,* 71(2), 67–75.

Walker, S. (2001). Tracing the contours of postmodernism. *British Journal of Social Work,* 31(1), 29–39.

Waller, B.N. (1991). *Freedom without responsibility.* Philadelphia: Temple University Press.

Ward, H., Munro, E., & Dearden, C. (2006). *Babies and young children in care,* London, Jessica Kingsley.

Watson, D. (ed.) (1985). *A code of ethics for social work.* London: Routledge & Kegan Paul.

Webb, S.A. (2003). Local orders and global chaos in social work. *European Journal of Social Work,* 6(2), 191–204.

Webb, S.A. (2006). *Social work in a risk society: Social and political perspectives.* Basingstoke: Palgrave Macmillan.

Webb, S.A. (2007). The comfort of strangers: The emergence of social work in late Victorian England (Part One). *European Journal of Social Work,* 10(1), 39–54.

Webb, S.A. (2008). Modelling service user participation in social care. *Journal of Social Work,* 8(3), 269–90.

Webb, S.A. (2009). Against difference and diversity in social work: The case of human rights. *International Journal of Social Welfare,* 18, 306–17.

Webb, S.A., & McBeath, G.B. (1989). A political critique of Kantian ethics in social work. *British Journal of Social Work,* 20(1), 125–46.

Weber, M. (1918). *Politics as a vocation.* Retrieved on 15.09.08 from: http://www.ne.jp/asahi/moriyuki/abukuma/weber/lecture/politics_vocation.html

Weber, M. ([1919]1948). Science as a vocation. In H.H. Gerth & C. Wright Mills (eds), *From Max Weber: Essays in sociology.* London: Routledge, pp. 129–56.

Weber, M. (1921 [1978]). *Economy and society.* 2 vols. Berkeley: University of California Press.

Wetzel, J. (2005). Personal communication, New York, 6 September.

Wijkström, F. (2001). Neue Schwerpunkte oder neue Rolle? Der Schwedische nonprofit-sektor in den 90er jahren [New emphases? The Swedish nonprofit sector in the 1990s]. In E. Priller & A. Zimmer (eds), *Der dritte Sektor international: Mehr Markt – weniger Staat?* [The third sector internationally: more market – less state?]. Berlin: Edition Stigma, 77–99.

Wilkes, R. (1981). *Social work with undervalued groups*. New York: Tavistock.

Williams, B. (1985). *Ethics and the limits of philosophy*. London: Fontana.

Williams, C., & Soydan, H. (2005). When and how does ethnicity matter? A cross-national study of social work responses to ethnicity in child protection cases. *British Journal of Social Work*, 35, 901–20.

Williams, F. (2001). In and beyond New Labour: Towards a new political ethics of care. *Critical Social Policy*, 21(4), 467–93.

Wilson, B. (1982). *Religion in sociological perspective*. Oxford: Oxford University Press.

Wilson, S.J., Lipsey, M.W., & Soydan, H. (2003). Are mainstream programs for juvenile delinquents less effective with minority youth than majority youth? A meta-analysis of outcome research. *Research on Social Work Practice*, 13(1), 3–26.

Wollheim, R. (1984). *The thread of life*. New Haven: Yale University Press.

Wuthnow, R. (2004). *Saving America? Faith-based services and the future of civil society*. Princeton: Princeton University Press.

Yahya, H. (2002). *Islam denounces terrorism*. Bristol: Amal Press.

Younghusband, E. (1978). *Social work in Britain, 1950–1975*. London: Allen & Unwin.

Zijderveld, A.C. (1970). *The abstract society: A cultural analysis of our time*. New York: Doubleday.

Zijderveld, A.C. (1999). *The waning of the welfare state: The end of comprehensive state succor*. New Brunswick, NJ: Transaction.

Index

AASW (Australian Association of Social Workers) 22–3, 28, 66
Abbott, A. 23
abortion 193
Abu Ghraib Prison 3
Adams, P. 35, 36
Addams, J. 64
adoption 66–7, 103–4
Adoption and Children Act (UK) 67
Adorno, T.W. 176, 181
advocacy 106, 144
African Americans 75, 137
African Charter on Human and People's Rights 140
Africans Unite against Child Abuse (AFRUCA) 68
Ahmad, F. 190, 192
AIDS case study 56–8
Albanian/Greek racism 137
Amato-von Hemert, K. 65
ambivalence, moral 120, 124–5
American Convention on Human Rights 140
American Declaration of Independence 152
American Psychological Association (APA) 28
Anscombe, G.E.M. 8–9
anti-discriminatory practice 29, 143, 144
anti-oppressive practice 163
  advocacy 144
  excluded people 162–3
  inequality 134, 160–1, 171
  managerialism 165
  personal/structural issues 164–5
  racial discrimination 133
  in UK 164
  values 4–5, 41
anti-racism 133, 135–6, 140–3
APA (American Psychological Association) 28
apartheid 140
AR v *Homefirst Community Trust* 103
Aristotle
  generalization 3
  golden mean doctrine 112
  human flourishing 8, 11–13
  naturalistic theories of ethics 9, 11–13
  Nicomachean Ethics 220
  teleology 8
  truth 4
  utilitarianism 8
  virtue 117
  virtue ethics 9, 109–10, 111–13
  wisdom/prudence 115
Arnstein, C. 178
ASAP (Australian Association of Psychologists) 28
Ashencaen-Crabtree, S. 189, 193
assimilation 86, 90
Atherton, C. 127
attachment theorists 81, 82
attentiveness 77
Aubrey, C. 164
Augustinian ethics 196, 198, 203
Aupers, S. 184, 213
Australia
  crtical social work 164
  Indigenous people 23
  racism 137
  religious organizations 69
  social workers/codes of ethics 25
Australian Association of Psychologists (ASAP) 28
Australian Association of Social Workers: *see* AASW

authoritarianism 84
authority 10–11
autonomy 32, 43, 44

BAAF (British Association for Adoption and Fostering) 67
Baba, I. 193
Balkan states 137
Banks, S. 24, 27–8, 29, 30, 35, 46, 53, 113, 181, 203
Barise, A. 192
Barnardo's 62–3
BASW (British Association of Social Workers) 20, 26, 27, 36
Battin, M. 70
Baudrillard, J. 91
Bauman, Z.
  assimilation 90
  ethical responsibility 94
  moral ambivalence 120, 124–5
  morality 89, 121, 123–4, 125, 128
  postmodern ethics 72, 122, 124, 130–1
  postmodern turn 91
  proximity 92–3
  utilitarianism 130
Bell, D. 208
beneficence 43
Bentham, J. 8, 125, 129
Beresford, P. 180
Besecke, K. 211
betrayal 109, 115
Beyond Racial Divides (Dominelli, Lorenz and Soydan) 144
BHA (British Humanist Association) 62, 63, 69
Bicultural Code of Practice, NZASW 27
Biestek, F.P. 11, 20, 184, 199
  Casework Relationship 197, 203–5
binary divisions 85, 88, 160
bioethical principles 43
black women 163
blame 219
Blanchot, M. 91
Blaug, R. 102
Bolland, K. 127
Bonhoeffer, D. 202
borders 88, 90, 91
Boros, L. 201, 206
Borrmann, S. 18
Bowles, W. 45
Bowpitt, G. 205, 215
Braye, S. 164
Brill, C.K. 30
British Association for Adoption and Fostering (BAAF) 67
British Association of Social Workers: *see* BASW
British Humanist Association: *see* BHA
British Journal of Social Work 205
British Muslims 190, 191–2
Buddhist ethics 197
Bunge, M. 52, 54
Burke, A. 164
Burke, B. 46
burqa 194
Burr, J. 192
Butler, J. 89–90

Campbell, C. 209, 210, 214
Canada 21, 22, 164
Canadian Association of Social Workers (CASW) 21, 22
Canda, E. 66
Canterbury, Archbishop of 191
care
  duty of 48
  as favour/right 184
  literature on 80–2
  see also caring
care ethic 73
  African American 75
  elements of 77
  feminism 43, 71
  moral agency 53
  moral/political practice 76–80
  policy 75–6
Carey, M. 180
caring 73, 76
  citizenship 77, 78, 79
  gender differences 77
  giving/receiving 73, 80, 82
  love 130
  as moral impulse 32
  Other 130
  phases of 76–7
  psychosocial perspective 81
case management 56

Casework Relationship (Biestek) 197, 203–5
caseworkers and clients 204
CASW (Canadian Association of Social Workers) 21, 22
categorical values 3
Catholic Church 67–8, 69, 213
Catholic Office for the Protection of Children and Vulnerable Adults (COPCA) 68
Catholic Social Science Review 215
Catholic Social Workers National Association (CSWNA) 62
causality 87
Centre for Human Rights, UN 140
Chapman, T. 192
Charitable Choice 69
charity 64, 133, 184, 214
Charity Organization Society 14, 215
Cheetham, J. 143
Chenoweth, L. 45
child abuse, by clergy 67–8
child neglect 103
child protection 84, 98, 102–6, 145, 205–6
child protection guardian 104–6
child protection register 103
Children's Society 62–3
children's views 84, 106
Chodorow, Nancy 74–5
Christian Ethicks (Traherne) 199, 201–2
Christianity
  bias 213
  ethics 183, 184, 196
  humility 199–200
  social work values 61, 196–7
  spiritual perspective 7
  virtues 199
  see also humanism, Christian
citizen participation 134, 173–4, 175, 176, 179, 180
citizen-controlled services 178
citizenship
  active/passive 73–4, 134, 177
  caring 77, 78, 79
  ethical dilemma 180–2
  marginalized people 182
  modern 217
  non-participation 175–6
  self-determination 134
  social justice 161–2
  types 160, 176–7, 179
civil society 173, 174–5, 180
Civilization and Ethics (Schweitzer) 198
Clark, C.L. 33–4, 113
clergy, child abuse 67–8
clients
  agency 161
  autonomy 21
  Code of Conduct 38
  diversity 5
  Internet use 178
  self-determination 9–11, 21, 175
  and service providers 162–3, 177
  and social workers 27, 28, 117, 144, 204
  voice 84
Clifford, D. 46
Cnaan, R. 69
code of ethics: *see* ethical codes
codes of conduct
  controversial 16
  and ethical codes 17–18, 32
  GSCC 31, 35–40, 110
  lighthouse metaphor 33–4
  moral development 39, 40
  regulation 36
  service users 38
codification 19, 31–2, 34–5, 121
Cohen, B.-Z. 65
Cold War 151–2
collectivism 21, 150, 152
collegial relations 48
Collingridge, M. 28
Collins, P.H. 75
Commission to Inquire into Child Abuse 68
commitment, ethical 220–1
commodification 95
communication 95–7, 101, 103
communicative action 96–7, 105–7
communitarianism 43, 108
community 111, 174, 187
  see also Muslim community; *Ummah*
Community Care Special Edition 38, 39
community development 156, 157, 172
community psychiatric nurse 103, 104
community-based cultural education 64

community-based service providers 178
compassion 72, 93, 119
competence 77
comprehensive model (Miner) 45
confidentiality
  AASW 28
  collective/individualistc 21
  conflicting interests 48, 55–6, 58
  contingent/absolute 161
  danger to self/others 24, 53
  ethical codes 25
  laws 24–5
  NASW 24, 28
  privacy 56
  religious confession 70
  as right 10
  as value 20
Congress, E. 17, 20, 25, 28, 45
Connor, S. 123
conscience 118, 130
consequences 42, 43
consequentialism 1, 8–9, 12, 13, 24, 53
constructed rights approach 155–6
consuetude 33
consumerism 177, 178, 212
contextuality 45–6, 50, 181
Convention Against Discrimination in Education, UNESCO 140
Convention on the Rights of the Child 140
COPCA (Catholic Office for the Protection of Children and Vulnerable Adults) 68
co-production of outcomes 173
Council on Social Work Education (CSWE) 66, 142, 143
counselling services case study 47–50
counter-culture 208
Cowburn, M. 35, 193
Crabtree, S.A. 65
crime prevention studies 145–6
critical reflective practice 41, 181
critical social work literature 164, 179
critical theory 21, 176, 181
Cross, T. 144
Crusades 188
CSWE (Council on Social Work Education) 66, 142, 143
CSWNA (Catholic Social Workers National Association) 62
Cultural Awareness in the Human Services (Green) 143
cultural competence 20, 23, 135, 144
cultural differences 140–1, 144, 150
cultural rationalization 210
Cumberlege Commission Report 67

Dahl, S. 164
Dahme, H.-J. 179
Dalrymple, B. 164
Daly, M. 79
Davies, M. 164
de Anda, D. 145
de Gruchy, John 200
Dean, R. 144
decision-making: *see* ethical decision-making
defensive practice 33, 115
dehumanization 93–4
deontology
  Kant 1, 8, 9, 13, 24, 53, 110
  lying 13
  moral realism 55
  principle-based ethics 33
  professional ethics 113
  and utilitarianism 43
  and virtue ethics 12
dependence 171
depression 167
Derrida, J. 91
desensitization 220
deterrence culture 40
detraditionalization 209
devaluation 160, 162
Developing Cross-Cultural Competence (Lynch and Hanson) 143
Devore, W. 143
dialogue 45, 101, 106–7, 118
difference 86, 140–1, 144, 150
  see also diversity; Other
dilemma: *see* ethical dilemma; moral dilemma
dirty hands, moral 219, 220
disability, people with 167–71
disability movement 79
Disability Team 167
disciplinary practice 31, 75, 180

discourse ethics
  child protection 102–6
  disorders of 97
  ethical decision-making 102
  Habermas 72, 95–7, 104–5, 121–2
  relativism 101
discourse model, perspective-taking 98
discrimination 141, 176, 180
  positive/negative 22–3
disempowerment 168
disenchantment 209–10
disorders of discourse 97
disvalues 11
diversity 5, 17, 44, 135–6
Dobbelaere, K. 207
Dolgoff, R. 46, 53
domestic violence 103, 193
Dominelli, L. 23, 134, 144, 163, 164, 165, 193
Douki, S. 193
dualist thinking 160
Dubois, B. 66
duty
  conflict 219
  moral worth 114
  and obligation 7–8, 9, 43, 150
  responsibility 126
  rights 150
  virtue 118–19

Ellis, K. 32
emergency protection order 103
emic perspective 210–11
empathy 74–5, 86
empowerment 100, 161, 164, 181
ends and means 72, 87, 114
England 29, 35
Enlightenment
  human rights 153, 157
  humanism 158
  questioned 150
  secularization 215
  subjectivity 88–9
  truth 121
entitlement/needs 163
Equality Act (UK) 67
Erasmus, D. 197, 198
esotericism 207, 208
essentialism 75, 120, 129
ETHIC model 45
ethic of care: *see* care ethic
ethical codes 19, 23–4
  CASW 21, 22
  and Code of Conduct 17–18, 32
  confidentiality 25
  cross-cultural comparisons 27–8, 29
  development of 19–20
  efficacy 34
  GSCC 34
  laws 24–5
  liberal-humanist 33
  NASW 20, 21, 24, 26–7, 141
  non-naturalistic 9–11
  NZASW 21
  principle/character based 24
  professional ethics 17
  self-determination 25, 28
  as tool 128
  universality 15, 24
ethical decision-making 42, 43
  context 45–6, 50
  discourse ethics 102
  ethical dilemma 41
  Habermas 97–100
  literature on 44–7
  models for 18, 45–7, 48–9
  in practice 50
  problems 83
  rational choice 17
  social work practice 47–50
  terms 7–8
ethical dilemma
  citizenship 180–2
  conflicts of interest 11
  defined 48, 51, 53
  ethical decision making 41
  moral realism 57
  social work practice 55–8
  see also moral dilemma
ethical grid 45
ethical principles screen 46
Ethical Statement of Principles, IFSW 20, 26, 28, 29, 44, 141
ethics 1
  adherence to 220
  Aristotle 9–13, 220
  Augustinian 196, 198, 203
  Christianity 183, 184, 196

ethics (*cont.*):
  Islam 183–4, 185, 186–7, 194
  Islamism 187–8
  language of 7–9
  liberal-humanist 33
  and logic 4
  and morality 8–9, 120
  naturalistic theories 9, 11–13, 54
  neo-Aristotelian 13
  New Age 183, 184
  non-naturalistic theories 9–11
  as process 88
  of responsibility 81–2, 85–6, 87–8, 90, 94
  Thomist 196, 203
  and values 20
  see also ethical codes; ethical decision-making; ethical dilemma; normative ethical order; professional ethics
Ethics and Social Welfare journal 46
Ethnic Sensitive Social Work Practice (Devore and Schlesinger) 143
ethnicity 139, 145, 176
  see also race
ethnocentrism, avoided 190
etic perspective 211
eudaimonia 12, 112, 119
  see also human flourishing; well-being
eupraxia 32
European Citizenship and Participation of Marginalised Network 176
European Convention on Human Rights 106, 140
European Social Charter 140
evaluations 16, 108–9, 221–2
Everitt, A. 110
Evers, A. 177–8
evidence-based interventions 146, 147
exclusion: *see* social exclusion
exploitation paradigm 76

faith 60–4
  social work literature 63–5
  social work practice 7, 18, 60–70, 197
  see also religion
faith-based agencies 62–3, 68–9
Faith-Based-Initiative 69
Faizi, N. 193
family group conference 102
fathering 77
Featherstone, B. 71, 77, 79
female circumcision 193–4
feminism
  care ethic 43, 71
  ethical decision-making 45, 49
  gendered caretaking 73, 77
  social policy 78–9
fiduciary relationship 27
Fikree, F. 193
Fisher, B. 76
Flexner, A. 17, 19
Fook, J. 127, 181
Foucault, M. 217
  disciplines 31, 75, 180
  ethics/power 18
  pastoral power 130
  similitudes 88
The Fragility of Goodness (Nussbaum) 223
Francis of Assisi, Saint 203
Franklin, D.L. 64
fraternity 204–5
freedom 23, 87
Freeman, C. 137
Freire, P. 161
French Revolution 152
Freud, S. 14
Frister, R. 2
Frogget, L. 81
fundamentalism 60, 61–2, 155
Furedi, F. 217, 218
Furness, S. 65–6

Gallagher, A. 113
Garcia, J.G. 45
gender factors
  caring 73, 77
  dependence 171
  discrimination 176
  empathy 74–5
  human rights 150
  identity formation 81
  moral frameworks 74–6
  oppression 163
General Social Care Council: *see* GSCC
generalizability 3, 116
Germany 29, 178–9
  see also Nazi Germany

Giddens, A. 78
gifts, accepting 37
Gilligan, C. 74–6, 79
Gilligan, P. 7, 65–6
Giordano, J. 144
Glaser, K. 45
globalization 137
gnosis 207
Gnosticism 211
golden mean doctrine 112
Goldstein, H. 71
good enough concept 113
good life concept 111–12, 117
Goode, H. 68
Graham, M. 144
gratification 97
Gray, M. 64, 69, 72, 100–1, 102, 113, 127, 128, 129, 144, 183, 213
Greek/Albanian racism 137
Green, J. 143
Green, R.G. 142–3
GSCC (General Social Care Council)
  Code of Conduct 31, 36, 110
  ethical code 34
  public confidence 35
  registration 36–8, 39–40
  religious beliefs 66
Guantánamo Bay camp 3
Guardian-ad-Litem agency 104–6
guilt 219
Guttmann, D. 64–5

Habermas, J.
  communication 95–7, 101, 103
  communicative action 95, 96–7, 105–6
  discourse ethics 72, 95–7, 104–5, 121–2
  ethical decision-making 97–100
  ethical theory 120–2, 129
  Justification and Application 97
  knowledge 121
  Moral Consciousness and Communicative Action 97
  moral discourse 97–100
  morality 121
  normative ethical order 95, 100, 120–1
  Other 106–7
  strategic action 97, 105
  values 120–1
Haeurwas, S. 202
Haj-Yahia, M. 193
Halstead, M. 193
Handy, C. 59
Hanson, M. 143
Harden, J. 45
Hardiker, P. 110
Harrington, D. 46
Harris, J. 64
Harvey, D. 122
Hayes, D. 102
health and safety policies 37
Healy, K. 32
Heelas, P. 209, 211, 213
Hekman, S. 75
Helsinki Final Act 140
Henery, N. 215
hijab 194
Hill, M. 45
Hinduist ethics 197
Hippocratic Oath 19
HIV case study 56–7
Hobbes, T. 125, 153
Hodge, D. 66, 190
Hodgson, L. 180
holism 52, 212–13, 215
holistic practice *166*, 167–71
Holland, T. 25
Hollis, F. 10
Hollway, W. 80–2, 84
Hölscher, D. 127, 128
homosexuality 61, 193
Honneth, A. 100, 102
Houston, S. 72, 100, 102
Houtman, D. 184, 211, 213
Hugman, R. 32, 52–3, 55, 101, 127
human flourishing 8, 11–13, 111, 112
  see also eudaimonia; well-being
human needs 54, 55, 59, 163
human rights 148, 158
  anti-racism 140–1
  community development 157
  constructed rights approach 155–6
  critical theory 21
  deductive approach 157
  Enlightenment 153, 157
  fundamentalism 155

human rights (*cont.*):
gender 150
IFSW 157
inabrogability 149
inalienability 149
individual/collective 150
indivisibility 149
law-based 154–5
legitimacy 153
public/private sphere 151
secular traditions 150
social justice 29, 44, 133–4
social work values 23, 29, 41
spirituality 150
state obligations approach 153
three generations of 151–2
universality 22, 149, 150
Human Rights and Social Work manual 54, 140–1
human rights discourse 149–52
human rights forums 155
human rights from below 156
human rights legislation 102, 153–6
humanism
Christian 198, 199–200, 202, 203–5, 204, 205
Enlightenment 158
secular 184, 204–5
humanity, nature of 148–9, 158–9
humility 199–200, 205–6
Hursthouse, R. 109
Husain, F. 65, 189
Hvinden, B. 177, 181

IASSW (International Association of Schools of Social Work) 54, 163–4
Ibn al-Athir 188
ideal speech situation 96–7, 102
identity 81, 139, 185, 186, 209–11
Ife, J. 133–4, 157
IFSW (International Federation of Social Workers)
Ethical Statement of Principles 20, 26, 28, 29, 44, 141
human rights 157
Human Rights and Social Work manual 54, 140–1
against racism 135
immigration status 23
In a Different Voice (Gilligan) 74–6
independence 27, 168, 170
Indigenous people 23, 27, 28, 137
Indigenous social work 129, 164
Indigenous Social Work around the World (Gray) 144
individualization 20, 203–4
individuals
community 111, 174
empowerment 100
freedom 23
inner life 183, 211
intellect/agency 72
moral spheres 52
subjectivization 176, 181–2
inequality
anti-oppressive practice 134, 160–1, 171
eradication of 161
power 144, 161
social construction 171, 202
structural 134, 168
systemic 172
value perspectives 133
informed consent 10, 70
inner life 183, 211
see also spirituality
intentions/consequences 87
interdependence 79, 170–1
interests, conflicts of
confidentiality 48, 55–6, 58
ethical dilemma 11
identity 185
interference, freedom from 10
interhuman aspect 85, 90
International Association of Schools of Social Work: *see* IASSW
International Convention on the Suppression and Punishment of the Crime of Apartheid 140
International Conventions 26, 140, 143
International Conventions on the Elimination of All Forms of Racial Discrimination 140
International Covenant on Civil and Political Rights 140
International Covenant on Economic, Social and Cultural Rights 140

International Federation of Social Workers: *see* IFSW
Internet 178, 180
intersubjectivity 82, 86, 88, 89
intolerance 44
intuition 212
The Invisible Religion (Luckmann) 211
Iraqi prisoners of war 3
Ireland 68
Irfan, S. 193
Irigaray, L. 91
Iser, M. 101
Isichei, E. 200
Islam 185
  British Muslims 190, 191–2
  community 187, 192–4
  diversity within 63–4, 191
  ethics 183–4, 185, 186–7, 194
  Five Pillars of Faith 186–7
  homosexuality 193
  identity 186
  prohibitions 193
  self-esteem 190
  social work 65, 189–92
  social work values 196–7
  spiritual perspective 7
  tithing 187
  welfare/non-discrimination 190
  women's movement 187
Islamism 185, 186, 187–8
isolation 168

Jayaratne, S. 25
Jesuits 201, 205
Jihad 185, 188
Johansson, H. 177, 181
Jordan, W. 197, 200
Judaism 196–7
Judeo-Christian perspective 64, 197
judgementalism 44
just practice 164
justice 43, 75–6
Justification and Application (Habermas) 97

Kant, I.
  deontology 1, 8, 9, 13, 24, 53, 110
  ends and means 72, 114
  non-naturalistic ethics 9–11
  virtue ethics 112
Kellner, D. 122
Kessl, F. 179
Khan, P. 165
Kilpatrick, A. 25
Kjørstad, M. 91, 92, 93
Klein, M. 82
knowledge 44, 121
Koenig, T. 35, 36
Kohlberg, L. 74
Kristjánsson, K. 11, 12–13
Kugelman, W. 25

labelling 105
Lago, C. 144
laws/ethical codes 24–5
Levinas, E.
  compassion 93
  ethics of responsibility 71–2, 86–7, 90, 94, 125–6
  interhuman aspect 85, 90
  intersubjectivity 89
  Other 82, 85, 89, 92, 127
  proximity 92–3
Lewicka, K. 193
Lewis, J. 79
liberal-open approach 62–3
libertarian citizenship 177, 179
life, value of 2–3
life maps 66
lifeworld 88, 95, 102
Lipsey, M. 145–6
Lipsky, M. 32
Locke, J. 152, 153
Loewenberg, F.M. 46
Lorenz, W. 144
Lovat, T. 100–1, 102, 113, 127, 128, 183–4
love
  caring for Other 130
  of enemies 201–3, 205
  meekness 202
Lovett, L. 45
luck 114–15
Luckmann, T. 211, 214
Luke's Gospel 200
Lum, D. 143
Luther, M. 198

lying 13, 109, 117
Lynch, E. 143
Lyotard, J.-F. 91

McAuliffe, D. 18, 25, 28, 45
McBeath, G. 100, 113
McGee, H. 68
McGoldrick, M. 144
MacIntyre, Alasdair 52, 116–17
McLaughlin, K. 35, 40
Mahamud-Hassan, N. 193
The Making of a Counter Culture (Roszak) 208
malfeasance 37
Malik, R. 190, 193
managerialism 158, 165, 170, 178
Māori people 27
marginalized people
  citizenship 176, 182
  clients/social workers 144
  inclusion 161
  sociocultural forces 92
  voice of 155
Marshall, T.H. 177, 217
Marx, K. 174
Mascini, P. 213
Maslow, A. 54
Matthies, A.-L. 134
Mattison, M. 45
Meagher, G. 32
meaning/identity 209–11
meekness 200–1, 202, 204, 205–6
Meleyal, L. 39
Methodist sick-visitors 214–15
Mexico 139
micro-ethics 128
migrant status 22, 25
Miley, K.K. 66
Mill, J.S. 8
Miner, M.H. 45
minority groups 16, 145–6
Miranda, J. 146
Mission Australia 69
modernity 85, 88, 124, 217
modernity, late 209–11
Moore, A. 109
moral agency 14, 53, 72, 83, 113–14
Moral Boundaries (Tronto) 77–8, 81
Moral Consciousness and Communicative Action (Habermas) 97
moral continuum 41, 43
moral development 39, 40, 74–6
moral dilemma 2, 18, 219
moral discourse 97–100
moral judgements 66–7, 71, 219
moral luck 114–15
moral panic 39
moral philosophy 7–9, 43–4
  see also ethics
moral realism 51–3, 54–5, 57, 59
moral spheres 51–2
moral worth 79–80
morality
  Bauman 121, 123–4, 125, 128
  discursiveness 123–4
  and ethics 8–9, 120
  evaluations 16
  Habermas 121
  idealized 15–16
  mindset 8, 32
  non-rational 123–4, 125
  personal 121
  relativism 3
  sexuality 196
  social life 81, 130–1
  social work 13–16
  values 15, 136
Moroccan/Spanish racism 137
motivation 111
Mouffe, C. 122
Ms magazine 74
Munro, E. 205
Murdoch, I. 130
Muslim community 186–7
  female circumcison 193–4
  religionization of problems 192–3
  somatization of problems 192
  veiling 194
  women's movement 187
Muslim social workers 191
Muslim Youth Helpline 193
mutuality 96

NAACSW (North American Association of Christians in Social Work) 62
Nagel, A.-K. 69
Nagel, T. 223

Narey, M. 63
NASW (National Association of Social Workers) 19
  confidentiality 24, 28
  core values 28
  ethical codes 20, 21, 22, 23, 24, 26–7, 141
  social workers' attitudes 142–3
National Conference on Charities and Corrections 17
National Youth Agency 190–1
natural law 14, 196, 203
natural rights 148, 152–3
naturalistic theories of ethics 9, 11–13, 54
Nazi Germany 136, 140
Nealon, J. 89
neglect of children 103
Nelson, P. 35
neo-Aristotelian ethics 13
neo-Marxism 129
New Age 207
  consumerism 212
  counter-culture 208
  emic perspective 210–11
  ethics 183, 184
  etic perspective 211
  personal experience 212–13
  public sphere 213–14
  social work 214–15, 217–18
  spiritual perspective 7, 183–4, 197
New Right 175, 197
New Testament ethics 196
New Zealand 35, 164
New Zealand Association of Social Workers: *see* NZASW
Nietzsche, F.W. 3, 101
noble savage concept 152
Nolan Report 67
non-discrimination 20, 22–3, 25
non-governmental organizations 174, 180
non-judgemental attitude 20, 22–3, 202–3
non-maleficence 43
non-naturalistic theories 9–11
non-profit organizations 174, 180
Nordic countries 179
normative ethical order 15, 71, 76, 95, 100, 120–1
North American Association of Christians in Social Work (NAACSW) 62
(North) American Association of Social Work 19
Norwegian studies 67, 92
Nozick, R. 117
Nussbaum, M. 3–4, 223
NZASW (New Zealand Association of Social Workers) 21, 27

object relations theory 74
obligations
  to client 219–20
  and duties 7–8, 9, 43, 150
O'Boyle, C. 68
Obrecht, W. 54
O'Melia, M. 66
oppression 160
  dynamics of 165
  gender 163
  power inequalities 144
  processes 162
  types 167–8
Orme, J. 31
Other
  being for/with 126–7
  compassion 72
  encountering 85
  Habermas 106–7
  Levinas 82, 85, 89, 92, 127
  proximity 92–3
  responsibility to 85
  self 85, 89–90, 114, 120, 126–7
Othering 160, 161–2
Otto, H.-U. 179
Ozanan, F. 203

panopticon 39
Park, Y. 144
participation
  Banks 181
  citizenship 134, 173–4
  human rights from below 156
  self-determination 181
  subjectivization 176, 182
participationism 178, 179
particular/universal 122
Parton, N. 83, 127

paternalism 11, 21, 44, 84, 177
patriarchy 150
Payne, M. 64
Pearce, J. 144
Pearson, D. 68
Perlman, H. H. 10, 20
persecution concept 90
personal experience 212–13
perspective-taking, discourse model 98
phantasy, Kleinian 82
Phillips, M. 164
Phoca, S. 13
Pinker, R. 164
pity 92–3
Plante, T. 67–8
Plato 9
pluralism 5, 15, 128, 223
political ethics of care 78–80
politics 11–12, 111–12
Portugal 213
positionality 123
positivist world view 158
postcolonial theory 123
postcolonialism 61
postmodern ethics 120, 127
  Bauman 72, 122, 124, 130–1
  moral relativism 122–3
  moral responsibility 125–7, 130
  positionality 123
  universals 127–8
postmodern turn 91
power 18, 130, 139, 144, 161
Preston-Shoot, M. 164
privacy 10, 56
private practice in social work 29–30
privatization, welfare provision 179
privilege 155, 162
proceduralism/holism 166
process-oriented model 48–9
professional ethics 1–2
  bleach-effect 15–16
  deontology 113
  ethical codes 17
  integrity 22
  proletarianization 34
  religion 69–70
  values 19
  virtue 100
professionalism 37–8, 86, 165, 177–8, 179
proletarianization 34
Protestantism 208
proximity/Other 92–3
psychosocial perspective 80–2
public sphere 108, 129, 151, 213–14
Putnam, R. 175

Quakers 200

race 133
  biological 138
  sexism 163
  as social construction 138–9, 146
  social workers' attitudes 142–3
Race Relations Act (UK) 140
Race Relations (Amendment) Act (UK) 140
racial discrimination 133, 137, 138
racism 135, 136–7, 146
  see also anti-racism
Radical Islam 185
Rankin, P. 66
rational-cognitive models 45
Rawls, J. 117
Reamer, F. 34, 45, 128
recognition theory 100, 102
record-keeping 37
Reeser, L. 45
reflective model 45, 49
Registered Partnership Act (Norway) 67
registration
  GSCC 36–8, 39–40
  New Zealand 35
  refused 38
  regulation 31–2
  Scotland 35
regulation 31–2, 36
Reichert, E. 157
Reid, J. 35
relativism 3, 101, 122–3, 125
religion 60
  confession 70
  and faith 64
  moral issues 66–7
  postcolonialism 61
  professional ethics 69–70

religionization of problems 192–3
religious organizations 61, 69
Renaissance 208
Rennie, G. 31
The Reproduction of Mothering (Chodorow) 74–5
respect for persons 15, 20, 21, 201
responsibility
care 77
duty 126
ethical 71–2, 85–6, 87–8, 90, 94
as first philosophy 85, 89
individual 72
intentions 87
moral 87, 120, 121, 125–7, 130
to the Other 85
self-determination 86
social 23
social work 91–2
unconditional 127
responsiveness 77
retribution, fear of 40
Rhodes, M.L. 29, 53
Rice, D. 26
Richmond, M. 64
rights
conflicting 150–1
cultural 154
duties 150
equal 61
individual 150
natural 148, 152–3
non-human 149
social 182
social justice 11
see also human rights
rights-based social work 43, 134, 163–4
risk assessment policies 37
risk regulation 31
risk-aversion 35, 36, 39
Robinson, W. 45
Rose, N. 217
Rossiter, A. 34
Roszak, T. 208
Rothman, J. 48
Rousseau, J.-J. 152
Rushdie, S. 16
sacred, inner life 211
SACSSP (South African Council of Social Service Professions) 27
Salvation Army 69
same-sex couples/adoption 66–7
Sandel, M. 117
Sanderson, T. 69
Schillebeeckx, E. 199–200
Schlesinger, E. 143
Schweitzer, A. 198
Scotland 35
secularization 209, 215
Seedhouse, D. 45
Segal, L. 75
self
generalizability 116
mundane/sacred 211
narcissism 92
Other 85, 89–90, 114, 120, 126–7
relational 83
spiritual 216–17
virtue 117–18
self-determination
Abbott 23
citizenship 134
clients 9–11, 21, 175
empowerment 161
ethical codes 25, 28
HIV/AIDS 56
Indigenous people 28
interdependence 79
participation 181
paternalism 44
responsibility 86
social work values 20
self-fulfilling prophecy 105
self-interest 125, 126
self-knowledge 217
self-reflection 15, 44, 123
self-spirituality 211–12, 215, 216–17
senstivity 11, 143–4
service users: *see* clients
Sevenhuijsen, S. 76, 78, 81
sexism 163
Sexual Orientation Regulations (UK) 67
sexual relationships 27, 28
sexuality 196
Sharia 191, 192
Sheridan, M. 65

Sheriff, S. 190, 192
sick-visitors 214–15
Sidgwick, Henry 8
Sikhism 63–4
Slote, M. 114
Smedley, A. 138–9
Smedley, B. 138–9
Smith, C. 32
Smith, D. 52–3, 55
Smith, N. H. 221
social control 83–4
social exclusion 118, 133, 134, 162–3
social justice 148
  Abbott 23
  citizenship 161–2
  human rights 29, 44, 133–4
  injustice 133
  minority groups 16
  positionality 123
  rights 11
  social work 21, 41, 121, 130
  Third Way 78
social perspectives 133, 134
social policy 78–9, 184, 217
social reform 133
social work 159
  as agency 189, 194
  Christianity 61, 196–7
  as conjectural settlement 64
  as constitutive socio-ethical good 222–3
  Flexner on 17
  Islam 189–92
  moral philosophy 43–4
  morality 13–16
  New Age 214–15, 217–18
  postmodernism 127–8
  private practice 29–30
  religious origins 64–5
  responsibility 91–2
  self-spirituality 216–17
  social control 83–4
  social justice 21, 41, 121, 130
  structural 164
  values 3, 20–3, 51–2, 110, 196–7
  virtue 113
  virtue ethics 110–11, 119
Social Work and Ethnicity (Cheetham) 143
Social Work Christian Fellowship (SWCF) 62
Social Work for the Activating State (Dahme) 179
Social Work Practice and People of Color (Lum) 143
social work students 35, 83–4
social workers
  authority of 10–11
  and clients 27, 28, 117, 144, 204
  decision-making 83
  desensitization 220
  egalitarianism 204
  ethnicity 145
  humility 205–6
  managerial support 170
  meekness 205–6
  non-directive 10
  obligation 219–20
  racial attitudes 142–3
  registration 31
  self-reflection 44
  training 16, 118, 141–3
  values 4, 18, 42–3
  virtuous 3, 113, 114, 116
sociologists of religion 214
Socrates 15
somatization of problems 192
Sonnenberg, K. 29
South African Black Social Workers' Association 27
South African Council of Social Service Professions (SACSSP) 27
Southern California, University of 141–2
Soydan, H. 133, 144, 145–6
Spain 137, 139
Spalek, B. 65, 189
Spano, R. 35, 36
Spicker, P. 10
spirit posesession 61, 68
spiritual perspectives 7, 183–4, 197
spiritual turn 207, 209–11, 210, 213
spirituality 60
  fragmented 211–12
  holism 212–13
  human rights 150
  and religion 64
  in social work 66, 183

Squires, J. 122–3, 129
Stacks, C. 75
state obligations approach 153, 157
Staub-Bernasconi, S. 182
Steinman, S.O. 45
stereotyping 44, 142–3, 162
Stobart, E. 68
Stocker, M. 114
Stolen Generations 137
strategic action 97, 105
subjectivity 82, 88–9, 113, 124–5
subjectivization 176, 179, 181–2
Swanton, C. 115
SWCF (Social Work Christian Fellowship) 62

Tascón, S. 71, 94
Taylor, C. 88–9, 221, 222
teleology 1, 8, 12
them–us dichotomy 160, 161–2
  see also Other
Third Way 78, 175, 177, 178, 181
The Third Way (Giddens) 78
Thomist ethics 196, 203
Thomson, J. 144
The Times 191
Timms, N. 11, 20, 118, 197
tithing in Islam 187
tokenism 44
torture 3
totalitarianism 93
tracking harms model 45
Traherne, T. 197, 198–9, 201–2
transcultural integrative models 45
Tronto, J. 75, 76, 77–8, 81
truth 4, 121

Ummah 187, 188
  see also Muslim community
uncertainty, moral 124
UNESCO 140
United Kingdom 137, 164, 179, 190, 191–2
  see also England; Scotland
United Nations Centre for Human Rights 140
United Nations Conventions/Charters 26, 140, 143, 154
United Nations Declaration of the Rights of the Child 153
United Nations Human Rights Commission 54
United States of America
  just practice 164
  Muslim-sensitive provisions 193
  New Right 197
  private practice in social work 29–30
  racial discrimination 137, 138
  social work ethical code 19
Universal Declaration of Human Rights 140, 153, 154, 156, 164
universality
  ethical codes 15
  human needs 54, 55
  human rights 22, 149, 150
  natural rights 148
  and particular 122
  postmodern ethics 127–8
  self-evident 15
  values 3, 8, 23, 42, 129
universalizable concepts 75, 123–4
universalization principle 98–9
user involvement 173
  critical perspective 180
  empowerment 181
  professionalism 177–8
  self-determination 175
  UK 179
  welfare politics 182
  see also participation
user-based service providers 178
user-controlled welfare research 178
utilitarianism
  Aristotelian 8
  Bauman 129, 130
  Bentham 8, 125, 129
  defined 1, 12
  and deontology 43
  ethical codes 24
  greater good 110, 115
  modified 128
  social work 43, 53

values
  anti-oppressive practice 4–5, 41
  assumptions 15
  categorical 8

values (*cont.*):
conflicting 16, 24
contingency 16
diversity 17
and ethics 20
as goods, circulating 16
Habermas 120–1
instrumental 54
intrinsic 51, 54
morality 15, 136
personal 223
pluralism 5, 15
professional 19, 223
social work 3–4, 20–3, 29, 41, 51–2, 61, 110, 129, 133
social workers 4
sources 223
universal 3, 8, 23, 42, 129
Van Berkel, R. 178
veiling 194
vice/virtues 109
Vincent de Paul, Saint 203
violence 103, 193, 202
see also domestic violence
virtue
Aristotle 117
Christianity 199
communication 101
duty 118–19
intellectual/moral 112
professional 100
self 117–18
social work 3, 113, 114, 116
vice 109
virtue ethics
Aristotle 9, 109–10, 111–13
defined 12–13, 108
and deontology 12
evaluation 109
individual workers 45, 72, 101
Kant 112
lying 13
moral agency 113–14
social work 100–1, 110–11, 115–18, 119
voice
of children 84, 106
of client 84
inner 212
of marginalized people 155
privileged 155
voluntary organizations 180
vulnerability 79

Walden, T. 25
Walker, S. 127
Watson, D. 26
Webb, B. 133
Webb, S.A. 35, 72, 100, 113, 182
Weber, M. 87, 209–10
Webster, P. 17–18
Weeks, J. 122–3
welfare politics 175, 177, 182
welfare provision 68–9, 179
Welfare Reform Act (USA) 69
welfare state 79, 134, 178–9, 182
welfarism 177–8, 179
well-being 111, 161, 168
see also eudaimonia; human flourishing
Wetzel, J. 22
Whiting, R. 184
Williams, B. 114–15, 128
Williams, F. 75–6, 77, 78–80, 84
Wilson, B. 207
Wilson, S.J. 145–6
Wollheim, R. 15
women, oppressed 163
women's movement, Muslim 187
Woodhead, L. 209, 213
workfare 92
World Conference against Racism 137
Wright, R. 13

Yahya, H. 187–8
Yellow Bird, M. 129